WITHDRAWN
REDWOOD

HORACE WALPOLE

A Biography

HORACE WALPOLE

A Biography

By R. W. KETTON-CREMER

CORNELL UNIVERSITY PRESS

Ithaca, New York

First published 1940
by Duckworth & Co Ltd

Second (revised) edition published 1946
by Faber and Faber Ltd

Third edition published 1964
by Methuen & Co Ltd

First printing Cornell University Press 1966

Library of Congress Catalog Card Number: 66–11431

PRINTED IN THE UNITED STATES OF AMERICA
BY W. F. HUMPHREY PRESS, INC.
BOUND BY VAIL-BALLOU PRESS, INC.

To

WILMARTH SHELDON LEWIS

and to the memory of

ANNIE BURR LEWIS

with love and gratitude

Contents

Illustrations

In this drawing Rowlandson has taken certain liberties with the architectural details of Strawberry Hill, in the same spirit in which he has peopled his foreground with monks and other figures more likely to be encountered at Paris than at Twickenham. It is reproduced as an agreeable and unusual fantasy on Strawberry Hill, rather than as an exact rendering of the northern aspect of the house.

"Went early this morning in company with Mr. George Dance, and Mr. Samuel Lysons, of the Temple, to Lord Orford's at Strawberry Hill, where we breakfasted with his Lordship. In the forenoon Mr. George Dance made a drawing of his Lordship's profile, an excellent resemblance. Lord Orford is now in his seventy-sixth year, infirm in his body, but lively and attentive in mind." (*The Farington Diary,* i. 1. July 13, 1793.)

Author's Note

IT is a great satisfaction to me to know that the revised version of my biography of Horace Walpole is to be made available to American readers. When the first edition was published, in the spring of 1940, the fate of European civilization was at stake and the situation of Great Britain appeared almost hopeless. In those dark days the reception of a book, even though it was the result of five years of work, seemed hardly to matter. Nevertheless I remember with particular gratitude the cordial letters and appreciative comments that arrived from friends and colleagues across the Atlantic.

The study of the eighteenth century is today being pursued, in amity and comradeship, by an ever-growing number of American and British scholars. My book is another example, although a modest one, of that Anglo-American co-operation which has been of such incalculable value in our troubled world. It could never have been undertaken without the encouragement and assistance of a great American scholar, Wilmarth Sheldon Lewis. My debt to him, and to his unrivalled collection of Walpole material at Farmington, Connecticut, is recorded in the Preface and should be evident to the reader on nearly every page. I owe a great deal also to the help of other American friends in the field of eighteenth-century scholarship. I am therefore especially gratified that the press of a famous American university is publishing this new edition of my book.

R. W. K.-C.

Preface

THIS book was completed in the summer of 1939, and first appeared during the inauspicious spring of 1940. A revised edition was published in 1946. The present edition includes some further corrections and adjustments, but no substantial alterations have been made.

The original preface is now out of date. It referred to my use of material, then unpublished or neglected, which has since been incorporated in the Yale Edition of Horace Walpole's Correspondence; and it contained a few other passages, explanatory and apologetic, which no longer seem relevant. But time has only enhanced the debt which I expressed to the founder and editor of the Yale Edition, Mr. W. S. Lewis.

I was an almost untried writer when I hesitatingly approached Mr. Lewis in 1935, and told him of my ambition to write a biography of Horace Walpole. With the utmost kindness and generosity, he at once invited me to make use of the unrivalled collection of Walpole material at his home at Farmington in Connecticut, where the first volumes of the Yale Edition were already in preparation. On two visits to the United States in 1936 and 1939, I was privileged to make what use I desired of the manuscripts, books and works of art that Mr. and Mrs. Lewis had assembled. I have never been able fully to express to them my affectionate thanks for their kindness during those happy weeks at Farmington.

In addition to this unrestricted use of his collection, I had the assistance of Mr. Lewis's privately printed monographs on Walpole; and his longer study, *The Genesis of Strawberry Hill,* was of the greatest service to me. Above all I had the constant benefit of Mr. Lewis's criticism and advice, and of his revision of the completed manuscript of my book.

Since then, a quarter of a century has passed. The Yale Edition has now reached its thirty-first volume, and will probably extend to fifty volumes or even more. It has been universally acclaimed as one of the major feats of scholarship achieved in our time. For more than thirty years Mr. Lewis has concentrated his thoughts and energies upon this great work. He has never embarked upon the definitive biography of Walpole which at one time he contemplated, and which would automatically have superseded my own. But he has distilled his lifelong study of Walpole into the six Mellon Lectures delivered in Washington early in 1960, and published in this country by Rupert Hart-Davis in the following year. I can only call the attention of my readers to this masterly book, and express once more to Mr. Lewis my homage and my gratitude.

I received great kindness also, when preparing the original edition of this book, from other owners of Walpolian material, who allowed me to quote from manuscripts in their possession or to reproduce portraits from their collections. In particular I would like to thank the Marquess and Marchioness of Cholmondeley, the Earl and Countess Waldegrave, and Lord and Lady Walpole for their interest and assistance. The hereditary connection of their families with Horace Walpole will become apparent in the course of my book, and their houses are richly endowed with his relics. My thanks are also due to the Society of Antiquaries of London, and to the authorities of the Harvard University Library, for permission to use manuscripts belonging to them.

Three men who greatly helped me are now dead. My friend Hugh Gatty, Fellow and Librarian of St. John's College, Cambridge, read every chapter and made many valuable suggestions. The advice of another friend, Leonard Whibley, was especially welcome in the passages dealing with Gray. The poet and scholar E. H. W. Meyerstein, who is now receiving something of the recognition that was denied him during his life, spared the time to read and improve the pages in which the Chatterton episode is discussed.

In my second edition I was able to make use of Dr. A. T. Hazen's *Bibliography of the Strawberry Hill Press* (1942); and I have now verified some further points with the aid of his *Bibliography of Horace Walpole* (1948). I am grateful also to Mr. Lewis's assistants on the Yale Edition, Dr. Warren Hunting Smith, Dr. George L. Lam, and Mr. Ralph S. Brown, for the help they gave me.

Where a letter has been printed in the Yale Edition, I have of course used that text; and I am indebted to Mr. Lewis and to the Yale University Press for permission to do so. Where a letter has not so far appeared in the Yale Edition, I have used the text of Mrs. Paget Toynbee's editon of *The Letters of Horace Walpole* (1903–5) and of Dr. Paget Toynbee's three supplementary volumes to his wife's great work (1918–25), by permission of the Oxford University Press.

Finally, my thanks are due to the Very Rev. V. McCarthy, C.M., formerly Principal of St. Mary's College, Strawberry Hill, and to his successors in that office for their friendly help. The precincts of the College incorporate the entire structure of Walpole's house, which is preserved as a separate entity and cherished with pious affection. It survived the perils of 1939–45 practically undamaged. Incendiaries came through the roof of the Gallery, and were promptly extinguished; the blast from flying bombs shattered some of the painted glass in the Library. Otherwise Walpole's house, a byword for its fragility even in the eighteenth century, has borne with equanimity the ordeals of a more brutal age. Strawberry Hill evidently shares with its creator that quality of "Herculean weakness" which enabled him to outlive almost all of his contemporaries; and long may it yet flourish in the careful hands which now have charge of it.

R. W. K.-C.

June 1963

HORACE WALPOLE

A Biography

I

Introductory

I

HORACE WALPOLE has now emerged from the clouds of critical disapproval which hung around him during much of the last century. For many years it was customary, while admitting the transcendent merits of his letters, to regard their author as the embodiment of malice, affectation and triviality. Much of his serious achievement was dismissed as insignificant; his character was maligned, his integrity as a historian was constantly aspersed, his private caprices as an architect and collector were subjected to the earnest inspection of Victorian moralists. Macaulay's famous essay[1] fixed a caricature of Walpole in the public mind; and the fact that its outlines were based upon the truth does not make it less of a caricature. It was a brilliant distortion of Walpole's personality, drawn by an unsympathetic mind and accepted by an unsympathetic age. Other critics, forgetting Macaulay's generous treatment of certain aspects of Walpole, seldom mentioned him without a sneer at his pettiness, or his inconsistency, or the lack of high seriousness displayed in the building and adornment of Strawberry Hill. The present age looks upon him with a more friendly eye. But traces of the old prejudices still linger; and a biography of Walpole must still assume, to some extent, the nature of a justification or a defence. This book is no exception, It attempts to show Walpole as a kindlier, wiser, more consistent and more straightforward man than our forbears would allow him to be; and it tries to give full value to the extent and variety of his achievement.

[1] *Edinburgh Review* (October 1833).

II

Walpole realized, in his early manhood, how admirably and almost uniquely he was qualified to record the history of his own times for the benefit of posterity. He knew that his health and his private inclinations would prevent him from taking an active part in affairs; but having once determined on his *rôle* as spectator and chronicler, he carried it out with triumphant success, to the immense enrichment of that audience of future centuries which was always in his thoughts. To his other merits as a chronicler, he added a vivid and unflagging consciousness of the service he was doing for posterity. Again and again, the reader of his letters and memoirs is reminded, by allusion or direct invocation, that it is he himself whom Walpole is deliberately and openly addressing. "My care that posterity may know all about it" is his main emotion on hearing of the death of Pelham.[2] "I have everything in the world to tell posterity," he reflects when discussing the numerous preoccupations of his outwardly idle life.[3] His political memoirs and journals, which he kept industriously for the great part of his life, are full of appeals and whispered asides to this unseen audience. His more perceptive friends realized the elaboration and the self-consciousness of the display. "I can figure no being happier than Horry," wrote Gilly Williams. *"Monstrari digito praetereuntium* has been his whole aim. For this he has wrote, printed and built."[4]

He developed his plans for the enlightenment of posterity with great care and forethought. He set down, in his historical *Memoirs,* a formal narrative of political occurrences; and at the same time, in private letters to his friends, he provided an illustrative commentary which could enlighten posterity as to the subtleties and undertones, the anecdotes and manners and social trivialities, which formed the background to the march of great events. Some of his correspondences were evidently designed at first to serve as rough material and useful memoranda for a more serious type of history. But he never underestimated the value

[2] *Lewis,* xx. 414 (Walpole to Mann, March 7, 1754).

[3] *Toynbee,* iv. 403 (Walpole to Conway, June 28, 1760).

[4] *Jesse,* i. 310 (Gilly Williams to George Selwyn, October 19, 1764). The quotation is from Horace, *Odes* IV. iii. 22.

of the letters themselves; and in time he came to regard them as of equal importance with the *Memoirs,* and as likely to rank higher in the favour of the great non-specialist mass of posterity—as indeed they emphatically do. I have attempted in this book to show with what subtlety he organized the whole scheme of his correspondence. He selected with great care the friends whom he proposed to favour with his letters; he saw to it that each particular branch of his activities and interests—politics, literature, antiquarianism, social life—should be regularly depicted in a series of letters addressed to an appropriate correspondent; and if, by death or disagreement, he lost one of these "key" correspondents, the gap was filled with as little delay as possible, so that the narrative of events should not suffer. It is impossible to exaggerate either his solicitude for posterity, or the skill with which he ensured that his varied records should reach posterity in the most complete and attractive form.

III

One of the difficulties which confront a biographer of Walpole is his remarkable versatility. He was active in so many fields—in politics, social life, literature, architecture, antiquarianism, printing, *virtù;* and it is not easy to include them all in the compass of a single volume. Even more intimidating is the tremendous bulk of material, published and unpublished, that Walpole left behind him. His correspondence alone runs to nineteen very substantial volumes in the Toynbee edition, and in Mr. Lewis's Yale edition may probably exceed fifty volumes. His literary works, printed in his lifetime or posthumously, together with the *Memoirs of the Reign of George II,* the *Memoirs of the Reign of George III,* and the *Last Journals,* swell the total of his writings to a very formidable figure indeed. Specialists in Walpole's various branches of activity must forgive my necessarily inadequate treatment of those subjects in which their particular interest lies.

Macaulay dwelt with particular severity on Walpole's frivolous and amateurish attitude to politics. "After the labours of the print-shop and the auction-room, he unbent his mind in the House of Commons. And, having indulged in the recreation of making laws and voting millions, he returned to more important pursuits, to researches after Queen Mary's comb, Wolsey's red hat, the pipe which Van Tromp smoked during his last sea-fight, and the spur which King William struck into the flank of Sorrel." In this book I have treated Walpole's political career in some detail, and have tried to show the injustice of Macaulay's view. Walpole was an enthusiastic politician, constantly present in the House throughout his twenty-seven years in Parliament, listening to every speech and taking copious and reliable notes for his *Memoirs.* Although his physique and voice prevented him from speaking regularly, he was always busy behind the scenes; and there was always some more conspicuous politician—Fox, Rigby, and above all Conway—who relied on his advice and through whom he could make his own views felt. If it is thought that I have said too much about Walpole's political opinions and intrigues, my excuse is that insufficient attention has been paid to them in the past.

IV

When a man deliberately consigns to posterity some thousands of his own private letters, he is subjecting his character and conduct to the searching criticism of generations of future readers. In the course of a life, every one is guilty of inconsistencies, contradictions, changes of opinion, breaches of friendship; but these appear both more numerous and more flagrant if they can be found assembled together in an index. Macaulay described Walpole as "the most fickle, the most inconstant of men"; and contrasted, among other examples, his opinions on the institution of monarchy with his actual conduct towards royal persons. But Walpole lived to see his eightieth year; and it was hardly inconsistent to profess a mild republicanism under George II, and yet to be horrified and outraged, forty years later, by the execution of Marie Antoinette. Similarly, when he knelt at the door of Strawberry Hill to kiss the hand of the silly young Duke of York, Lady Louisa Stuart has explained, "with the good leave of a swarm of magazine critics that never saw his face," that this action was not a piece of inconsistent servility on the part of one who often proclaimed his indifference to kings. "He probably had a politic view quite unsuspected by the aforesaid critics: that of warding off too close an intimacy, and preventing the illustrious young gentleman from skipping in and out of his house at pleasure."[5] Lady Louisa Stuart, that remarkable survival of the eighteenth century, could understand and respect Walpole's behaviour; but the less sympathetic age into which she survived had forgotten the subtleties of conduct and motive by which his life was regulated. Its "magazine-critics" were already interpreting him, in harsher and cruder terms, to their contemporaries; and their interpretation of his character is still sometimes accepted in the present age.

Walpole had faults and absurdities, and the most has been made of them. He could be petty and malicious. He had a feminine element which occasionally rose to the surface in the form of violent jealousy or spite. He gossiped with old ladies for days on end; he was fond of china and goldfish and little dogs; he committed every architectural absurdity in the building and adornment of his house; he stuck sweet peas in his hair and sang to a roomful of dowagers at their card-tables; he could never quite forget, however familiarly he met them in social life, that Reynolds was a painter and Garrick a player. How often this solemn and perfectly veracious catalogue of his shortcomings has been repeated!

Less attention has been paid to the qualities of kindness, loyalty, and tolerance which were pre-eminent in Walpole. Madame du Deffand ended her *Portrait* of him with the words: "Vos sentiments sont nobles et généreux, vous faites le bien pour le plaisir de le faire, sans ostentation, sans prétendre à la reconnaissance; enfin votre âme est belle et bonne."[6] This was no loving exaggeration on the part of the old Frenchwoman, whose picture of Walpole was remarkably frank as well as perceptive. Walpole's essential kindness of heart was constantly being revealed in his actions, just as Pinkerton, not always a friendly critic, observed it in "the placid goodness of his eyes."[7] From relating some malicious story in a letter, or drawing a savage portrait of a politician in his *Memoirs,* he would turn to acts of unostentatious charity. His notes to his deputy at the Exchequer, Grosvenor Bedford,

[5] *Coke,* i. lxxxvi-vii (introduction by Lady Louisa Stuart).

[6] *Lewis,* viii. 72. [7] *Walpoliana,* xl.

are filled with little commissions of this kind. Would Mr. Bedford inquire if the persons mentioned in certain advertisements were genuine objects of charity, and if so would he leave a guinea for each of them? Would he send one of the Exchequer porters with two guineas for the sick prisoners in Southwark Jail, and one for those in the Marshalsea Prison?[8] He was unfailingly sympathetic and considerate towards the poor, the unhappy and the obscure. It was not the act of a selfish man to remain in London through a sweltering August, watching the last illness of old Mrs. Leneve, who had been his mother's and sister's companion.[9] He displayed the same unselfish spirit when he discovered, late in life, that a hitherto unknown natural daughter of his father was living in poverty, and maintained his half-sister—unattractively described by Cole as of a "squab, short, gummy appearance, rather undersized and snub-faced"—in comfort at Strawberry Hill until she died.[10] The world, of course, could know nothing of this goodness and decency and quiet generosity. By the unkind irony of circumstance, Walpole was regarded by many of his contemporaries as a mean and cold-hearted personage, because of his supposed responsibility for the death of Chatterton. He had never set eyes on Chatterton, and could in no imaginable way be blamed for his suicide; yet the belief in his guilt persisted to the end of his life and for many years afterwards.

He hated injustice and persecution, and every sort of bigotry and intolerance. When Admiral Byng, a man with whom he had no personal acquaintance, was condemned to death in order to satisfy popular clamour, he made tireless efforts to save him. He had a fervent sense of family loyalty, and not only towards the splendid memory of his father; his attempts to help the fatuous nephew who sold the pictures of Houghton and wrecked the estate, and the drudgery and ingratitude to which he submitted in the process, are striking proofs of his determination that the glory of the family should be maintained. His loyalty towards his friends was of the same order. From two or three he became

[8] *Toynbee,* v. 246, vi. 23 (Walpole to Bedford, September 24, 1762; February 29, 1764).

[9] *Lewis,* xxi. 416 (Walpole to Mann, August 8, 1759).

[10] *Ibid.,* ii. 370–2 (Cole's Account of his Visit to Strawberry Hill, October 29–31, 1774).

estranged, from no apparent fault of his own; with two, Gray and Mason, he quarrelled and was later reconciled; otherwise no man can ever have had a wider, a more varied or a more faithful circle of friends.

In personal relationships, throughout his life, Walpole endeavoured to shun emotion and to cultivate detachment. He used often to repeat one of his favourite *bons mots:* "This world is a comedy to those who think, a tragedy to those who feel."[11] He had his share of tragedy; a mind so sensitive could not hope to escape: and the things that he felt most deeply in his life—his mother's death, his devotion to his cousin Henry Conway, the love for Mary Berry which delighted and distracted his old age—bore witness to the truth of his saying. He preferred to regard the world as a comedy; and it flowed past him gaily and agreeably, full of amusement and interest, for almost eighty happy years. He had chosen to be a spectator, and he never regretted his choice.

[11] *Works,* ix. 369 *(Detached Thoughts). Toynbee,* ix. 403 (Walpole to Lady Ossory, August 16, 1776).

II

Parentage, Childhood and Schooldays (1717-35)

I

THE Walpoles are a family of great antiquity. They are said to have owned land at Walpole, in Norfolk, in the eleventh century or even earlier; and in any case their acquisition of the nucleus of their estate at Houghton, also in Norfolk, dates from the thirteenth century.[1] But until the sudden emergence of Sir Robert Walpole as one of England's greatest Prime Ministers, they had farmed their land and carried out their local and, occasionally, their Parliamentary duties in comparative obscurity. There were a few remarkable exceptions: a vigorous mediæval prelate; a Jesuit martyr under Elizabeth; a marriage (much emphasized at Strawberry Hill) with the romantic family of the Robsarts. Otherwise the Walpoles lived quietly upon their gradually increasing estates for generation after generation, laying up those stores of experience, of caution, of shrewdness, of sheer practical ability which one of their descendants was to expend upon the guidance of England.

Sir Robert Walpole's grandfather and father were still true to this type. They sat in Parliament for King's Lynn or Castle Rising, and their infrequent speeches were heard with respect. But their main interests lay in the vigorous, obstinate, litigious Nor-

[1] See "The Origin of the Walpoles" in *Family Origins and other Studies* by the late J. Horace Round. This short essay is probably the most authoritative account of the early pedigree of the Walpole family. Dr. Round could not discover any proof that the Walpoles of Houghton were descended from the Walpoles of Walpole. "We fail to find either at Houghton or Walpole any proof of the Walpole pedigree before John de Walpole, who was living apparently about the middle of the thirteenth century" (p. 52).

folk of the seventeenth century, with its bustling trade at Norwich, its crowded shipping at Yarmouth and Lynn, its busy market-towns and prosperous villages: the Norfolk where Sir Thomas Browne wrote *Urn Burial* and *The Garden of Cyrus,* and dedicated them to the country gentlemen whom he doctored: the Norfolk which had been almost solid for the Parliament against the King, and which presently welcomed the King's son at its great houses—Oxnead, Blickling, Raynham, the vanished palace of the Howards in Norwich—in one of the most successful progresses ever undertaken by an English sovereign through his realm.

II

Robert Walpole was born on August 26th, 1676. He was the third son and fifth child of Robert Walpole of Houghton, Member of Parliament for Castle Rising, and his wife Mary Burwell, a Suffolk lady. He was educated at Eton and King's College, Cambridge: and was removed prematurely from the latter seat of learning by his father, who intended "that Robert should become the first grazier in the country."[2] So the younger Robert Walpole supervised the sale of his father's cattle each market-day at Swaffham or Fakenham, while the elder Robert Walpole attended to his Parliamentary duties. During a winter session of three months his entire expenses in London amounted to sixty-four pounds seven shillings and five pence. "He little thought," Horace Walpole was to write some fifty years later, "that what maintained him for a whole sessions, would scarce serve one of his younger grandsons to buy Japan and fans for princesses at Florence."[3]

The elder Robert Walpole died in 1700; and the younger Robert Walpole succeeded, at the age of twenty-four, to the estate at Houghton, by now of a very considerable extent, and to the representation of Castle Rising. Shortly before his father's death he had somewhat broken the Walpole tradition by marrying, not a gentlewoman of East Anglia, but the daughter of a wealthy Baltic timber merchant, John Shorter of Bybrook in Kent, the son of Sir John Shorter, Lord Mayor of London in 1688. Catherine

[2] *Coxe* i. 5.

[3] *Lewis,* xvii. 506 (Walpole to Mann, July 21, 1742).

Shorter brought him a very handsome dowry, and in the course of time bore him six children. The eldest son, Robert, was born in 1701; a daughter Mary in 1705; and a second son, Edward, in 1706. Another son, William, died in infancy, and a second daughter, Catherine, also died young. And the youngest child of all, Horatio—a name which from his earliest years was usually contracted to Horace—was born at his father's house in Arlington Street on September 24th, 1717.

By the time of the birth of his youngest child, Robert Walpole had been Secretary at War during some of Marlborough's most important campaigns; had been sent to the Tower on a charge of corruption; had become, on the accession of George I, the most powerful man in Parliament; and, mainly as a protest against the King's foreign policy, and to the King's extreme surprise and indignation, had lately resigned the Seals of First Lord of the Treasury and Chancellor of the Exchequer. To such a position of influence had already risen the young man in whom his father had hoped to behold Norfolk's most prominent grazier.

III

It might have been expected that Horace Walpole's singular lack of resemblance, alike in physique, in manners and in interests, to his father and brothers would have caused much comment in the gossip-haunted society in which he moved. He was indeed an unexpected type to emerge from the jovial country-loving generations of the Walpoles, and the worthy commercial stock of the Shorters. But in no contemporary letter of a friend or enemy, in none of the pamphlets or lampoons directed against his father or against himself, is there any whisper of a doubt as to his paternity. It was Lady Louisa Stuart, retailing in the eighteen-thirties the gossip which had descended from her grandmother Lady Mary Wortley Montagu, who first set down in writing a new and, at first sight, plausible story. "In a word, Horace Walpole himself was generally supposed to be the son of Carr Lord Hervey, and Sir Robert not to be ignorant of it. One striking circumstance was visible to the naked eye; no beings in human shape could resemble each other less than the two passing for father and son; and, while their *reverse* of personal likeness provoked a malicious whisper, Sir Robert's marked neglect of Horace in his infancy tended to confirm it."[4] Lady Louisa, it should be observed, did not attribute this story entirely to her grandmother, who had died, incidentally, when she was a child of five. She related it as a fact known apparently to every one except Horace Walpole himself; as if the son of a bitterly hated statesman, and a man who was himself the object of much ridicule and malice, would have been allowed to remain ignorant of a circumstance so rich in potential humiliation and insult. In spite of the protestations of her grand-daughter, one is inclined to give Lady Mary the responsibility for the legend. It would have been easy for her, a resentful old woman brooding in Venice or Brescia on her brilliant youth, to associate Horace Walpole with the fragile, febrile, erratic Herveys rather than with

> the lively eyes and rosy hue
> Of Robin's face, when Robin first I knew.[5]

Her early hatreds lasted sourly into old age; and she had been at enmity with Horace Walpole's mother, and a close friend of her rival, Sir Robert's mistress Maria Skerrett. Admittedly, Catherine Walpole's occasional gallantries seem to have been well known to the world and accepted by her husband. "Sir Robert it is likely is not very sorry," wrote Lord Egmont in his diary at the time of her death: "she was as gallant, if report be true, with the men as he with the women, nevertheless they continued to live together and take their pleasures their own way without giving offence."[6] But there is no contemporary evidence whatever for the suggestion that Lord Hervey was the father of Horace Walpole; and none to show that Sir Robert believed Horace not to be his own son, and neglected him in infancy on that or any other account.

Furthermore, Mr. Romney Sedgwick has pointed out that the delicate and eccentric strain in the Hervey family appears to have been transmitted through a Lady Bristol who was the mother of John Lord Hervey, the celebrated "Lord Fanny," but not of his

[4] *Montagu* i. xcii-iii. Lady Louisa Stuart contributed an admirable set of "Introductory Anecdotes" to her nephew Lord Wharncliffe's edition of Lady Mary's letters and works, which was first published in 1837.

[5] *Ibid.*, ii. 500 *(On Seeing a Portrait of Sir Robert Walpole).*

[6] *H.M.C., Egmont MSS,* ii. 431 (August 24, 1737).

half-brother Carr Lord Hervey, the supposed father of Horace Walpole.[7] Mr. Sedgwick has also suggested that some confusion may have arisen over the rumours, which certainly were current and probably were well-founded, about the parentage of the third Earl of Orford, the only child of Sir Robert's eldest son.[8] The second Lady Orford had a well-known *liaison* with Sir George Oxenden; and even Horace Walpole himself, that pattern of family loyalty, in moments of temper would speak of his nephew's dubious legitimacy.[9] Taking into account Mr. Sedgwick's arguments, the complete silence of Walpole's contemporaries as to any doubt of his birth, and the extremely slender foundations of Lady Louisa Stuart's story, it may be assumed with some confidence that Sir Robert was his father.[10]

Lady Walpole seems to have been an attractive, extravagant, rather weak and unambitious woman. Long before Horace's birth, she had begun to lose her husband's affections; and whether or no their mutual complaisance was so great as rumour suggested, she must have keenly resented her husband's preoccupation with "Moll Skerrett," which dated from a few years earlier. She had to spend most of her time between the house in Arlington Street and another house in Chelsea, where the family retired during the summer; while Miss Skerrett accompanied Sir Robert to the half-finished splendours of Houghton, or entertained his friends at his hunting-lodge in Richmond Park. Gay made use of the situation in *The Beggar's Opera,* in which Macheath's embarrassment between Polly and Lucy, and his song *How happy could I be with either,* delighted the Opposition. This neglect caused Lady Walpole to devote to her youngest child the principal share of her time and her affection; to which he responded with that passionate love for her which Lady Louisa Stuart pronounced to be "so

[7] *Hervey,* xiv.

[8] *From Anne to Victoria,* "Horace Walpole" by Romney Sedgwick. See also *Hervey,* 742.

[9] *Toynbee,* xi. 405: "the late Countess's most doubtful son" (Walpole to Mann February 26, 1781). *Farington,* i. 149.

[10] I would, however, draw attention to the discussion of this matter by Dr. J. H. Plumb in *Sir Robert Walpole: the Making of a Statesman* (1956), 257–9. Dr. Plumb considers that the doubts as to Horace's paternity "may not have been without substance."

much the most amiable point in his character."[11] And in spite of Miss Skerrett and the problematical Lord Hervey, and other mistresses and lovers now forgotten, there seems to have been a reasonable degree of harmony between his equable and tolerant parents. There is every indication in his earliest letters, those laborious scrawls which he sent home from his first school, of a happy and normal family life. "Dear mama I hop you are wall and I am very wall and I hop papa is well and I begin to slaap and I hop all wall and my cosens liks thers pla things vary wall and I hop Doly phillips is wall and pray give my Duty to papa...and I am very glad to hear by Tom that all my cruatuars ar all wall."[12]

IV

Sir Robert Walpole had a younger brother, Horatio, after whom the subject of this book was named. He was one of Sir Robert's most stalwart and reliable supporters, and undertook successful embassies in Holland and France in addition to his work in Parliament. His fine house at Wolterton in Norfolk was under construction at the same time as his brother's new mansion at Houghton. In 1720 he married a lady named Mary Lombard, by whom he had several children, the eldest of whom was also christened Horatio. The elder Horatio retained, to a much greater extent than Sir Robert, the provincial accent and manners of Norfolk: he was uncouth in person, and his wife was even more homely. Horace Walpole joined from an early age in the ridicule which was lavished on this extremely able Ambassador and his family; but in later years he grew more friendly with his cousins of this branch.

Two of Sir Robert's sisters married Norfolk gentlemen, Sir Charles Turner of King's Lynn and Anthony Hamond of South Wootton. A third sister, Dorothy, later married Lord Townshend, a middle-aged widower. This match was of great importance to Sir Robert, as Townshend was one of his most valued colleagues in Parliament, and the only man with an influence equal to his own in Norfolk. The alliance between Houghton and Raynham

[11] *Montagu,* i. xcii.

[12] *Toynbee,* Supplement, i. 1 (Horace Walpole to Lady Walpole, undated [1725]).

Prince of Wales. He was received by the Prince with a coldness that amounted to dismissal, and told to take his orders from the Speaker, Sir Spencer Compton. A multitude of enemies awaited his final fall. His son Horace, walking in procession at Eton to the proclamation of the new King, was suddenly overcome by the thought of the old monarch in the blue riband and snuff-coloured clothes, and burst into a flood of tears: "though I think they partly fell because I imagined it became the son of a Prime Minister to be more concerned than other boys." The spectators, he afterwards supposed, must have imputed these tears to some rumour of his father's impending disgrace: but he had heard nothing of such a possibility.[16] And in any case he need have had no apprehensions for his father. The new Queen had long ago realized the unique abilities of Sir Robert Walpole. They had been for some years on terms of alliance and friendship; and when she told her husband that his new minister, Sir Spencer Compton, had been reduced to sending for the fallen minister, Sir Robert Walpole, to assist him in the composition of the King's first speech in Council,[17] George II began to modify the instinctive hatred with which he regarded any man whom his father had delighted to honour. After a period of anxious suspense, and much intrigue and bargaining on all sides, the influence of Queen Caroline began to prevail. At this vital moment, Walpole undertook to produce a Civil List of far greater emolument, both to the King and Queen, than anything that his rivals could venture to put forward. The King's lingering prejudices were finally overcome; and he urged Walpole, in the warmest terms, to become the chief of his Ministers. Less than a month after the old King's death, Walpole found himself back in office, and in a stronger position than before; and he embarked, secure in the confidence of the King and the firm and active support of the Queen, on the period of his most effective statesmanship and his most unchallenged power.

VI

There is a singular placidity, an almost pastoral air, about the life which Horace Walpole and his circle of intimate friends ap-

[16] *Ibid.*, 276. [17] *Ibid.*, 294–5, *Hervey*, 25–6.

pear to have led at Eton. They regarded with unconcern the daily rough and tumble in which their more normal school-fellows were involved. The Eton through whose "watery glade" they sauntered so demurely was also the scene of tremendous fights and savage floggings, of occasional riots and rebellions, of permanent and bloody warfare against townsmen and bargees. Walpole and his friends dismissed all such things as barbarisms beneath their notice, and rejoiced in the completeness of their detachment. "Dear George, were not the playing fields at Eton food for all manner of flights? . . . At first I was contented with tending a visionary flock, and sighing some pastoral name to the echo of the cascade under the bridge: how happy should I have been to have had a kingdom, only for the pleasure of being driven from it, and living disguised in an humble vale. As I got further into Virgil and *Clelia,* I found myself transported from Arcadia to the garden of Italy, and saw Windsor Castle in no other view than the *capitoli immobile saxum*. . . . I can't say I am sorry I was never quite a school-boy; an expedition against bargemen, or a match at cricket, may be very pretty things to recollect; but thank my stars, I can remember things that are very near as pretty. The beginning of my Roman history was spent in the Asylum, or conversing in Egeria's hallowed grove; not in thumping and pummelling King Amulius's herdsmen."[18] The Eton of the eighteenth century, the brutal, rowdy, vigorous nursery of so many great men, becomes a sanctuary in which a group of delicate and retiring boys found a peace and security which they remembered to the end of their days.

> Ah happy hills, ah pleasing shade,
> Ah fields belov'd in vain,
> Where once my careless childhood stray'd,
> A stranger yet to pain!
> I feel the gales, that from ye blow,
> A momentary bliss bestow,
> As waving fresh their gladsome wing.
> My weary soul they seem to soothe,
> And, redolent of joy and youth,
> To breathe a second spring. . . .[19]

[18] *Lewis,* ix. 3–4 (Walpole to George Montagu, May 6, 1736).
[19] Gray, *Ode on a Distant Prospect of Eton College,* 11–20.

Horace Walpole's tutor at Eton was the Reverend Henry Bland, the eldest son of Doctor Bland, the Master of the School. It would appear, from a letter written a few years later, that he displayed towards his tutor the same calm detachment with which he regarded the majority of his school-fellows. "I remember when I was at Eton, and Mr. Bland had set me any extraordinary task, I used sometimes to pique myself upon not getting it, because it was not immediately my school business. What! learn more than I am absolutely forced to learn! I felt the weight of learning that; for I was a blockhead, and pushed up above my parts."[20]

This show of happy idleness, and also the touch of obstinate pride which maintained it in defiance of Mr. Bland, are very characteristic of Horace Walpole. After all, he was the Prime Minister's son; and if his tutor thought fit, for that reason or any other, to promote him beyond his deserts, he would not gratify his tutor by a display of unnecessary diligence. Eton and Windsor, their tranquil meadows surrounding the ancient buildings, were the home of beauty and dignity and tradition. They were always to be associated in Walpole's thoughts, not with Mr. Bland and his extraordinary tasks, but with vague Virgilian musings, with the dreaming of gentle pastoral nonsense, on the banks of the placid Thames, by privileged and sentimental youths. And they were always to be connected very intimately with the pleasures of friendship. For Walpole's Eton friendships were numerous and warm, and some of them lasted as long as life.

His earliest friends were probably his cousins, Francis and Henry Seymour Conway, whose mother was the sister of Lady Walpole. He became strongly attached to both these cousins, and especially to Henry Conway, whose military and political career he afterwards followed with passionate interest, and towards whom he felt a more consistent and lasting devotion than he was able to extend to any other person. Other friends, all more or less of his own age and standing, were Charles Lyttelton, who developed into an amiable clergyman of antiquarian tastes, and died Bishop of Carlisle; George Selwyn, the celebrated wit and gambler; and George Montagu, a man of pleasant humour and overmastering indolence, who was one of Walpole's most favoured

[20] *Toynbee*, ii. 29 (Walpole to Conway, June 29, 1744).

correspondents for the greater part of his life. Another future correspondent, the antiquary William Cole, was also friendly with him at Eton, and used to be invited to his home at Chelsea.[21] Walpole established, with Lyttelton and Montagu, a sort of schoolboy confederacy which they called the Triumvirate.[22] But the Triumvirate was second in importance to another confederacy known as the Quadruple Alliance, which he formed with three less aristocratic and more intellectual boys, Thomas Gray, Richard West and Thomas Ashton.

Walpole was younger by about a year than the other members of the Quadruple Alliance. He was decidedly their social superior; they all came from middle-class and rather impecunious homes, and homes (at any rate those of Gray and West) which for one reason or another were divided and unhappy. They were studious, retiring, rather moody youths; and they were naturally attracted by the vitality and assurance of the younger boy, and were mildly flattered, even in the democratic atmosphere of Eton, by the friendship of Sir Robert Walpole's son. Gray and West, dazzled by Walpole's charm, and struck by the contrast between his background of wealth and power and their own depressing circumstances, came to feel for him a devoted attachment which was no less warmly returned. Ashton was probably well aware, even at that early age, of his chances of future advancement through the influence of the Walpole family.

Thomas Gray was the only child of a London scrivener and his wife; the latter ran "a kind of India warehouse" with the aid of an unmarried sister. His father was a violent and eccentric character, who refused to pay anything towards the boy's education: and his school expenses were paid by Mrs. Gray and her sister out of the profits of their shop, with some additional help, probably, from one of their brothers, who was a tutor at Eton. His holidays were spent miserably at home, or rather forlornly at the houses of his more kindly uncles and aunts. Eton, and the friendships which he made there, gave him the earliest and the most unclouded happiness that he was to know.

West seems to have been in a rather similar position. He was the

[21] *Cole,* 54.

[22] *Lewis,* ix. 4 (Walpole to Montagu, May 6, 1736).

only son of a distinguished lawyer who became Lord Chancellor of Ireland, and his mother was a daughter of Bishop Burnet. His father died when he was ten years old; and his mother, whom he loved devotedly, entered upon a love affair with her late husband's secretary. This *liaison* does not seem to have been known to West until he reached manhood; it is said that his early death was caused by his discovery of it. But his childhood under such circumstances cannot have been a happy one; and he also found consolation at Eton and in the company of his friends. He was a shy, pale, delicate boy, and was thought at Eton to be the most promising scholar and poet of the Quadruple Alliance.

Ashton was the son of a Lancaster schoolmaster. His character was a curiously unendearing one, and in the end he behaved with treachery both to Walpole and Gray. His letters, with their irritating blend of jauntiness and servility, support the accepted view that he was a decidedly unpleasant person. And yet he must have possessed some qualities which gained him the affection and confidence of Walpole and Gray, who were fastidious even in their youth, during a period of fifteen or twenty years. The exact nature of these qualities will never be known: but they were gradually obliterated by ambition and self-interest, until the "Dear Child" of Walpole's earlier letters came to be contemptuously dismissed as "a Mr. Ashton, a clergyman."[23]

The Quadruple Alliance was a much more romantic affair than the Triumvirate. There was nothing really very pastoral about George Montagu or Charles Lyttelton. But Gray and West were poets by temperament and by habit; and all four friends were literary and sentimental and intellectually precocious. They studied the English poets as well as Virgil and Propertius, and exchanged verses of their own making; they were deeply read in English plays and French romances, and found magnificent titles for one another in those flowery pages. Gray was Orosmades; West and Ashton were Favonius and Almanzor; Walpole received the name of Celadon, borne by many shepherds of poetry and romance.

They formed a loyal and united group, and their friendship endured long after their schooldays. Their correspondence reveals

[23] *Ibid.*, xx. 164 (Walpole to Mann, July 25, 1750).

how firmly the conception of the Quadruple Alliance persisted, in spite of vicissitude and separation. It broke up eventually: Walpole and Gray quarrelled; West died; Walpole and Gray were reconciled, but each found it necessary to terminate his friendship with Ashton. But throughout their University days, and beyond them, the Alliance stood fast.

West seems to have left Eton during 1733. The other three friends remained until the following year. Walpole has recorded that he finally left Eton on September 23rd, 1734, the day before his seventeenth birthday. In 1735 he joined Gray and Ashton at Cambridge; while West, who had been sent to Christ Church, wandered disconsolately through the groves of Oxford, dreaming of his friends. There is a very moving note in a poem which he wrote in the Walks of Magdalen, and sent in a letter to Walpole.

> The thought which still my breast invades,
> Nigh yonder springs, nigh yonder shades,
> Still, as I pass, the memory brings
> Of sweeter shades and springs.
>
> Lost and inwrapt in thought profound,
> Absent I tread Etonian ground;
> Then starting from the dear mistake,
> As disenchanted, wake...
>
> Oh! how I long again with those,
> Whom first my boyish heart had chose,
> Together through the friendly shade
> To stray, as once I stray'd.
>
> Their presence would the scene endear,
> Like paradise would all appear,
> More sweet around the flowers would blow,
> More soft the waters flow.[24]

[24] *Ibid.*, xiii. 110–1 (West to Walpole, August 20, 1736).

III

Cambridge (1735-9)

I

GRAY began residence at Peterhouse in October 1734. Ashton had been admitted a scholar at King's in August. They were lonely and depressed at Cambridge; and the more sociable Walpole, when he presently joined them at the University, was struck with their friendless state. "Orosmades and Almanzor are just the same; that is, I am almost the only person they are acquainted with, and consequently the only person acquainted with their excellencies."[1] Gray in particular, ever critical and fastidious in his contacts with his fellow-men, found Cambridge very tedious, and sought consolation in an elaborate correspondence with Walpole. His letters used to arrive with the greatest frequency, sometimes two and three in a week—letters overflowing with wit and affection; railing endlessly at the pedantry and dullness, the "hogsheads of liquor and quantities of Tobacco," which weighed so heavily upon Cambridge; filled with exuberant and childish terms of endearment, many of which Walpole thought fit to expunge in later years. They show clearly how intense was the devotion which Walpole had inspired in Gray. And when Walpole finally appeared at Cambridge, the delight of "a long ungainly mortal at King's College, and a little, waddling Freshman of Peterhouse" knew no bounds.

Walpole began his residence as a Fellow-Commoner of King's on March 11th, 1735. He remained at Cambridge for almost four years; but his periods of actual residence there were brief and irregular. Nevertheless the details given in *Short Notes of My Life*

[1] *Lewis,* xiii. 94 (Walpole to West, November 9, 1735).

show that for some while he took Cambridge fairly seriously. "My public tutor was Mr. John Smith; my private, Mr. Anstey: afterwards Mr. John Whaley was my tutor. I went to lectures in civil law to Dr. Dickins, of Trinity Hall; to mathematical lectures to blind Professor Saunderson, for a short time; afterwards, Mr. Trevigar read lectures to me in mathematics and philosophy. I heard Dr. Battie's anatomical lectures. I had learned French at Eton. I learnt Italian at Cambridge of Signor Piazza. At home I learned to dance and fence; and to draw of Bernard Lens, master to the Duke and Princesses."[2] His attempts to learn mathematics with Professor Saunderson were not a success. After a fortnight, the old Professor announced that it was cheating him to take his money, as there was no possibility that he would ever learn any mathematics. Walpole has recorded that he wept with mortification, and engaged a private instructor; but at the end of the year he was forced to own that the Professor had been right. And certainly his Strawberry Hill account-books, piously edited by Dr. Paget Toynbee, contain some of the shakiest arithmetic that has ever been committed to paper. Nor can he have benefited greatly from the instructions of another of his tutors. According to Cole, "excessive Drinking, high and luxurious Eating, and other riotous Behaviour was the daily and Common Way of Life with Mr. Whaley," who was so fastidious that he could seldom bear to dine in Hall, never drank any wine that did not come from France, and eventually became "sleek and fat as a Mole."[3]

Beyond the list of his tutors, few memorials have survived of Walpole's life at Cambridge. He contributed a Latin poem to the *Gratulatio* published by the University on the marriage of the Prince of Wales in 1736. He went through a phase of religious excitement, and used to go with Ashton to pray with the prisoners in Cambridge gaol.[4] He exchanged commiserating letters with West about their "two barbarous towns o'er-run with rusticity and mathematics,"[5] and later visited him at Oxford, which he found "one of the most agreeable places I ever set my eyes on." He did not in any way share Gray's vehement dislike of Cambridge; he was able to come and go as he pleased, no shadows of an academic

[2] *Ibid.*, 6–7 *(Short Notes of My Life).*

[3] *Cole*, 75. [4] *Restitua*, iii. 50.

[5] *Lewis*, xiii. 94 (Walpole to West, November 9, 1735).

life were gathering around him, and he was able to regard the place and its inhabitants with his customary detachment. But he expressed no affection for Cambridge until many years afterwards, when he would experience on his occasional visits an after-dinner wistfulness for the pleasures of a cloistered life.

Only one person at Cambridge exerted any influence on Walpole's intellectual development—Doctor Conyers Middleton, the celebrated and unorthodox theologian. Middleton's personal qualities attracted many of the young men of Walpole's generation, even such pillars of orthodoxy as Gray and Cole; but Walpole himself readily accepted the sceptical conclusions to which Middleton's writings ultimately led, and adhered to them with little variation till the end of his days. In a lifetime of controversy and pamphleteering, Middleton had assailed a number of the essential doctrines of the Church in which he was a beneficed clergyman. Most of his brethren of the cloth regarded him as little better than an infidel; but he was ambitious for preferment, and eagerly cultivated the friendship of such politicians as were in sympathy with his religious views. He corresponded regularly with Lord Hervey, and had dedicated to that nobleman his *Life of Cicero* in terms of such fervent eulogy that Pope was inspired to remark how

> Narcissus, praised with all a parson's power,
> Looked a white lily sunk beneath a shower.[6]

But Sir Robert Walpole was a greater man than Narcissus, and Middleton was careful to ensure the friendship of his intelligent young son. His polite flatteries of Horace brought him no very tangible reward. No Deanery or fat Crown living resulted from his delicate suggestion that the young man should inform Sir Robert that "you have a client, who, in the decline of life, would be proud to receive from him, what he never received, or asked before from any minister, some mark of public favour, proper to his character and profession."[7] But, in spite of the failure of his hopes, Middleton remained on the friendliest terms with Horace Walpole even after Sir Robert's fall. Walpole, for his part, always retained his affection and respect for Middleton; and his religious

[6] *Dunciad,* Book IV. 103–4.

[7] *Toynbee,* Supplement, i. 6 n. (Middleton to Walpole, December 25, 1736).

views, the vague and tepid deism which was his creed, his impatience with all devotional enthusiasm whether Papist or Methodist, his hatred of superstition and bigotry, may be entirely attributed to his early preceptor.

Probably the most important event during his years at Cambridge was the visit he paid to his father at Houghton in the summer of 1736. Sir Robert's magnificent new house had been completed in the previous year, and his love of hospitality could at last be fully gratified. Horace had never visited his ancestral county before, and looked forward with some alarm to a period of uproarious jollity at Houghton. Gray sent shuddering condolences: "You are in a Confusion of Wine and Bawdy and Hunting and Tobacco; and heaven be praised, you too can pretty well bear it. . . . I imagine however you'll rather chuse to converse with the living Dead, that adorn the Walls of your Apartments, than with the Dead living, that deck the middles of them, and prefer a picture of Still-life to the realities of a noisy one."[8] But in fact Walpole was delighted with Houghton, and not only with its incomparable pictures. He was almost alone during the first week of his visit, and had time to enjoy the unexpected beauty of the woodlands and wide heaths, the vast spreading landscapes and blue distances of Norfolk; and to linger in the "charming garden all wilderness, much adapted to my romantic inclinations." In the second week he had friends of his own to stay; and throughout his time at Houghton he was spared any contact with his two aversions, hunting and country gentlemen.[9] But the visit was something of a landmark in his life because it gave him an opportunity to appreciate for the first time, and in their true perspective, the personality and achievement of Sir Robert Walpole. Hitherto he had only known him as a distant and preoccupied statesman, and had resented on his mother's behalf the presence in the background of Miss Skerrett. But at Houghton he had visible proofs of his father's greatness in that noble house, filled with a collection of works of art unsurpassed in England, and surrounded with a stately park and vast plantations, which rose where a small country manor-house had stood a few years before among its enclosures and heaths and stony pastures. In this splendid setting,

[8] *Lewis*, xiii. 104 (Gray to Walpole, July 15, 1736).

[9] *Toynbee*, i. 19 (Walpole to Lyttelton, July 27, 1736).

Sir Robert was at his best; his geniality, his wisdom, his unruffled kindliness and good humour were more than ever apparent when he was at Houghton. And the atmosphere of horses and hounds and bawdy jokes and huge draughts of "hogan," which hung round him and which blended so curiously with his other background of a great man ruling a great nation, gave precisely the toughening effect of which his youngest son's character stood in need. Horace Walpole had the good sense to appreciate his father and to learn from him; and there can be no doubt that his love and admiration for Sir Robert, which grew stronger with every year, began at this time. "As fine as [Houghton] is," he wrote to him at the close of the visit, "I shou'd not have felt half the satisfaction, if it had not been your doing: I wish all your other Actions cou'd afford you as much ease to enjoy their Success, as Those at Houghton do: But as I know how little leisure you have, I will not detain you by endeavouring to express in a long letter, what the Longest cou'd never do, my Duty and Admiration."[10]

II

A great deal of criticism was directed at Houghton when it was first built. Since Sir Robert Walpole had risen to affluence by his own exertions, it was almost automatically condemned on the grounds of vulgarity and ostentation, as the grandiose work of a *parvenu*. Since he was a politician, his foes asserted that the expense of its erection and furnishing was fraudulently defrayed out of the public funds. Since he was fond of women and high living, the pamphlets of the Opposition were filled with exaggerated descriptions of the orgies that took place beneath its roof. And since he employed Thomas Ripley, a carpenter whom he had promoted and who had married one of his servants, as his architect (though not until after the death of Colin Campbell, who was responsible for the original design); and since Ripley's reputation was gravely lowered in the eyes of posterity, together with the reputations of his clients, by a single contemptuous couplet of Pope,[11] it has often been assumed that Houghton was

[10] *Ibid.*, Supplement, i. 4–5 (Walpole to Sir Robert Walpole, July 27, 1736).

[11] Heav'n visits with a Taste the wealthy Fool,
And needs no Rod but Ripley with a Rule.
Moral Essays, Epistle IV (Of the Use of Riches), 17–8.

an architectural monstrosity. Even at the present day, biographers of the Walpoles sometimes accept the prejudices of Pope and the onslaughts of *The Craftsman* as legitimate criticism of Houghton.

Houghton is a magnificent house; but it is quite unjust to condemn it for ostentation. Beside the palaces of Vanbrugh, or the vast Palladian structures raised later in the century, its scale might almost be described as modest. There is nothing in the design to mark it as the fulfilled ambition of a wealthy *parvenu;* it is simple, massive, dignified, and every foot of its surface is remarkable for a sober perfection of detail and finish. And the vast sums which Sir Robert spent on it were not, as his enemies loved to allege, cynically diverted from the public moneys of the nation. We shall not have a complete picture of his financial transactions until the appearance of the concluding volume of Dr. J. H. Plumb's great biography. But it seems clear that the building and decoration of Houghton were achieved on borrowed rather than on peculated money, to such an extent that Sir Robert died forty thousand pounds in debt.

In only one of the contemporary subjects for complaint against Houghton was there any substantial truth. The accusations about the riot and drinking and dissipation that went on beneath its roof were well founded. It might have been argued that this was Sir Robert Walpole's personal affair; but it is certain that among the causes of his eventual unpopularity was the resentment excited by the echoes of the Houghton Congresses, those uproarious summer meetings at which his political friends and hangers-on joined with the squires and parsons of Norfolk in protracted and undignified *saturnalia.* Lord Townshend, his staid brother-in-law, who had bitterly resented the eclipse of Raynham by the rising magnificence of Houghton, used to mark his disapproval of these jovial functions by retiring from Norfolk directly they began.[12]

It is said that Sir Robert Walpole occasionally envied his brother Horatio's mansion of Wolterton, where Ripley had achieved admirable results upon a smaller scale than Campbell had laid down for him at Houghton. But Houghton, in its spacious magnificence, was the perfect expression of Sir Robert; and it is hard to believe that he could have ever wished it smaller by a

[12] *Hervey,* 85. "... this fabric of fraternal discord."

single foot. The house matched the man. There was something of his personality in all its features and in all its furnishings—in the solemn massive east front; in the more ornate west front which faced the gardens; in the astonishing Hall and its famous lantern, which was so often ridiculed in *The Craftsman;* in the Marble Parlour, with its cool alcoves and granite cistern, refinements to aid deep drinking and heavy dining on a hot day; in the bed-chambers with their superb tapestries and marvellous embroidered bed-hangings; in the velvet, the gilding, the friezes and doors and chimneypieces; and above all in room after room filled with pictures from floor to ceiling, the Gallery, the Saloon, the Carlo Maratt Room, and all the other rooms with their profusion of pleasant family portraits, indifferent hunting scenes, and unrivalled masterpieces by every painter whose work was admired by the *cognoscenti* in the reign of George II.

III

In the summer of 1737 Lady Walpole died. Her son Horace described, in a touching letter to Charles Lyttelton, the calmness and courage which she displayed before her death; and how he hastened back to Cambridge in the following month "out of a house which I could not bear."[13] His love for his mother was the most powerful emotion of his entire life. It had profound and familiar reactions on his character, and the whole of his psychological history was dominated by it. Her death was the first and the greatest sorrow he was to know; and the indifference of the rest of the family was an additional source of grief to him. He alone mourned her and remembered her, and raised to her memory the monument in Westminster Abbey with its lines of lovingly exaggerated eulogy. Sir Robert displayed his indifference by marrying six months later his mistress Maria Skerrett. She seems to have been an able and charming woman, and probably a better intellectual companion for Sir Robert than his first wife. Horace Walpole never spoke of her with anything approaching personal dislike, and he was sincerely attached to Mary, her daughter by Sir Robert, who now became a member of the Walpole household. But he is known to have resented strongly this

[13] *Toynbee,* i. 24–5 (Walpole to Lyttelton, September 18, 1737).

hasty supplanting of his mother by the woman who had been her open rival for so many years.

The second Lady Walpole, however, died in childbirth only three months after her marriage. Sir Robert was overwhelmed with grief. A second great blow was the death, later in the same year, of his old ally and friend Queen Caroline. "My dear Sir Robert," she had said before she died, "you see me in a very indifferent situation. I have nothing to say to you, but to recommend the King, my children and the kingdom to your care."[14] Her death was a deep personal sorrow to him; the loss of her cool and sensible advice, and of her unfailing support of his measures, was a political disaster, and an immense encouragement to the increasing army of his opponents. The King remained faithful to him; but deprived of the Queen and of Miss Skerrett, the two most important influences on his later life, Sir Robert was left in a lonely position from which to face the gathering hostility of the nation. Most of the political talent of the country was ranged against him; many of his friends and supporters, though still forming a large majority in Parliament, were sycophants of little ability; and his history from this year onwards begins to assume the character of a gallant and almost single-handed struggle against very formidable odds.

Politics mattered little then to Horace Walpole, who could not remember a time, except during the anxious weeks at the King's accession, when his father had not been in a position of almost absolute power. He was occupied with his own affairs. He saw little or nothing of his brothers; Robert was married, Edward was occupied with his mistress and increasing family of bastard children. His sister Mary had married Lord Malpas in 1723, and had died abroad in 1731; he had scarcely known her. But he spent a great deal of time with his cousins, Francis and Henry Seymour Conway, and became very fond of their sister Anne. His affection for her—one cannot call it by any stronger name—lasted for several years, and was a matter of common knowledge to his friends. "You long prodigiously to see me and Miss Conway," West wrote to him when was on his travels:[15] and as late as 1744 his tutor, John Whaley, inquired in a set of complimentary verses

[14] *Hervey*, 898.

[15] *Lewis*, xiii. 234 (West to Walpole, November 10, 1740).

"Flows from thy Pen the sweet spontaneous line
While Seymour's look supplies the absent Nine?"[16]

In spite of this lengthy and public attachment Walpole never showed any intention of marrying Anne Conway, who became the wife, in 1755, of an elderly gentleman named John Harris.

Gray's reaction to the news of this love-affair was one of surprise: surprise that Walpole should be in love, and also that he should be taking the matter so calmly. "I confess, I am amazed: of all likely things this is the last I should have believed would come to pass: however, I congratulate you upon being able at this time to talk of Clytemnaestra, and Mrs. Porter; I wish, you have not admired this last-mention'd Gentlewoman long enough to catch a little of her art from her, for if I'm not mistaken, you are a very different person behind the Scenes, and whatever face you set upon the matter, I guess—but perhaps I guess wrong; I wish I may for your sake; perhaps you are as cool as you would seem: either way I may wish you joy; of your Dissimulation, or Philosophy: ...I don't wonder at the new study you have taken a likeing to; first because it diverts your thoughts from disagreeable objects, next, because it particularly suits your Genius, and lastly, because I believe it the most excellent of all sciences, to which in proportion as the rest are subservient, so great a degree of estimation they ought to gain...."[17]

"It particularly suits your Genius." It is unlikely that Gray was writing in an ironic mood; yet he must have known Walpole well enough by this time to realize that nothing suited his genius less appropriately than the passion of love. The cool and detached manner in which his friend had confided the affair cannot have been really surprising to Gray; nor can he have been genuinely amazed that the charms of Anne Conway should have been discussed in the same letter, and almost in the same tone, as the histrionic powers of Mrs. Porter. He may even have perceived in the light of his own affection for Walpole, that Walpole's admiring devotion to Henry Conway outweighed any sentiments he might feel towards Conway's sister.

One cannot tell. It is impossible, from a few hints in a few let-

[16] *Toynbee,* Supplement, iii. (Whaley to Walpole, December 4, 1744).
[17] *Lewis,* xiii. 151–2 (Gray to Walpole, February 23, 1738).

ters, to form a coherent picture of Walpole's early attachments to women—to Anne Conway, to Elisabetta Grifoni presently in Florence, to Elizabeth Evelyn after his return to England. He was not seriously in love with any of them. He would often be attracted to women, and they to him, but he would never allow any human being to disturb the detachment in which he had chosen to move through life. One cannot tell whether Miss Conway and Miss Evelyn were in love with him; Madame Grifoni certainly was, and probably for a few weeks she was his mistress. But if the English-women were in love with him, there is no doubt that they shared the experience which, at the close of those few weeks, befell the Florentine. All three were confronted by the same polite and obstinate detachment.

The relationships about which Walpole felt most strongly, and which really influenced his life, were those into which the element of physical passion did not enter—his love for his mother, for Conway, for Mary Berry. He was a natural celibate. Conversation and social life, pictures and books, the adornment of his house and the occasional presence of his friends, were all he required for happiness. Before he was twenty years of age, an older friend, Sneyd Davies, perceived this, and was struck with the contrast between Walpole and his exact contemporary John Dodd of Swallowfield. The two young men were close friends, had been together at Eton and King's, and differed completely in character and outlook. Davies wrote a poem *On Two Friends, Born the Same Day,* containing a description of Walpole which remained perfectly applicable throughout his life.

> The one, of nature easy, and compos'd,
> Untost by passions, and in arts repos'd;
> The other, of a keen impatient soul,
> Wing'd in the race, and stretching to the goal:
> One calm as Theodosius to desire;
> The other glowing with Varanes' fire:
> This pleas'd to wander in Pierian glades,
> Where the rill murmurs, and the laurel shades;
> The other warm'd in what his heart approves,
> The chace, the mistress, or the friend he loves.[18]

[18] *Nichols,* i. 591.

The frigid Theodosius, incidentally, outlived the fiery Varanes by fifteen years. In 1782 Walpole mentioned to Cole, in a slightly unfeeling postscript, that "my old friend, and your acquaintance, Mr. Dodd, died last Sunday—not of cold water. He and I were born on the very same day, but took to different elements. I doubt he had hurt his fortune as well as health."[19]

IV

Horace Walpole, incongruous though it may seem, had been intended by his father to follow the profession of the law, and had in fact been entered at Lincoln's Inn in 1731.[20] Even so late as his Cambridge days, his elders had not abandoned the hope that he would embark upon a legal career. "My nephew Horace has been a good deal out of order," his uncle Horace wrote at the beginning of 1738. "He has his choice to take a turn abroad and stay some time at The Hague, or to study and stick to the Common Law. He has not yet declared his opinion."[21] But young Horace had not the slightest intention of studying the law; and when he finally decided to travel, it was on a very different scale from this projected holiday trip to The Hague.

He ceased to reside at Cambridge towards the end of 1738, though for a long while his appearances there had been infrequent. He finally left the place "in form," without taking a degree, in the following year. Sir Robert had assured to him an adequate and impregnably secure income for life by obtaining from the King his appointment to certain patent places under the Crown, the duties of which were performed by deputy. Soon after his mother's death he had been made Inspector of the Imports and Exports in the Custom House, an office which he resigned on being appointed Usher of the Exchequer a few months later. On coming of age he took possession of the places of Comptroller of the Pipe and Clerk of the Estreats. And it was arranged that the Cornish borough of Callington should return him to Parliament when an opportunity arose. In the meantime, he decided to

[19] *Lewis,* ii. 299 (Walpole to Cole, February 14, 1782).

[20] *Ibid.,* xiii. 5 *(Short Notes of My Life).*

[21] *H.M.C., Buckinghamshire MSS.,* 10 (Horatio Walpole to Robert Trevor, January 3/14, 1737/8).

travel; and he asked Gray to accompany him. They were to live upon terms of absolute equality in every respect. He also drew up a will by which he left to Gray everything he then possessed in the world.

Gray had left Cambridge, where his attacks of depression and melancholy had steadily become more frequent, about the same time as Walpole. Some time before, he had ceased to read for a degree, and had drifted on at Peterhouse, always deep in study, but making no attempt to prepare himself for a career, until circumstances had made it imperative for him to think about earning his living. It was suggested that he and West should study law together in the Inner Temple. The project filled them both with horror; but Gray got so far towards fulfilling it as to leave Cambridge, and he was living at his father's house in Cornhill when Walpole's proposal was made.

He accepted the offer with gratitude. It delivered him from the immediate bondage of the law-courts, and promised a long period of interest and amusement in the company of the friend whom he idolized. He had written, a few years before, that Walpole was the only person who could uproot him from the stagnant way of life into which he had fallen at Cambridge. He was still, as in his Eton days, irresistibly drawn to Walpole, that embodiment of those qualities of charm, high spirits, wit and worldliness which he always sincerely admired and knew he was not fated to attain. And Walpole now uprooted him to some purpose. It was with every prospect of harmony and enjoyment that the two friends left England in March 1739.

But it was impossible that this harmony should remain unbroken. They had not lived, since their Eton days, in closer intimacy than was allowed by rather irregular residences in different colleges at Cambridge; now they were proposing to encounter together, for months at a time, the exhaustion, annoyance, discomfort and boredom that travel in the eighteenth century involved. They had hitherto met in the comparative democracy of an English school and university; now they were to enter foreign societies in which Walpole was received with the regard due to the son of the most powerful man in England, and Gary was tolerated as his obscure companion. Gray was profoundly devoted to Walpole, and Walpole was sincerely attached to Gray; the gulf that divides love from affection lay between them. And Gray was not blindly adoring. He was critical of his idol, and irritated by his faults; and he was extremely outspoken. Walpole resented his frankness. Many years afterwards, when his friend was dead, he wrote to Mason: "We had not got to Calais before Gray was dissatisfied, for I was a boy, and he, though infinitely more a man, was not enough so to make allowances."[22] There can be no doubt that their friendship was subjected, almost from the commencement of the tour, to those stresses and embarrassments which culminated in a disastrous quarrel two years later.

[22] *Lewis,* xxviii. 114 (Walpole to Mason, November 27, 1773).

IV

The Grand Tour (1739-41)

I

WALPOLE and Gray left Dover at noon on Easter Sunday, March 29,[1] 1739, and reached Calais by five o'clock in the afternoon. Gray suffered a good deal from the "pretty brisk gale" which assisted their progress: and their landing at Calais was accomplished in a snowstorm. Travelling by way of Boulogne, Amiens, and Saint-Denis, where they were shown the royal tombs and relics by a jovial and irreverent Benedictine, they reached Paris on the night of April 4, and with some difficulty found their lodgings, which were at the Hôtel de Luxembourg in the Rue des Petits Augustins. Here they were presently joined by Walpole's cousins, Lord Conway and his brother Henry, and by Lord Holdernesse, another of the many young Englishmen of their own age who were then in Paris. These three supped with them and remained till two in the morning. Next day they dined with Lord Holdernesse, where all the guests were English with the agreeable exception of the author of *Manon Lescaut;* and afterwards saw an elaborate spectacular ballet on the story of Pandora, which was staged in the *Grande Salle des Machines* in the Tuileries. The following day they dined with Lord Waldegrave, the British Ambassador, and afterwards went to the opera. These two days were typical of their stay in Paris. They were almost embarrassed by the civilities of their fellow-countrymen: "all the English are

[1] This date, as all dates mentioned during the continental tour of Walpole and Gray, is given according to the "New Style." The date of their crossing according to the "Old Style," which continued in force in England until 1752, was March 18. The date of March 10 given by Walpole in his *Short Notes of My Life* is proved incorrect both by his letters and by Gray's.

acquainted and herd much together," wrote Gray, "and it is no easy matter to disengage oneself from them, so that one sees but little of the French themselves."[2] And when they could escape from the other Englishmen, they were occupied from morning till midnight with sight-seeing and theatre-going. They visited Versailles and Chantilly, were astonished at the excellence of the French actors and at the mediocrity of the Opera, and wrote all their impressions with great liveliness and volubility, to West and Ashton in England. Occasionally a note of dissatisfaction appears in Walpole's letters; his French was not readily understood, he did not seem to be making sufficient contact with the people, he was on the whole a little disappointed with Paris. But Gray, contrasting the novelty and variety of his experiences with the dreary prospects which life had held for him a few months before, was abundantly happy. He could entertain himself, he told West, for a whole month merely with the common streets and the people in them.[3]

At the beginning of June they left Paris for Rheims, intending to remain there till they had perfected themselves in the French language. They were accompanied by Henry Conway, whose brother had spent a good deal of time at Rheims, which ensured them a welcome from the people of fashion in the town. But they found the provincial *noblesse* of Champagne extremely dull and formal, the town of a melancholy aspect, and nothing worthy of praise except the incomparable food and wine. There was one exceptional party, charmingly described by Gray in a letter to his mother, when supper was laid beside a fountain in the garden, and the whole company—"men and women of the best fashion here"—danced and sang till four o'clock in the morning, and then paraded through the streets of the city, the more weary in their coaches and the others dancing before them.[4] But this was an impromptu burst of gaiety, and Walpole's attempt to give an entertainment of the same sort in the following week found no support. The town reverted to diversions impatiently described by Walpole in a parody of the idiom he had come to Rheims to acquire: "the comedians return hither from Compiegne in eight

[2] *Gray, Walpole, West and Ashton,* i. 212 (Gray to Ashton, April 21, 1739).
[3] *Ibid.*, 206 (Gray to West, April 12, 1739).
[4] *Gray,* i. 113–4 (Gray to Mrs. Gray, June 21, 1739).

days, for example; and in a very little time one attends the regiment of the king, three battalions and an hundred of officers; all men of a certain fashion, very amiable, and who know their world."[5] They had intended to go southward later in the summer, but stayed on at Rheims until September, in expectation of a visit from their Eton friends George Montagu and George Selwyn. On September 9 they arrived at Dijon. The town, the countryside, the society were all charming: and everything they saw in Burgundy increased their regret that they had wasted so much time in Champagne. They remained at Dijon only a few days; and on September 18 Gray was writing to West from Lyons, an unwelcome contrast with its roar of traffic, narrow streets and enormous barrack-like houses. In a short time they set out again, in order to accompany Conway to Geneva, where he proposed to stay for some while. They took the road through Dauphiné and Savoy, which was longer and more arduous than the direct route, in order to visit the Grande Chartreuse. This excursion was their first introduction to mountain scenery; and to Gray, at any rate, it was perhaps the most exciting and impressive event in the whole course of their travels. Walpole's next letter to West was addressed with romantic unexpectedness "from a Hamlet among the Mountains of Savoy." It proceeds with the same consciousness of romance: "Precipices, mountains, torrents, wolves, rumblings, Salvator Rosa—the pomp of our park and the meekness of our palace! Here we are, the lonely lords of glorious desolate prospects. . . . Yesterday I was a shepherd of Dauphiné; to-day an Alpine savage; to-morrow a Carthusian monk; and Friday a Swiss Calvinist."[6] The letter was resumed from Aix on the 30th, the visit to the Chartreuse having taken place on the intervening day. They left the main road at Echelles, and climbed the narrow winding six-mile track to the monastery on mule-back, returning to the village the same night through the descending clouds. They were pleased by the decency and order of the monastery, by its unique position and by the friendliness of the brothers; it was the road leading to it that astonished and awed them. "But the road, West, the road! winding round a prodigious mountain, and surrounded

[5] *Lewis,* xiii. 178 (Walpole to West, July 20, 1739).
[6] *Ibid.,* 181 (Walpole to West, September 28, 1739).

with others all shagged with hanging woods, obscured with pines or lost in clouds! Below, a torrent breaking through cliffs, and tumbling through fragments of rocks! Sheets of cascades forcing their silver speed down channelled precipices, and hasting into the roughened river at the bottom! Now and then an old foot-bridge, with a broken rail, a leaning cross, a cottage, or the ruin of an hermitage! This sounds too bombast and too romantic to one that has not seen it, too cold for one that has. If I could send you my letter post between two lovely tempests that echoed each other's wrath, you might have some idea of this noble roaring scene, as you were reading it. Almost on the summit, upon a fine verdure, but without any prospect, stands the Chartreuse. We staid there two hours, rode back through this charming picture, wished for a painter, wished to be poets! Need I tell you we wished for you?"[7] Such was Walpole's description of that amazing landscape; on Gray it made a far more profound impression. "In our little journey up to the Grande Chartreuse," he wrote to West six weeks later from Italy, "I do not remember to have gone ten paces without an exclamation, that there was no restraining: not a precipice, not a torrent, not a cliff, but is pregnant with religion and poetry. There are certain scenes that would awe an atheist into belief, without the help of other argument."[8] And when he was returning to England alone, nearly two years afterwards, he made a second visit to the monastery, and wrote there his noble *Alcaic Ode*. The place and its associations moved him very deeply, both as a poet and as a religious man. Walpole's admiration of it was wholly visual, the admiration he would have bestowed on an unusually grand and theatrical painting by Salvator Rosa. He would have made nothing of Gray's almost Wordsworthian conception of mountain landscape as "pregnant with religion and poetry"; and indeed such a conception was at that time unique.

After spending a few days at Geneva, and seeing Conway settled there, they returned to Lyons, where they found a letter from Sir Robert Walpole, suggesting that they should travel in Italy instead of spending the winter in the south of France, as they had intended. This permission to extend and prolong their tour was

[7] *Ibid.*, 182 (Walpole to West, September 28–October 2, 1739).

[8] *Gray, Walpole, West and Ashton*, i. 259–60 (Gray to West, November 16, 1739).

an unexpected and most welcome concession on the part of Sir Robert. "You may imagine I am not sorry to have this opportunity of seeing the place in the world that best deserves it," Gray wrote to his father. Also the old Pope, Clement XII, was gravely ill; and they would therefore in all probability be able to witness in Rome the excitements of a Conclave and the splendours of a Papal Enthronement. They left Lyons at the end of October, and after eight days of exhausting and exciting travel arrived safely at Turin.

Winter had come, and they could hardly have crossed the Alps at a more unpleasant time of the year, or in more disagreeable circumstances. Owing to the cold and foggy weather, the scenery never attained the beauty and sublimity of those memorable landscapes around the Grande Chartreuse; and Mont Cénis, where the most striking scenes were to be observed, "carried the permission mountains have of being frightful rather too far; and its horrors were accompanied with too much danger to give one time to reflect upon their beauties."[9] The first few days of the journey were uneventful; but on the sixth day the ascent of the mountains began, and the first of their misfortunes took place. "I had brought with me a little black spaniel of King Charles' breed; but the prettiest, fattest, dearest creature! I had let it out of the Chaise for the air, and it was waddling along close to the head of the horses, on the top of one of the highest Alps, by the side of a wood of firs. There darted out a young wolf, seized poor dear Tory by the throat, and before we could possibly prevent it, sprang up the side of the rock and carried him off. The postilion jumped off and struck at him with his whip, but in vain. I saw it and screamed, but in vain; for the road was so narrow, that the servants that were behind could not get by the chaise to shoot him. What is the extraordinary part is, that it was but two o'clock, and broad sunshine. It was shocking to see anything one loved run away with to so horrid a death."[10]

Next day they reached Lanslebourg, at the foot of Mont Cénis, over which ran the only road into Italy. Here the chaise was taken to pieces and loaded on mules; and the travellers, wrapped in bear-skins, with muffs, masks, hoods and boots of fur, were carried

[9] *Ibid.*, 261 (Gray to West, November 16, 1739).
[10] *Lewis*, xiii. 189–90 (Walpole to West, November 11, 1739).

up the six-mile ascent of the mountain in low chairs swung from poles. Twelve men and nine mules were required to transport them, their servants and their baggage. At one of the most dangerous points of their journey, there was another alarming occurrence; their "Alpine Savages" got drunk and started fighting amongst themselves at the very edge of a fearful chasm, with the travellers tossed to and fro by the conflict, helplessly muffled and pinioned in their chairs. The wide plain at the summit of Mont Cénis was deep in snow and often obscured by clouds; and the final descent, another six miles, was even steeper than the climb up to the mountain, and far more terrifying from the inconceivable speed at which their bearers covered the ground. Most of the few people they encountered were hideously afflicted with goitre. "Such uncouth rocks, and such uncomely inhabitants!" Walpole lamented: "My dear West, I hope I shall never see them again!"

They did not remain long at Turin, but went on to Genoa. A rapturous letter from Gray to West describes their delight in that lovely city, with its marble palaces and churches, its terraced gardens and orange-groves sloping down to the crowded shipping of the bay, and the radiant blue of the Mediterranean stretching endlessly beyond. After a week at Genoa they continued their travels, to Piacenza, Parma, Reggio, Modena, and Bologna, where they spent several days. They then crossed the Apennines, which they found "not so horrid as the Alps, though pretty near as high,"[11] and arrived at Florence on December 16. They were met at the city gates by the servant of Mr. Mann, the acting British resident, who conducted them to his master's house.

II

Horace Mann was related to the Walpole family, and Sir Robert had appointed him two years before to act as assistant to Mr. Fane, the British Minister at the Court of Tuscany. Mr. Fane spent little time in Florence, finding it more convenient to draw his salary and leave his work to Mann. In 1739 Mann was therefore in the position of *chargé d'affaires;* but early in the following year he succeeded Mr. Fane as Minister.

[11] *Gray,* i. 134 (Gray to Mrs. Gray, December 19, 1739).

His post at Florence was one of considerable responsibility. The last of the Medici, the Grand Duke Gian Gastone, had died in 1737; and Francis, Duke of Lorraine, had surrendered his own duchy of Lorraine to France in exchange for the throne of Tuscany and the hand of Maria Theresa. His regent in Florence was the Prince de Craon, a nobleman of Lorraine who had been his tutor and had married one of his father's mistresses. This lady, who as Princesse de Craon ruled Florentine society, had first attracted the notice of the old Duke of Lorraine when driving turkeys in a field; she and her husband were a good-natured but not a dignified couple. It was Mann's duty to flatter and conciliate them, and to keep both the Lorraine and the Florentine elements in the state favourable to the policy of England. And above all it was his business to watch the movements of the Stuart party at Rome, and to defeat any intrigues they might set on foot in Tuscany. For with the growth to manhood of the Pretender's sons, the Stuart court was becoming active once more, and was causing some anxiety to Sir Robert Walpole and his government.

At the time of Horace Walpole's first visit to Florence, Mann was thirty-three years old, a bachelor, something of an invalid, fastidious, affected, but very skilful and pertinacious in the complicated duties of his post. It is uncertain whether he and Walpole had ever met in England; but at Florence they immediately became close friends, in spite of the considerable difference in their ages. Only three days after their arrival, Gray was describing Mann to his mother as "the best and most obliging person in the world." There was every reason for Mann to wish to oblige Horace Walpole, since his own position and prospects depended entirely upon Sir Robert. But quite apart from this, there was a remarkable similarity in their tastes and outlook, and a warm friendship sprang up between them. A large part of Mann's time was occupied with civilities to the English travellers who passed through Florence in an unending stream; and Walpole (and Gray for that matter) formed a most welcome contrast to the "travelling boys" or "flights of woodcocks," the young bucks in "jemmy frocks and frightful staring hats," the "Johns" who were indignant when he only gave them coffee to drink after dinner, the parsons whom he forgot to ask to say grace, the naval captains and merchants up from Leghorn, the ladies who wished to be introduced into the

Florentine assemblies, the ladies who wished to acquire *cicisbei* for the duration of their stay, and all the other uncongenial people who trespassed upon his leisure hours.

Walpole and Gray were different indeed from his usual guests. There was a bond of unconventionality in their very manner of travelling. Most young men of Walpole's age and wealth were accompanied through Europe by a tutor-companion, usually a clergyman, almost always their superior in age and their inferior in social position. These tutors were sometimes the trusted friends and mentors of the young men in their care; more often, perhaps, their presence was faintly resented as a reminder of parental authority, and as a check on the normal pleasures and extravagances of manhood. It is characteristic of Sir Robert Walpole's broad-mindedness that he allowed his youngest son to travel about Europe unaccompanied except by a young man of his own age. And when Walpole and Gray arrived at Florence, charming, independent, uncontrolled by any middle-aged bear-leader in wig and bands, it is not surprising that Mann welcomed them with pleasure.

In Florence, as in Paris, Gray was happier than Walpole. He was enraptured with the treasures of painting and sculpture which generations of the Medici had assembled in the palace of the Grand Duke; and the innumerable palaces and churches filled him with delight. Walpole was more exacting. "I don't know what volumes I may send you from Rome," he wrote to West; "from Florence I have little inclination to send you any. I see several things that please me calmly, but *à force d'en avoir vu* I have left off screaming Lord! this! and Lord! that! To speak sincerely, Calais surprised me more than anything I have seen since. I recollect the joy I used to propose if I could see the Great Duke's gallery; I walk into it now with as little emotion as I should go into St. Paul's. The statues are a congregation of good sort of people, that I have a great deal of unruffled regard for. The farther I travel the less I wonder at anything: a few days reconcile me to a new spot, or an unseen custom; and men are so much the same everywhere, that one scarce perceives any change of situation. The same weaknesses, the same passions, that in England plunge men into elections, drinking, whoring, exist here, and show themselves in the shapes of Jesuits, *cicisbeos,* and

Corydon ardebat Alexins. . . ."[12] Walpole was led to adopt this despondent tone by the social torpor which brooded over Florence during the winter months. He had paid a gloomy visit of ceremony to Gian Gastone's sister, the widowed Electress Palatine, who still lived mournfully on in Florence, the last of her illustrious house: she had received him under a great black canopy, and had bestowed upon him a few frigid words of goodwill. He had attended the formal assemblies given by the Prince de Craon and other notables, and had witnessed the celebrations in honour of the birth of Maria Theresa's son. This seems to have been the sum of his social activities. But the Florentines were reserving their energies for Carnival; and the festivities of that season broke down his reserve. He adored masquerades, and was to adore them till the end of his life; and he found that masquerades in Florence were conducted with a courtesy and consideration that he had looked for in vain in England. "Here they do not catch at those little dirty opportunities of saying any illnatured thing they know of you, do not abuse you because they may, or talk gross bawdy to a woman of quality." In these circumstances the Carnival of 1740 was a period of delight to Walpole, a wild *crescendo* of balls and masquerades and music, until Ash Wednesday solemnly dawned. "I have done nothing but slip out of my domino into bed, and out of bed into my domino. The end of the Carnival is frantic, Bacchanalian; all the morn one makes parties in mask to the shops and coffeehouses, and all the evening to operas and balls. *Then I have danced, good gods, how I have danced!*"[13]

Walpole was, in fact, essentially a man of pleasure in his early years; and the Carnival at Florence was the first of those periods of sheer frivolity in which he always liked to indulge. In London he had been little more than a boy, unhappy over his mother's death, not always in good health, rather uncertain of himself, with his most intimate friends on a different social level. At Paris he had also been ill at ease, compelled to associate with the English colony and unable to establish any contact with French society. But Florence was altogether different. He found precisely

[12] *Lewis*, xiii. 199 (Walpole to West, January 24, 1740).

[13] *Ibid.*, 201 (Walpole to West, February 27, 1740).

the type of society he was best fitted to enjoy—a society which was lively, talkative, and rather informal; and after the first hesitations he found himself perfectly at home in it. The Florentine friends and acquaintances, of whom he had made many during Carnival, appeared no less agreeable during the sober weeks of Lent. The Prince and Princesse de Craon, and their son the Prince de Beauvau, were friendly and hospitable. An eccentric Englishwoman, Lady Pomfret, settled at Florence with her husband and their two beautiful daughters, Lady Sophia and Lady Charlotte Fermor. Mann proved himself every day a more charming and more congenial friend. Walpole had perhaps never been so completely happy.

He occupied his more reflective hours in writing a rhymed *Epistle from Florence to Thomas Ashton, Esq., Tutor to the Earl of Plymouth.* (Ashton had lately obtained this position, probably by Walpole's recommendation.) This solemn and formal production, his first poem of any importance, might be described as an exercise in English history from the Whig point of view. It owes much to the writings of Conyers Middleton, as Walpole himself admitted;[14] but his short residence in Italy had filled him with a first-hand hatred of priestcraft which was all his own, and to which he gave expression on all possible occasions—in his letters, in his poems, and in conversation. His attitude was intemperate and excessive, but the Roman Church and the Stuart cause were then inextricably linked, and there were many circumstances in contemporary Italy to strengthen his conviction that

> The greatest curses any Age has known
> Have issued from the Temple or the Throne.

He therefore exhorted Ashton to inculcate in his young pupil a proper regard for Virtue and Liberty, and a proper horror of Bigotry and Tyranny: in short, "to build the free, the sensible, GOOD MAN," out of little Lord Plymouth. He shows considerable power in several passages, and particularly in his Hogarthian vision of a death-bed repentance:

> Some hoary hypocrite, grown old in sin,
> Whose thoughts of heav'n with his last hours begin,
> Counting a chaplet with a bigot care,

[14] *Toynbee,* Supplement, i. 45 (Walpole to Middleton, November 22, 1741).

HORACE WALPOLE (*circa* 1735)
From a painting by JONATHAN RICHARDSON at Chewton Priory, Bath
By kind permission of the Earl Waldegrave

HORACE WALPOLE (1741)
From a pastel by ROSALBA CARRIERA at Houghton Hall, Norfolk
By kind permission of the Marquess and Marchioness of Cholmondeley

travellers indulge. It is likely that in Rome, deprived of the amusements of a congenial society and the change of companionship that Mann could always provide, Walpole grew a little weary of Gray's solemn and indefatigable pursuit of learning. He resented his friend's preoccupation with worn inscriptions and shattered columns, with the stony banks which marked vanished cities and the grassy mounds above forgotten tombs. In one of his letters to Ashton occurs a passage completely expressive of the weary scorn felt by an amateur for a professional who had bored him. "By a considerable volume of Charts and Pyramids which I saw at Florence, I thought it threatened a Publication. His travels have really improved him; I wish they may do the same for any-one else."[17] This was far from the spirit in which they had set out from England; but such an outbreak of peevishness was not repeated in any other letters. There was an essential disloyalty in Ashton which encouraged this type of confidence.

They went on a long excursion to Naples and its neighbourhood, and returned to Rome to find the Conclave still at a deadlock. The summer heats were descending on the city: Walpole was frightened of "a horrid thing called *mal'aria,*" and longed for Mann's cool house above the Arno. Gray would have been willing to remain at Rome indefinitely, and was a little reluctant to leave; but Walpole was inexorable, and they returned to Florence early in July. The new Pope was not chosen until six weeks later.

IV

The house of His Majesty's Resident at the Court of Tuscany was Casa Mannetti, in the Via Santo Spirito. But during their second visit to Florence, Walpole and Gray lodged in Casa Ambrogi, a pleasant small house which lay between the Via de' Bardi and the Arno. Mann used Casa Ambrogi as a guest-house for his friends, and indeed seems to have spent as much time there as at his official residence. Walpole lived in the *piano terreno,* which had an open gallery facing upon the Arno. Gray occupied two small rooms close by. From some of the windows it was possible to fish in the river.

[17] *Lewis,* xiii. 219 (Walpole to Ashton, May 28, 1740).

Mann appears to have run his little legation almost single-handed. The English Government did not allow him an official assistant, and he had to make what use he could of an unsatisfactory Italian secretary, until Walpole after his return to England sent out to him a youthful and inexperienced clerk, who was also expected to wait at table. In consequence the minister was overworked at times of crisis; and he often had cause to complain that his salary and allowances were greatly in arrears. But the ordinary routine work of his post was not considerable, and he was able as a rule to forget his headaches and *épuisements,* and take a prominent and lively part in the social life of Florence.

If Walpole had been delighted with Florentine life during the winter Carnival, he was even better pleased with its summer gaieties. He was popular with all the Florentines, and was welcomed wherever he went. The days passed in happy idleness; nobody in Casa Ambrogi rose till noon; in the evening the whole town flocked to "the charming bridge"—the Ponte Vecchio—and lingered there throughout the warm soft nights, supping, listening to music, talking, intriguing. And there would be operas, masquerades, assemblies, balls: *conversazioni* in moonlit gardens, among the nightingales and the orange-flowers, and *cocchiate,* serenades to which people listened in their coaches. There were also visits to the Gallery, visits to churches and private collections, some further pursuit of the study of *virtù;* but it was the idle, easy-going, unmalicious atmosphere of the city that Walpole found so charming. "As, by the absence of the Great Duke, Florence is become in a manner a country town, you may imagine we are not without our *démêlés,*" he wrote to Conway; "but for a country town I believe there never were a set of people so peaceable, and such strangers to scandal. 'Tis the family of love, where everybody is paired, and go as constantly together as paroquets. Here nobody hangs or drowns themselves; they are not ready to cut one another's throats about elections or parties; don't think that wit consists of saying bold truths, or humour in getting drunk."[18]

'Tis the family of love, where everybody is paired. . . . It is impossible to enter here into a detailed explanation of the theory

[18] *Toynbee,* i. 83–4 (Walpole to Conway, September 25, 1740).

and practice of *cicisbeatura* in eighteenth-century Italy. There was a convention by which a married woman was attended on public occasions by some other man, her *cicisbeo* or *cavaliere servente,* who was regarded by her husband and by the world in general as her accepted escort and gallant. No speculation about the more intimate developments of this arrangement was ever permitted; each little group of husband, wife, and *cicisbeo* was expected to settle the matter privately and without scandal. Some families adhered firmly to the original custom, by which the *cicisbeo* was an escort and nothing more; others very definitely did not. As the husband was customarily the *cicisbeo* of some other woman, the harmony of the house was in any case seldom impaired.[19]

Horace Walpole became the *cicisbeo* of one of the most beautiful women in Florence, Elisabetta Capponi, the wife of a certain Marchese Grifoni. Little is known about her and her husband—Mann once contemptuously referred to him as "her chucklehead"[20]—and still less, thanks to the decorous rules of *cicisbeatura,* about Walpole's relationship with them. But it seems probable that he was Madame Grifoni's lover, and was generally believed to be so by his English and Florentine friends. It was not, so far as he was concerned, a lasting or indeed a very passionate attachment. He was writing to Mann about his mistress in a tone of indifference within a very few months of his departure from Florence. But from Mann's letters in reply it is evident that her

[19] Mann's letters to Walpole give numerous details about *cicisbeatura* as practised in Florence. One passage is perhaps worth quoting as showing the complications and difficulties of the convention, and also as an example of Mann's epistolary style. "For the common transactions of the town, they are all confined to the knowledge of what cicisbeos have been displaced, and what new establishments have been made. The great news of this kind is that Madame Acciajuoli, who immediately after the departure of her joined cicisbeos Mr. Pelham and Millbanke took to Jacky Langlois, whom the town thought an unworthy successor, has now turned him off for a young Marquis Pucci, who succeeded Lord Rockingham with the Siristori, whom that Pucci has abandoned abruptly without a just cause, consequently has offended against *le legge d'amicizia,* as Madame Acciajuoli has done likewise to her friend the young and handsome Siristori in debauching her *cavaliere servente* from her. These are the circumstances that employ the attentions of the gay Florentine world. An English traveller frequently deranges the whole harmony of cicisbeship." (*Lewis,* xx. 284 [Mann to Walpole, November 26, 1751].)

[20] *Ibid.,* xvii. 229 (Mann to Walpole, December 19, 1741).

love for him was deep and genuine, and persisted long after he had ceased to write to her or even to send the most perfunctory messages of affection through his friend. Walpole seldom came well out of a relationship in which his personal detachment was called in question. But during those intoxicating months in Florence, when he was flushed with popularity and youthful vanity, he regarded it as a final triumph to be the accepted gallant of the lovely Grifona.

Occasionally his contentment was ruffled by a group of women of a very different type. His eldest brother Lord Walpole [21] had married a wealthy Devonshire heiress named Margaret Rolle, who after living with him for some years, and bearing him a son, had quarrelled violently with the whole Walpole family and had left England, to proclaim her woes to the rest of Europe. She had now settled in Florence with her lover of the moment, a Mr. Sturgess, and was also engaged in an intrigue with Count Richecourt, one of the Lorraine nobles who composed the Council of Regency. She was ill-tempered, malicious, and, to judge by her portraits, very unattractive; her brother-in-law Horace loathed her. She had violent intellectual pretensions, and struck up a warm friendship with Lady Pomfret, who was also addicted to learning and to the composition of enormous poems. To swell "the rhapsody of mystic nonsense which these two fair ones debate incessantly,"[22] a more talented blue-stocking presently arrived in the person of Lady Mary Wortley Montagu. Though outwardly polite to this dilapidated old wit, Walpole disliked her and probably feared her. The descriptions of her in his letters are merciless; but in her own letters she always referred to him with perfect good-nature, and it does not appear that her gossip about his birth was prompted by personal malice towards him.

Apart from this forbidding trio, everyone in Florence was friendly and likeable. Lady Pomfret's daughters were always charming. It has been said that Walpole was in love with Lady Sophia Fermor at this time; but it appears from an unpublished note among the papers at Chewton Priory that, greatly as he admired Lady Sophia's beauty, he liked Lady Charlotte better

[21] Sir Robert Walpole's eldest son had been created Baron Walpole of Walpole in 1723.

[22] *Lewis,* xiii. 227 (Walpole to West, July 31, 1740).

than her sister. In any case Lady Sophia had a devoted *cicisbeo,* a Florentine gentleman named Uguccioni, whom she preferred to any of her English admirers. A host of Florentine ladies, the Antinori, the Galli, the Albizzi, the Pucci, the Tesi, make brief appearances in the letters of Walpole and Mann. A well-known physician of the city, Doctor Cocci, was intimate with Mann, and they saw something of the unpleasant but learned *virtuoso* Baron Stosch. There were plenty of young English travellers—Lord Lincoln, who presently fell vainly in love with Lady Sophia Fermor; his tutor Joseph Spence, later well known as an antiquarian and writer, and for his collection of anecdotes of Pope and his circle; Edward Coke, son of the builder of Holkham; Sir Francis Dashwood, in years to come the leader of the famous orgies at Medmenham Abbey. And during Walpole's second visit to Florence two other Englishmen came to Casa Ambrogi who require more than a passing mention: John Chute and Francis Whithed.

John Chute was the youngest in his generation of the family which owned that beautiful house, The Vyne in Hampshire. He was of the same age as Mann, and was at this time wandering about Europe accompanied by a young cousin, Francis Whithed, whose estate was also in Hampshire. Whithed emerges from Mann's letters as a silent and rather colourless young man, obediently following in the wake of his elder cousin, and quietly attached to a Florentine woman named Lucchi, by whom he had a daughter. Chute, like Mann, was something of an invalid—short-sighted, nervous, enfeebled by a melancholy diet of milk and turnips, which he adopted to avert the dreadful attacks of gout to which he was a life-long victim. In manner he was affected and extravagant. Mann describes how a party of ordinary English travellers "disliked his fan extremely" at a dinner at Casa Mannetti; and his early letters to Walpole also give the impression that he was a fatuous *petit-maître*. Actually nothing could be farther from the truth. Under an elaborate mask of affectation, he was kindly and generous, able and courageous, as Walpole's letters to him, and his subsequent appearances in Walpole's life, abundantly show.

V

The brilliant and happy summer of 1740 drew to a close. The Emperor Charles VI died in October, and the recently acquired Tuscan subjects of his son-in-law somewhat unwillingly put an end to all their public gaieties. Even the winter Carnival, in which Walpole had taken such delight in the previous year, could not be held. The town settled into a quiet routine of cards and private music. Each Monday there was "a select set and a sixpenny pharo-table" at Casa Mannetti. The Pomfrets gave a similar entertainment on Thursdays. Sir Francis Dashwood had a concert every Wednesday.[23]

Such diversions were not very absorbing; and the absence of any other occupation seems to have increased the rapidly growing friction between Walpole and Gray. For two years they had weathered the vicissitudes and irritations of travel reasonably well; but the differences between them in temperament, in tastes, and in rank, were proving too powerful. From the first, Gray had been rather resentful that they should have left Rome and settled down to a life of complete idleness at Florence—"an excellent place to employ all one's animal sensations in, but utterly contrary to one's rational powers,"[24] as he told West. He gave his rational powers some employment in the composition of his poem *De Principiis Cogitandi;* and he made a large collection of manuscript music; but Walpole had little interest in music, and still less in the philosophy of Locke as expounded in Gray's Latin hexameters. Such things only strengthened his conviction that Gray was becoming a pedant and a bore. And there is no doubt that Gray's character was rapidly altering; the shyness, the indolence and the melancholy which he had so often revealed in youth, and which the excitement and novelty of travel had for a time driven away, were now threatening to dominate his nature completely. He knew it perfectly well: he described the process to West, whom he had not seen for two years, in one of the remarkable passages of self-analysis which occur now and then in his letters. "Methinks I ought to send you my picture (for I am no more what I was, some circumstances excepted, which I hope I

[23] *Hartford-Pomfret,* i. 176.

[24] *Gray, Walpole, West and Ashton,* i. 327 (Gray to West, July 31, 1740).

need not particularize to you); you must add then, to your former idea, two years of age, reasonable quantity of dullness, a great deal of silence, and something that rather resembles, than is, thinking; a confused notion of many strange and fine things that have swum before my eyes for some time, a want of love for general society, indeed an inability to it. On the good side you may add a sensibility for what others feel, and indulgence for their faults or weakness, a love of truth, and detestation of everything else. Then you are to deduct a little impertinence, a little laughter, a great deal of pride, and some spirits. These are all the alterations I know of, you perhaps may find more. Think not that I have been obliged for this reformation of manners to reason or reflection, but to a severer schoolmistress, Experience. One has little merit in learning her lessons, for one cannot well help it; but they are more useful than others, and imprint themselves in the very heart."[25]

Walpole was probably unaware of these developments and changes in Gray's character. He only observed him becoming moody, low-spirited, unsympathetic to his pleasures and his idleness, and out-spokenly critical of them. He retaliated with the easy arrogance of a happy and successful young man wishing to humiliate a less fortunate friend. It was not difficult when the friend was as sensitive as Gray, and when he had been, and probably still was, deeply devoted to him. It is impossible to tell at what point the tension between them first became permanent, how rapidly it grew, how soon it was evident to the other occupants of Casa Ambrogi. The whole affair was extremely embarrassing to Mann and Chute, who liked both Walpole and Gray and were unwilling to lose the friendship of either. They stood helplessly by, watching pride conflicting against pride, unable to reconcile two people who had drifted into a position of hopeless incompatibility.

Walpole had planned to start homeward in the spring, first visiting Venice, and returning either through France, or by way of Germany and the Low Countries, as the state of the Spanish war dictated. At the end of April, therefore, he and Gray left Florence. He had spent there what were probably the happiest months of his life. But he never returned. He never saw Mann

[25] *Ibid.*, ii. 4 (Gray to West, April 21, 1741).

again, though they were to correspond with undiminished affection and freedom for forty-five years. And he never again saw Madame Grifoni. He took back to England, as tokens of remembrance, Patapan, the dog she had given him, and her portrait by Ferdinand Richter, which was to hang in his bedchamber at Strawberry Hill until the end of his life. This need not however be taken as a sign of romantic devotion, as he referred to the work in later years as "a frightful picture by a one-eyed German painter," and said that it made his beautiful *cicisbea* look like a surly Margravine.[26]

VI

In the year 1772, when Mason was writing the life of Gray, he consulted Walpole about the treatment of this delicate matter of their breach of friendship in Italy. Walpole, naturally unwilling to have his youthful quarrels publicly discussed, wrote a short passage for inclusion in the book, and in a private letter to Mason gave a more explicit account of the affair. There is every reason to accept his generous and candid account of the progress of their estrangement; but he passes in silence over the occurrence, whatever it was, that brought about the final quarrel. "I am conscious," he told Mason, "that in the beginning of the differences between Gray and me, the fault was mine. I was too young, too fond of my own diversions, nay, I do not doubt, too much intoxicated by indulgence, vanity, and the insolence of my situation, as a Prime Minister's son, not to have been inattentive and insensible to the feelings of one I thought below me; of one, I blush to say it, that I knew was obliged to me; of one whom presumption and folly perhaps made me deem not my superior *then* in parts, though I have since felt my infinite inferiority to him. I treated him insolently; he loved me, and I did not think he did. I reproached him with the difference between us, when he acted from conviction of knowing he was my superior. I often disregarded his wishes of seeing places, which I would not quit my amusements to visit, though I offered to send him to them without

[26] *Toynbee,* ix. 26 (Walpole to Mann, August 4, 1774). *Lewis,* xi. 153–4 (Walpole to Mary Berry, November 29, 1790). *Works,* ii. 452 *(Description of Strawberry Hill).*

me. Forgive me, if I say that his temper was not conciliating; at the same time that I will confess to you that he acted a more friendly part, had I had the sense to take advantage of it—he freely told me of my faults. I declared I did not desire to hear them, nor would correct them. You will not wonder that with the dignity of his spirit, and the obstinate carelessness of mine, the breach must have grown wider, till we became incompatible."[27]

In this uneasy mood Walpole and Gray set out from Florence. They were still outwardly on good terms, and in spite of their disagreements they certainly expected to remain together for the few months that were to elapse before they reached England. But any trifling accident would have been enough to bring about a definite breach between them; and such an accident presently happened. At first everything went well. They stopped for a few days at Bologna; Walpole wrote to Mann, and enclosed an affectionate letter of farewell to Madame Grifoni. (Before long all Florence had seen it, and pronounced it to be *la più bella cosa che si possa mai vedere.*)[28] Mann's first letters to Walpole contain friendly messages to Gray. Then the travellers went on to Reggio, where the annual Fair was in full swing. Walpole flung himself into its gaieties, amusing himself at the Fair in the mornings, going each evening to balls and masquerades, and hearing the opera from the Duchess of Modena's box. But at some time during all these revels, the growing antagonism between himself and Gray flared up violently. There was a furious quarrel, after which they parted. Gray went on to Venice, and left Walpole alone at Reggio.

Endless speculation has been lavished on the actual cause of their quarrel. Did Walpole open a letter from Gray to some one in England, because he suspected that it contained unflattering remarks about himself? It seems highly unlikely; and the story has come down on very doubtful authority.[29] But both Walpole and Gray had made slighting remarks about one another in their letters to Ashton and West; and four years later, when they were reconciled, Gray spoke of Ashton's share in the negotiations, and that "he I found was to be angry about the letter I had wrote

[27] *Lewis,* xxviii. 68–9 (Walpole to Mason, March 2, 1773).
[28] *Ibid.,* xvii. 37 (Mann to Walpole, May 9, 1741).
[29] *Works of Thomas Gray;* edited by Mitford (1816), ii. 174 n.

him."[30] Was this a letter of complaint against Walpole which Gray had sent to Ashton, the contents of which that unlovable person transmitted back to Walpole?[31] It is possible. Then what is the meaning of the letter written by Mann to Walpole on May 23rd, some days after the quarrel? "From a horrid uneasiness I find and in justice to Gray (for whom I have received no letter or wrote to, though I designed to have it done last Saturday but was prevented by my fever) I cannot help adding two or three lines to assure you that in the late affair except writing that letter he was not so much to blame as on the sight of it you might imagine. I take the greatest part of the fault on myself and I am convinced of his regard for you; nay I have been witness to his uneasiness and tears when he suspected you had less confidence in him than his inward and real friendship for you made him think he deserved. This I think myself bound in justice to tell you, as I believed him sincere. As to the oddness of his behaviour with C—, and the particulars you mention and Bologna, they indeed surprised me much, and would almost induce me to give another turn to the whole."[32] What was the letter referred to here? How had Mann become involved in the affair? It is really useless to speculate. We only know that the tension between Walpole and Gray had become so acute that any additional strain would bring about a violent quarrel; and that at Reggio something occurred which had precisely this effect.

After Gray's departure, Walpole continued to amuse himself at Reggio, scarcely finding time, between the gaming-tables and the masquerades, to write a mournful letter now and then to Madame Grifoni. Then he suddenly fell ill with a quinsy, and attempted to cure himself without the aid of a doctor. At this moment, most opportunely, Lord Lincoln and his tutor Joseph Spence arrived at Reggio. Lord Lincoln, still desperately in love with Lady Sophia Fermor, had followed her to Rome, and was now pursuing her to Venice. He and Spence heard that Walpole

[30] *Gray,* i. 226 (Gray to Wharton, November 14, 1745).

[31] *Tovey,* 9.

[32] *Lewis,* xvii. 50 (Mann to Walpole, May 23, 1741). The sentence mentioning "C—" was obliterated by Walpole from the original text of Mann's letter. It may have referred to Chute, or to Francesco ("Cecco") Suares, a Florentine acquaintance who was travelling in the party.

was ill, and found him "swelled to such a degree as I never saw anyone in my life." They do not seem to have realized that he was not being attended by a doctor; but in the middle of the night he sent for Spence, who found him very much worse and hardly able to speak. Spence was a good, gentle, solicitous little man, and very well able to look after Walpole. He summoned the best physician at Reggio, and dispatched an express to Mann at Florence, urging him to send their friend Doctor Cocchi immediately. After some very anxious hours, Walpole's condition began to improve; and he was soon well on the way to recovery. "You see what luck one has sometimes in going out of one's way," Spence wrote to his mother with pardonable satisfaction: "If Lord Lincoln had not wandered to Reggio, Mr. Walpole (who is one of the best natured and most sensible young gentlemen that England affords) would in all probability have been now under the cold earth."[33]

Mann was naturally most anxious about Walpole, but was presently reassured by the return of Doctor Cocchi. His next letter contained another plea on behalf of Gray. "It gives me too much uneasiness to think of the late affair and the despair G. is in, therefore I will not enter into any detail, I do beseech you only that you will reflect on what I wrote in my last and former letter about it, I can only say that you have it in you to do a most generous action, to forget and forgive. I would ask it on my knees if I was with you."[34]

It appears from another letter of Mann's that Walpole listened to his friend's entreaties and had an interview with Gray, at which he proposed a reconciliation. Gray returned from Venice to Reggio, listened to Walpole's offers of reconciliation, and scornfully and indignantly rejected them. Mann wrote on June 10th: "I conclude you are at Venice and that you have received my last letter of the 3rd Inst. . . . two days after the departure of that letter I received yours of the 2nd and to my greatest surprise read the account therein of the interview, which I fear has destroyed all the hopes of a reconciliation with which I flattered myself, for the reasons I mentioned at large in a former letter. I must own I wished it extremely and should have been happy to have been the

[33] Egerton MS. 2234, ff. 263–4 (Spence to his mother, May 29, 1741).

[34] Mann to Walpole, undated, end of May, 1741. (MS. at Farmington, unpublished.)

means of bringing it about. I was astonished to see the terms and the reproaches, and much more that he could withstand your entreaties to return with you to England. I am highly sensible my dear Sir this was done at my request and heartily thank you for this proof of your goodness. I cannot help repeating again how sorry I am it had no effect but I will not dwell on so disagreeable a subject or trouble you any more on this affair."[35]

After this unsuccessful interview, Gray returned to Venice. Walpole, now completely recovered, arrived there on June 9th.[36] On entering Venetian territory, he had a dispute about the duty to be paid on his collection of medals. "I am glad to hear you are got well to Venice," wrote Mann, "and so well off your quarrel. That you should think of fighting with a great gondolier or custom house officer! You forget surely how impertinent these are here."[37] Walpole always behaved with spirit on occasions of this sort, but his physical fragility was ample justification for Mann's relief that the brawl in the *dogana* did not proceed to blows. At Venice he rejoined Chute and Whithed, and lived in the same house with them. Certain evidence suggests that Gray was also an occupant of this house; yet it seems hardly possible that he and Walpole could have endured the embarrassment of meeting every day after a violent quarrel and an unsuccessful attempt at reconciliation. And another letter from Mann reveals such a picture of difficulty and confusion about supplying Gray with money, stranded and almost penniless as he was, that it seems more probable that he was living entirely apart from Walpole, and that the two did not meet during their stay at Venice. Walpole would never have been so ungenerous as to withhold money from Gray; but Gray, with his obstinate pride, would not accept a loan from a man with whom he had quarrelled bitterly. So Mann had to supply Gray with funds until he could receive credit from England for his homeward journey; and Gray never knew that the money he received from Mann was actually Walpole's, and was remitted by his orders. Mann's letter to Walpole was written on July 1st. "I wrote formerly to Gray to offer him what money he might want as you directed me and punctually followed your

[35] *Lewis,* xvii. 58–9 (Mann to Walpole, June 10, 1741).
[36] *Hartford-Pomfret,* iii. 221.
[37] *Lewis,* xvii. 64 (Mann to Walpole, June 17, 1741).

orders in not mentioning your name in it, so that I am persuaded he thinks it came from me. He has I hear taken up 40 zecchini of Mr. Smith (the English consul at Venice) to whom I wrote to furnish him. He (the latter) tells me Gray waits for credit from England. In the meantime Smith designs to draw on me for the 40 zecchini: perhaps his draft may be on the road but as yet the Bankers here have not received it. I have ordered it paid when it comes. This affair you see is delicate as I am unwilling to let Gray think he is obliged to me and yet I have wholly concealed it from him because you insisted upon it. I do not wish him to return it, yet I am ignorant what he designs to do when he receives his credit from England, or, in case he does not, whether he may take more. I gave Mr. Smith a general order to supply him, either upon his bills on England or upon me. Gray however had great delicacy in taking the first sum, but I believe he was wholly destitute of any, as before my letter reached him he had borrowed 10 zecchini to carry him to Reggio. Tell me what I shall do."[38] Only two of Walpole's letters from Venice are in existence; and those have been mutilated in such a way that any mention of Gray has disappeared. So it is impossible to know how Walpole and Mann finally solved the problem of supplying him with money in such a way as not to injure his pride. He left Venice later in July, and travelled homewards unaccompanied except by a *laquais du voyage,* visiting various places of interest on the way. He reached London on September 1st, about a fortnight in advance of Walpole.

For many eighteenth-century travellers, and especially for those of a learned and reflective cast of mind, Rome was the most memorable point of their Grand Tour. Young men in search of frivolity and pleasure usually found their greatest enjoyment in Venice. Walpole in happier circumstances would have delighted in the city of Longhi and Guardi, in the blazing pageantry of its public events, in its gondolas gliding along the shadowy canals, its balls and its masquerades. He would have appreciated the suggestion of the orient which lingered about Venice, the Byzantine splendours of Saint Mark's, the barbaric architecture of the ancient buildings, the Turks and Levantines who mingled with

[38] *Ibid.,* 82 (Mann to Walpole, July 1, 1741).

the European crowds on the Piazza. He always had a taste for oriental stories, Arabian tales, Persian and Chinese fantasies; and in Venice alone was the ordinary traveller of his day able to catch a fleeting impression of the romance and cruelty of the East.

But Venice held no charms for him. He never spoke of the city with any pleasure, either during his stay there or in later years. His recent illness, his quarrel with Gray, the embarrassment of Gray's presence in the city, his imminent return to England, all combined to depress him. He was not alone in Venice; the Pomfrets and Lord Lincoln were also there, and Chute and Whithed were living in the same house. The Doge died and was magnificently buried; his successor was chosen amid great rejoicing and splendour. Venice was at its gayest; but he remained unhappy. Lady Pomfret, in one of her pleasant rambling letters, describes how she and her daughters were sitting with some friends at a masquerade on the Piazza, in the cloaks, white masks and black hats which were the only masquerade dress allowed in Venice, and which Longhi's pictures have made familiar: and how Walpole came along without a mask, and how they called to him and told him who they were, and how he sat down with them and related a long story, just received in a letter from Mann, full of mistaken identities and moral dilemmas of the type which later formed the plots of *The Castle of Otranto* and *The Mysterious Mother*.[39] On that evening, at least, Walpole may have enjoyed himself.

He left Venice for Genoa on July 12th, travelling with Lord Lincoln and Spence. Lord Lincoln was still sighing for Lady Sophia Fermor; he rode on horseback most of the way, bowed down with melancholy. Walpole and Spence travelled in the chaise; on the last day of the journey they whiled away the time by counting the number of loaded mules they passed on the road. After spending a few days at Genoa, where they encountered Lady Mary Wortley Montagu again, they embarked in a *felucca* for Antibes. This method of travelling was uncomfortable and sometimes dangerous, but the route over the Alps was unbearably exhausting at the height of summer. Nevertheless, they were taking a considerable risk; for it appears from one of Mann's letters

[39] *Hartford-Pomfret,* iii. 233.

that they were closely pursued by some Catalan vessels. "I am charmed," wrote Mann, "with your account of yourself and that you escaped those three Catalan monsters. Jesus, if they had taken you! The reflection of the dangers you have run I vow frightens me: they would have exulted more had they got you in their ship than the noble Venetian. . . ."[40] It would certainly have been an odd development of the war between England and Spain, into which Sir Robert Walpole had been forced so strongly against his will, if his son had been made prisoner by these marauding Catalans.

After landing at Antibes, the party travelled to Paris by way of Toulon, Marseilles, Aix, Montpellier, Toulouse and Orleans. Walpole stayed a few days in Paris, and then went on alone to England. He landed at Dover on September 12th. There had been a little trouble over his medals at Calais, but at Dover the customs officers "respected Sir Robert's son even in the person of his trunks." Next day he was writing appreciatively to Mann from Sittingbourne about the populousness, gaiety and prosperity of provincial England. On September 14th he reached London, after an absence of almost two and a half years.

[40] *Lewis,* xvii. 132 (Mann to Walpole, September 17, 1741).

V

London and Houghton (1741-5)

I

SIR ROBERT WALPOLE was at Houghton at the time of Horace's arrival in England, but before long he was back in Downing Street. Father and son had not met for two and a half years. During all that time Sir Robert had been fighting a losing battle, and his political position had now become desperate. He was facing defeat; and he was facing it in comparative loneliness. His elder sons had their own establishments; and his household consisted only of Mary, his daughter by Maria Skerrett, and Mrs. Leneve, the elderly lady who looked after her. The return of his youngest son, affectionate, vital and voluble, was an event that brought unexpected pleasure to the weary and ageing statesman. He began to perceive that this frivolous young man, with his passion for operas and masquerades and his insatiable hunger for the scandal of forgotten years, was in reality the most faithful and devoted of his sons.

But it was a melancholy home-coming for Horace Walpole, recalled from the pleasures and flatteries of Italy to witness the twilight of his father's greatness. He could not help remembering how in former days, in London or in Norfolk, he had seen the great Prime Minister attended by a crowd of deferential followers, and had shrunk from the boisterous good cheer which always surrounded him. Now Sir Robert, at the head of a Government many of whose members were in open rebellion, was about to confront an Opposition of almost overwhelming strength. He was ill and dispirited, and he could not sleep. At the dinner-table, where he had once presided so splendidly, Horace would watch him sitting for hours at a time, speechless, gazing into vacancy.[1]

II

It was now two years since Sir Robert Walpole had been forced, against his own judgment, into the declaration of war against Spain. He had made every effort to avert the war; he regarded it as altogether foolish and unnecessary; but there was no resisting the passionate anger against Spain which an industrious Opposition, aided by the ear of Captain Jenkins, had aroused throughout the country. Instead of resigning, he had remained at the head of affairs. A variety of motives probably brought about his decision to be responsible for the conduct of a war of which he profoundly disapproved—sheer love of power, the conviction that he alone could guide the nation on the unwise course it had determined to take, the belief that he could soon find some way of bringing the miserable business to an end. But the war had dragged on indecisively, month after month. Prodigies of obstruction were performed by the Opposition; having forced Walpole into a war, they did everything they could to prevent him from bringing it to a successful conclusion. Their attacks culminated in the famous motion brought forward in both Houses of Parliament in February 1741, praying the King to remove Sir Robert Walpole "from his Majesty's presence and counsels for ever." Every phase of his public life, from the South Sea settlement to the Spanish war, was vindictively reviewed; and charges of corruption, incompetence, and unconstitutional conduct were showered upon him. On this occasion he had a great personal triumph; his speech in defence of his ministry completely split the Opposition vote, and the motion was thrown out by large majorities in both Houses. But the publicity given to the accumulated charges against him, and the universal dissatisfaction over the slow progress of the war, had their effect on the nation. A general election took place in the summer of 1741, and Walpole was returned with his majority dangerously reduced.

In this election the Cornish boroughs, or rather their owners, had been very prominent in the swing against Sir Robert. But

[1] *Lewis,* xvii. 171 (Walpole to Mann, October 19, 1741).

Horace Walpole was duly returned to Parliament by the docile electors of Callington, a borough which had been brought into the family by his eldest brother's marriage with Margaret Rolle. He never visited Callington; but he represented the place in Parliament for thirteen years.

III

Parliament was not due to meet until December. There was time for Walpole to renew old friendships, to encounter new people, to accustom himself to the altered social and political currents of London, before the fight began. He had expected to be unhappy in England, and had returned there with some reluctance. But, once in London, he seldom had time to repine for Italy. He had been welcomed into a set of youngish people, a frivolous, witty and somewhat rowdy group, which contained George Selwyn and Sir Charles Hanbury Williams, and which hailed as its presiding deity the celebrated Etheldreda, Lady Townshend. There were balls and operas and plays; there was his closet to be fitted up with the spoils of his travels—"such a mixture of French gaiety and Roman *virtù*!"—and there were discussions with Sir Robert about pictures which he had admired in Italy and which might be bought for Houghton. At the royal birthday he figured in Parisian clothes of remarkable splendour, which nearly arrived too late for the occasion, and had to be specially fetched from Dover (since there are advantages in being the son even of a falling Prime Minister) by a King's Messenger.

He thoroughly enjoyed this sort of life. But he was also fully aware of the historical importance of the juncture at which he had returned to England. He perceived the uneasiness beneath the social brilliance, the sense of imminent political crisis; he appreciated the drama of his own position, as a young man entering the world at the very moment of his father's fall from power. It was not unpleasant to strike attitudes for the benefit of Mann—"Trust me, if we fall, all the grandeur, the envied grandeur of our house, will not cost me a sigh. . . ."[2] He realized that the long period of his father's tranquil rule was over, that England was about to experience critical years of development and change, and

[2] *Ibid.*, 248 (Walpole to Mann, December 17, 1741).

that he himself was destined, both by character and by circumstance, to be an extremely well-informed spectator of the coming events, but never an actor in them.

He had been aware, from a very early age, of the outstanding merits of his own letters. As an undergraduate he had urged George Montagu, perhaps rather to the surprise of that casual young man, not to destroy his letters; and the pride with which he regarded them did not diminish with time. At the outset of his epistolary career he had only two outstanding interests, politics and social life; and he had in Horace Mann the ideal recipient for a series of letters which would form a political and social history of his own time. Mann was living far away in Florence; he was personally interested in political developments in England, since the security of his post in a great measure depended on them; he loved social gossip, and knew many of Walpole's friends in London; he was intelligent and responsive, and Walpole had a great affection for him. Nor would their correspondence be one-sided, for Mann himself wrote excellent letters, and his accounts of Florentine life, and of the English visitors to Florence, were always amusing and interestng to Walpole. They had exchanged frequent letters since Walpole left Florence; and their letters now developed into an astonishing correspondence which lasted without the slightest intermission for forty-five years, during the whole of which time they never met at all.

IV

When Parliament met at the beginning of December, Sir Robert Walpole's supporters believed themselves to be in a majority of about forty. Horace Walpole wrote with the optimism of inexperience that this was "a vast number for the outset: a good majority, like a good sum of money, soon makes itself bigger."[3] He was wrong. There were plenty of waverers in that deceptive majority, and plenty of opportunists. In the debate on the King's Speech, Sir Robert made an effective reply to Pulteney's opening attack; but the first of a series of election petitions was debated on the following day, and the Government's majority in the division dropped to seven. A few days later, in a division on the choice of

[3] *Ibid.*, 220 (Walpole to Mann, December 3, 1741).

a chairman for the Committee of Elections, Sir Robert's party was defeated by four votes. For the first time in twenty years his opponents had triumphed; and his son did not easily forget their roar of exultation. "It was not very pleasant to be stared in the face, to see how one bore it," he wrote. Immediately after the division, one of the doorkeepers in the House was grossly impertinent to him; and a member of his own party expressed approval of the man's action.[4] But it was not difficult to bear unpleasant trifles like these with equanimity, when Sir Robert himself, confronted with daily threats of impeachment and the Tower, was heartening all his friends by his unshakable courage and good spirits. He had recovered from the illness and depression of the autumn; and even the insistence of the Opposition on sitting on Saturdays, in order to deprive him of his week-end exercise of hunting in Richmond Park, made no impression on his health. "Damn him, how well he looks!" one of these amiable opponents was heard to remark.[5]

The Ministry carried on the struggle, with varying majorities and more than one defeat, until the Christmas recess. When Parliament met again in January, the position was at first the same. The majorities still fluctuated, there were occasional defeats, sick and dying men were summoned from their beds and dragged through the divisions. Sir Robert was still indomitable. His sons wished him to resign, and so preserve some measure of health for the years of his retirement; but after a long and strenuous sitting of the House, he could still enjoy a jovial supper in the small hours of the morning, while Horace crept from the supper-table exhausted to bed. At the close of the month, however, the end came. A decisive defeat occurred on an election petition; and Sir Robert's sons, his brother Horace, and some of his principal supporters united in urging him to resign. The King, with embraces and tears, took reluctant leave of his beloved Minister.

Sir Robert was immediately created Earl of Orford. The King also bestowed upon him a pension of £4,000 a year, which he would not accept.[6] His illegitimate daughter by Maria Skerrett

[4] *Ibid.*, 244 (Walpole to Mann, December 16, 1741).

[5] *Ibid.*, 247, 252 (Walpole to Mann, December 17 and 22, 1741).

[6] He was obliged to ask for this pension in the last year of his life, when the King, according to Horace Walpole, somewhat reluctantly granted it.

was given the rank of an earl's daughter, and his enemies lavished much self-righteous indignation on this proceeding. His friends and supporters crowded his house in a series of informal levées. Seldom has a Minister, defeated and threatened with impeachment, made so dignified an exit from office.

But the more vindictive of his opponents were still determined to break him. They realized that he would continue to be the "minister behind the curtain," and that the King, who, after all, had never known any other Minister during the fifteen years of his reign, would undoubtedly wish to consult him in secret. The King, indeed, had already insisted that Lord Wilmington, formerly Sir Spencer Compton and as much of a cipher in 1742 as in 1727, should take Walpole's place, instead of Pulteney, the Leader of the Opposition and the obvious claimant for the office; and this has always been attributed to the advice of Walpole himself. It was annoying enough for the Opposition that the man whom they had at last defeated should be driving about London instead of languishing in the Tower; it was really outrageous that he should coolly select the man who was to succeed him. So they began to agitate for a Committee of the House of Commons to inquire into the history of Walpole's administration, and into every detail of his public life. Meanwhile the object of their proposed inquiries retired to the pleasant air of Richmond, and his son Horace moved gaily about London, and appeared at a masquerade as Aurungzebe.

The motion for appointing a Secret Committee to inquire into the last twenty years of Sir Robert Walpole's administration was debated on March 9th, and to the general surprise it was defeated. Ten days later a second motion, for a Committee to inquire into his conduct of affairs for the last ten years, was passed by three votes. On this occasion Horace Walpole spoke in the House for the first time. He made a pleasant, rather diffident little speech, neatly phrased and full of becoming filial sentiments. William Pitt, later in the debate, simultaneously complimented young Walpole on his effort and scored a point for his own party, when he said "how very commendable it was in him to have made the speech, which must have made an impression upon the House; but if it was becoming in him to remember that he was the child of the accused, that the House ought to remember too that they are the children of their country."[7]

The Secret Committee was duly formed. Of its twenty-one members, only five could possibly be regarded as friendly to Sir Robert; the rest were all enemies. But no one in the Walpole camp was much perturbed about the Committee. Its formation coincided with some popular demonstrations against Sir Robert, which were paid for, according to his son, by certain of his leading opponents. And it was not altogether pleasant for Horace Walpole, on driving up to a procession in the street, to find that they were carrying "a mawkin in a chair"—an effigy of his young sister, the newly-created Lady Mary.[8] But the Secret Committee, after a truculent beginning, gradually and inconclusively faded out of existence before the year was over. Sir Robert quietly moved out of Downing Street into a small house in Arlington Street. His popularity began to return. Horace ventured to take him one night to Ranelagh—"it was pretty full, and all its fullness flocked round us: we walked with a train at our heels, like two chairmen going to fight; but they were extremely civil, and did not crowd him, or say the least impertinence—I think he grows popular already."[9] Early in August they went down together to Houghton.

V

For the next three years Horace Walpole continued to spend most of his time with his father, and this companionship was only ended by Lord Orford's death. A small house was rented for him next door to his father's house in Arlington Street. Here, and at Houghton, he watched the dignified close of the old Minister's life.

As his enemies had feared, Lord Orford retained complete influence over the King, and therefore a greater actual power than any other man in the nation. He saw his victorious opponents, who had been united only in opposition to himself, drift into hopeless discord and confusion. Pulteney had already made

[7] *Lewis,* xvii. 376–7 (Walpole to Mann, March 14, 1742).
[8] *Ibid.,* 390 (Walpole to Mann, April 8, 1742).
[9] *Ibid.,* xviii. 8 (Walpole to Mann, July 29, 1742).

an unexpected ascent to the House of Lords. In July 1743 Lord Wilmington died, and Lord Orford's friend and ally, Henry Pelham, succeeded him in office, in spite of the efforts of Carteret to obtain the nomination of Pulteney. Finally Carteret himself, the principal figure of a divided and ramshackle Cabinet, was driven to resign at the end of 1744; and Pelham was left in undisputed power.

In all these developments Lord Orford played a discreet but decisive part. He realized with pleasure that his power was undiminished; he enjoyed the many signs of his returning popularity: but his greatest happiness was in the long periods of retirement at Houghton. In a celebrated letter to one of his friends, he described the delights of rural seclusion. "This place affords no news, no subject of amusement and entertainment to you fine Gentlemen. Men of wit and pleasure about town understand not the language, nor taste the charms of the inanimate world: my flatterers here are all mutes, the Oaks the Beeches and the Chestnuts seem to contend, which shall best please the Lord of the Mannor: They cannot deceive, they will not lie. I in return with sincerity admire them, and have as many beauties about me as take up all my hours of dangling, and no disgrace attends me since sixty-seven. Within doors we come a little nearer to real life and admire the almost speaking Canvas, all the airs and graces of which the proudest of the ladies can boast, with these I am satisfied as they gratify me with all I wish and all I want, and expect nothing in return which I am not able to give."[10]

His son Horace did not share this idyllic view of Houghton. He never really enjoyed retirement; rural seclusion was insupportable to him without the presence of lively and congenial people. And the squires and parsons of Norfolk, the aldermen from Norwich and King's Lynn, were not lively and congenial. "Only imagine that I here every day see men, who are mountains of roast beef, and only seem just roughly hewn out into the outlines of human form, like the giant-rock at Pratolino! I shudder when I see them brandish their knives in act to carve, and look on

[10] Earl of Orford to—[General Charles Churchill?], June 24, 1743. From a contemporary MS. copy at Farmington. I have used this version in preference to that in *Coxe* (i. 762 n.), which seems to have been somewhat polished and corrected before publication.

them as savages that devour one another." They even interfered with his enjoyment of his father's pictures. "Why must I never expect to see anything but Beefs in a gallery which would not yield even to the Colonna!" Fits of melancholy would descend on him, when there seemed nothing to do but to play with Patapan and long to be in London, or, better still, back at Casa Mannetti with Mann and Chute. "Oh! my dear Sir, don't you find that nine parts in ten of the world are of no use but to make you wish yourself with that tenth part? I am so far from growing used to mankind by living amongst them, that my natural ferocity and wildness does but every day grow worse. They tire me, they fatigue me; I don't know what to do with them; I don't know what to say to them; I fling open the windows, and fancy I want air; and when I get by myself, I undress myself, and seem to have had people in my pockets, in my plaits, and on my shoulders! I indeed find this fatigue worse in the country than in town, because one can avoid it there and has more resources; but it is there too. I fear 'tis growing old; but I literally seem to have murdered a man whose name was Ennui, for his ghost is ever before me."[11]

But, in spite of his complaints, there were many pleasant features about the three summers which he spent at Houghton. There was the kindness and confidence of his father, and the affectionate irony with which he would ask him to come down to Norfolk. "All the disagreeable symptoms I had, are gone, and this I verily believe will make you partake in my pleasures, I know what would add to them when you can persuade y^{r}self to sacrifice the Joys of the *Beau-monde* to ye amusements of a dull rural life.

"But we all love to please our selves, and may it allways be in y^{r} power to make y^{r}self as happy as I wish you for I am most truly

"Yours most affectly

"Orford."[12]

There was the occasion when Patapan was attacked and shaken by a large pointer, and Lord Orford, who shared his son's attachment to Madame Grifoni's gift, remarked that "he never saw

[11] *Toynbee*, i. 372–4 (Walpole to Chute, August 20, 1743).

[12] *Ibid.*, Supplement, iii. 116 (Earl of Orford to Horace Walpole, July 14, 1744).

ten people show so much *real* concern."[13] There were visits to Wolterton, his uncle Horace's charming estate on the other side of the county, with its pleasant lake and woods. In the summer of 1744 he went coursing every morning, accompanied only by his footman, "who knows no more of it than I do," and he even proposed to go hunting when the season began.[14] It is not easy to picture Horace Walpole galloping across the windy commons towards Bircham and Anmer, or ineffectively pursuing hares over Coxford Heath. But his main pleasure and diversion was in writing. In the summer of 1742 he composed a *Sermon on Painting*, with special reference to individual pictures at Houghton, which was preached before Lord Orford by his chaplain. It was an admirable *pastiche* of the apostrophic and exclamatory sermons of the day. Next summer he wrote a long, rambling, and somewhat indelicate poem called *Patapan, or the Little White Dog*, a satire on various contemporary politicians.[15] And in August 1743 he completed *Aedes Walpolianae*, a detailed catalogue of his father's pictures, to which he prefixed an introduction discussing the merits of the various schools of painting.

The art-criticism of any period almost inevitably causes pain and bewilderment to future generations; and Horace Walpole's introduction to *Aedes Walpolianae* is no exception. It is not, perhaps, surprising that many of the world's supreme painters, from Giotto down to Rembrandt, were entirely passed over; Walpole had never visited Holland and Flanders, and the great galleries of Italy, which he knew intimately, displayed few works by the earlier masters. His omissions can be forgiven; but one is sometimes startled by his more positive judgments. His pages are filled with extraordinary opinions and baffling phrases. The Dutch painters were dismissed as "those drudging Mimicks of Nature's most uncomely coarsenesses." Andrea del Sarto's colouring was a mixture of mist and tawdry; the Landscapes of Titian, and the Architecture of Veronese, were equal to their Carnations; the colouring of the Florentine school was gawdy and gothic. There was some good criticism and sound appreciation scattered

[13] *Lewis*, xviii. 71 (Walpole to Mann, October 8, 1742).

[14] *Ibid.*, xxx. 81 (Walpole to Sir Charles Hanbury Williams, September 19, 1744).

[15] *Ibid.*, 287–306.

about the introduction, and almost too much of Walpole's habitual vivacity; but the general standard of the performance can best be judged by the paragraph of resounding nonsense with which it closes. "I shall conclude with these few Recapitulations. I can admire Correggio's Grace and exquisite Finishing; but I cannot overlook his wretched Drawing and Distortions. I admire Parmegiano's more majestic Grace, and wish the length of Limbs and Necks, which forms those Graceful Airs, were natural. Titian wanted to have seen the Antique; Poussin to have seen Titian. Le Sœur, whom I think in Drawing and Expression equal to Poussin, and in the great ideas of his Heads and Attitudes, second to Raphael, like the first wanted Colouring, and had not the fine Draperies of the latter. Albano never painted a Picture, but some of the Figures were stiff, and wanted Grace; and then his scarce ever succeeding in large Subjects, will throw him out of the List of perfect Painters. Dominichini, whose Communion of Saint Jerome is allow'd to be the second Picture in the World, was generally raw in his Colouring, hard in his contours, and wanted clearness in his Carnations, and a knowledge of the Chiaro Oscuro. In short, in my opinion, all the qualities of a perfect Painter, never met but in RAPHAEL, GUIDO, and ANNIBAL CARACCI."

The Description of the pictures is a more attractive performance than the Introduction. With care and pride Horace Walpole described the glorious collection which his father had assembled, and which he himself was to see so tragically dispersed. The Raphaels, the Titians, the Poussins, the Van Dycks, the Salvator Rosas, the Guido Renis, and the vaunted roomful of Carlo Marattis—he pointed out, for the benefit of the interested tourist, their merits and their faults, the little anecdotes and peculiarities which were attached to them. He added to the Description his own *Sermon on Painting,* and a poem by the deplorable Mr. Whaley, *A Journey to Houghton.* And he prefixed to it an engaging dedication to his father, in which he expressed his heartfelt admiration for that great man.

"Could those virtuous men your Father and Grandfather arise from yonder Church, how would they be amazed to see this noble edifice and spacious plantations, where once stood their plain and homely dwelling! How would they be satisfy'd to find only the Mansion-house, not the Morals of the Family altered!

"May it be long, Sir, ere You join Them! And oh! As You wear no stain from Them, may You receive no disgrace from

"Your dutiful

"and affectionate Son,

"HORACE WALPOLE."[16]

VI

If Walpole only occasionally found contentment at Houghton, he was almost invariably happy in London. At his first return from Italy, as the son of a declining and defeated Minister, a young man of delicate constitution and fastidious tastes, he felt a little out of place there.[17] But before long he had completely adapted himself to its conditions, and could write that "were I a physician, I would prescribe nothing but *recipe ccclxv drachm. Londin.*"[18] Balls and masquerades and concerts; card parties, water parties, parties at Ranelagh, parties at Vauxhall; the park: the Opera: the theatre. It was his life at Florence all over again, but on a larger scale, without a hint of provincialism or pettiness, and with a background of strenuous political activity.

Theatrical affairs were a topic of endless interest to Walpole. He became one of the thirty subscribers, or guarantors, of the Opera in the season of 1743, and duly regretted the two hundred pounds which he had subscribed.[19] He was not greatly impressed by the earlier performances of Garrick, the rising star; he much preferred to entertain old Mrs. Bracegirdle to breakfast, and to listen to her fading memories of earlier days of the stage. Once or twice he became incongruously involved in the quarrels and riots that suddenly blew up in the theatres. On one such occasion he rushed to the rescue of Lord Lincoln, who was being insulted by a drunken officer, climbed over the shoulders of three ladies, and

[16] Manuscript copies of *Aedes Walpolianae* were circulated for some years. Walpole issued a private edition, which contained a good many errors, in 1747; and published a corrected edition, from which the above quotations are taken, in 1752.

[17] *Lewis,* xvii. 270 (Walpole to Mann, January 7, 1742).

[18] *Ibid.,* xviii. 316 (Walpole to Mann, October 3, 1743).

[19] *Ibid.,* 293–4 (Walpole to Mann, August 14, 1743).

tumbled ingloriously into Lord Rockingham's lap.[20] Two years later he intervened in another dispute with more success, though with results hardly less embarrassing to himself. "The town has been trying all this winter to beat pantomimes off the stage, very boisterously; for it is the way here to make even an affair of taste and sense, a matter of riot and arms. Fleetwood, the master of Drury Lane, has omitted nothing to support them, as they supported his house. About ten days ago, he let into the pit great numbers of Bear-garden *bruisers* (that is the term), to knock down everybody that hissed. The pit rallied their forces, and drove them out: I was sitting very quietly in the side-boxes, contemplating all this. On a sudden the curtain flew up, and discovered the whole stage filled with blackguards armed with bludgeons and clubs to menace the audience. This raised the greatest uproar; and among the rest, who flew into a passion, but your friend the philosopher? In short, one of the actors advancing to the front of the stage to make an apology for the manager, he had scarce begun to say, 'Mr. Fleetwood——' when your friend, with a most audible voice and dignity of anger, called out 'He is an impudent rascal!' The whole pit huzzaed, and repeated the words. Only think of my being a popular orator! But what was still better, while my shadow of a person was dilating to the consistence of a hero, one of the chief ringleaders of the riot, coming under the box where I sat, and pulling off his hat, said, 'Mr. W., what would you please to have us do next?' It is impossible to describe the confusion into which this apostrophe threw me. I sank down into the box, and have never since ventured to set my foot into the playhouse. The next night, the uproar was repeated with greater violence, and nothing was heard but voices calling out, 'Where's Mr. W.? Where's Mr. W.?' In short, the whole town has been entertained with my prowess, and Mr. Conway has given me the name of Wat Tyler. . . ."[21]

His friends were for the most part young men of wealth and good family, some with political ambitions, some interested mainly in women or cards. George Selwyn, who was one day to shake a grey head over the gaming enormities of Charles Fox, was already famous as a wit and gambler. In the intervals of cards

[20] *Ibid.*, xvii. 411–2 (Walpole to Mann, April 29, 1742).

[21] *Ibid.*, xviii (Walpole to Mann, November 26, 1744).

and dice he had spent a few terms at Oxford, but was expelled in 1745 for enacting a silly and blasphemous parody of the Last Supper during a drunken party at an inn.[22] Another headstrong young gambler was Richard Edgcumbe, the son of Lord Edgcumbe of Mount Edgcumbe in Cornwall. Selwyn and Edgcumbe both remained Walpole's lifelong friends, and were his constant visitors at Strawberry Hill. Another friend was the poet and satirist Sir Charles Hanbury Williams, always a fervent partisan of Lord Orford and the brilliant and tireless assailant of his enemies. A series of pungent letters from Horace Walpole to Hanbury Williams still exists;[23] and the poet paid an agreeable tribute to his younger friend in his *Epistle to the Right Hon. Henry Fox,* where he speaks of

> my young Walpole, blest with truest taste,
> Adorn'd with learning, with politeness grac'd.[24]

Henry Fox and Richard Rigby, a pair of capable and determined politicians, were also prominent among Walpole's friends. And he was intimate with other youthful grandees of the day—Lord Lincoln, who consoled himself, after Lady Sophia Fermor's unexpected marriage with Carteret, with a first-rate political alliance with Miss Pelham; the second Lord Hervey, "the delicate Lord," who was more effeminate in appearance even than his father, but who showed, on the memorable occasion when Lord Cobham spat into his hat, that no man could insult him with impunity;[25] and several more.

But Conway remained his most intimate friend. He idolized his cousin, watched with anxiety the opening of his military career, and sat trembling at Houghton in expectation of the despatches after the battle of Dettingen. And in 1744 he showed that he was prepared to undergo on behalf of Conway sacrifices and exertions which he would certainly not have endured for any other human being. Conway, an impoverished young officer, had fallen in love with Lady Caroline Fitzroy, one of the daughters

[22] *Jesse,* i. 2, 3, 71–89, 93–9.

[23] Printed in *Lewis,* xxx.

[24] *Hanbury Williams,* ii. 145. *(Epistle to the Right Hon. Henry Fox, written in August 1745).*

[25] *Lewis,* xx. 123–4 (Walpole to Mann, February 25, 1750).

of the Duke of Grafton. His brother Lord Conway had married her sister Lady Isabella; but it was generally known that Lady Caroline, while rivalling her sister in beauty, made no pretence of equalling her in virtue. Horace Walpole, who admired Lady Caroline and was usually on the friendliest terms with her, deplored his beloved cousin's choice: yet he was so generous as to offer to share with Conway the whole of his fortune, if it would help him to bring about the marriage he desired. He was quite frank in his disapproval of the match: but he could not take the responsibility of advising Conway to break it off, and offered instead to supply the means of bringing it about. His places, he said in a letter to Conway, brought him in almost two thousand pounds a year; by living with his father, he had no real use for this income, and spent it extravagantly on trifles. Could it be expended better than in making happy his friend, his cousin, his nearest relation by the mother whose memory he adored? "I am sensible of having more follies and weaknesses, and fewer real good qualities, than most men. I sometimes reflect on this, though I own too seldom. I always want to begin acting like a man, and a sensible one, which I think I might be if I would. Can I begin better, than by taking care of my fortune for one I love? You have seen (I have seen you have) that I am fickle, and foolishly fond of twenty new people: but I don't really love them—I have always loved you constantly: I am willing to convince you and the world, what I have always told you, that I loved you better than anybody. If I ever felt much for anything (which I know may be questioned), it was certainly for my mother. I look on you as my nearest relation by her, and I think I can never do enough to show my gratitude and affection to her. For these reasons, don't deny me what I have set my heart on—the making your fortune easy to you. . . ."[26]

Walpole's admiration for Conway was not shared to any considerable degree by his more detached contemporaries. He appeared to them, for all his good looks and his high military reputation, as a cold, prudish, rather colourless man. As a soldier, his bravery and coolness became proverbial; but in social and political life he was not an outstanding figure. Even Walpole, in later years, had to admit his essential coldheartedness and lack of

[26] *Toynbee,* ii. 37–8 (Walpole to Conway, July 20, 1744).

generosity, of which he met with humiliating instances. At this time, however, nothing could have been more creditable than Conway's reception and refusal of the offer made in the letter just quoted. His reply was full of gratitude and of his sense of the sacrifice that Walpole was offering to make; but he absolutely refused to accept anything from his cousin. Walpole's fortune, he said, "is disposed of in a manner equally useful to society and honourable to yourself, by encouraging in your sphere those arts that humanize mankind, or by supporting those with your charity who are real objects of compassion. I am too sensible of my own incapacity to make half so good a use of it, and I should both rob them of the effects of your generosity, and you of the pleasure of exercising it."[27]

In any case, Conway did not marry Lady Caroline Fitzroy. Instead he married three years later a young widow, the Countess of Ailesbury, with whom he lived in complete happiness to the end of his days. Lady Caroline married Lord Petersham, who later succeeded his father as Earl of Harrington; and embarked on a career of cheerful gallantry. There were to be many glimpses of her, gay and disreputable, "gloriously jolly and handsome," in Walpole's letters in years to come.

VII

Three familiar names have been missing from this narrative since the time of Walpole's return from Italy, those of Gray and West and Ashton. How was the Quadruple Alliance weathering the years?

Ashton had been ordained, and in the spring of 1742 was living with Walpole in Downing Street. He soon began to be known as a rising young preacher, and Walpole was able to obtain for him, by an application to Henry Pelham, the Crown living of Aldingham in Lancashire.[28] West was in ill-health, and was living quietly at a friend's country house, Popes, near Hatfield. Gray, whose father had died in the previous autumn, had not yet settled down to live at Cambridge. Apparently Conway had made some attempt to reconcile him to Walpole, but without success.

[27] *Albemarle,* i. 399–403 (Conway to Walpole, August 5, 1744).

[28] *Toynbee,* i. 224 (Walpole to Henry Pelham, May 17, 1742).

One can hardly doubt that West, that gentle and kind-hearted person, would have made some attempt to reconcile Gray and Walpole, unless he considered that the circumstances of their quarrel made a reconciliation out of the question. Whether he made such an attempt is not known. Possibly the state of his health prevented it; indeed there is no evidence that he ever saw Walpole after the latter's return from Italy, though they exchanged affectionate letters. And although nobody seems to have realized it, he was actually in the last stages of consumption. The tone of his letters concealed his real condition from his friends: but on June 1st, 1742 he died at Popes, in his twenty-sixth year. Gray was not informed of his death, although he suspected it when one of his letters was returned unopened; he only found out the truth of his suspicions from seeing some memorial verses by Ashton which were printed in a newspaper. Ashton himself did not hear that his friend was dead until several days after the event.

West's lonely and unnoticed death was a great sorrow to the other members of the Quadruple Alliance, who were still united in their affection for him. Gray in particular was profoundly grieved. He had admired West's shy poetic talent, which had affinities with his own still latent genius; he had valued him greatly as a friend, especially perhaps since his own estrangement from Walpole. West's death, and in a lesser degree the quarrel with Walpole, directly inspired the *Ode on a Distant Prospect of Eton College,* which he wrote at this time. He also bewailed the loss of his friend in a beautiful sonnet. But West's death did nothing to repair the breach between his two closest friends; and for three more years Gray and Walpole were to remain estranged.

Another friendship of Walpole's lapsed soon after his return from Italy. He had sent Madame Grifoni a number of presents from England—some fans, a watch of particularly exquisite workmanship, a picture of Mary Queen of Scots:[29] and for two or three years he continued to write to her, though without any spontaneous enthusiasm. "Lord! I am horridly tired of that romantic love and correspondence!" he complained to Mann. "Must I answer her last letter? there were but six lines—what can I

[29] *Lewis,* xvii. 413–5 (Mann to Walpole, May 15, 1742).

HORACE WALPOLE (*circa* 1755)
by JOHN GILES ECKHARDT
By kind permission of the Trustees of the National Portrait Gallery

HORACE WALPOLE (1757)
From an engraving by JAMES MCARDELL of a painting by SIR JOSHUA REYNOLDS

say?"[30] His Italian was growing rusty; compliments and endearments no longer flowed easily from his pen.[31] Finally, in a despairing effort to recover his affections, she asked Mann if he thought Mr. Walpole would accept a present of hams, Marzolini cheeses and Tuscan wine. Mann discouraged this polite attention, much to Walpole's relief. "Jesus! how blank I should have looked at unpacking a great case of bacon and wine! My dear child, be my friend, and preserve me from heroic presents. I cannot possibly at this distance begin a new courtship of *regali*; for I suppose all those hams were to be converted into watches and toys...alas! I am neither old enough nor young enough to be gallant, and should ill become the writing of heroic epistles to a fair mistress in Italy—*No, no: ne sono uscito con onore, mi pare, e non voglio riprendere quel impegno più.*"[32] These ungallant sentiments form Walpole's last important reference to his *illustrissima*. So far as is known, he did not write to her after 1743. And he no longer included messages to her among the numerous commissions which he entrusted to Mann, and which ranged from the purchase of a Domenichino for Houghton to the acquisition for Lord Islay of a pair of Maltese cats of the largest possible size.

VIII

During the summer of 1744 Lord Orford had been unwell; and when he left Houghton that autumn, it was for the last time. By November the doctors were certain that his complaint was the stone. In spite of the protests of his youngest son, they made use of a specific of extraordinary violence, the Lixivium Lithontripticum, the cherished invention of Dr. Jurin, one of their number. A ferocious battle of pamphlets, in which the medical profession afterwards engaged, revealed all too vividly the effects of this remedy on the immense and unwieldy frame of the old statesman. Horace Walpole attended him throughout his last illness, and has left some notes of his father's words during the final agonizing night.

"Dear Horace this Lixivium has blown me up. It has tore me

[30] *Ibid.*, xviii. 63 (Walpole to Mann, September 25, 1742).

[31] *Ibid.*, 201, 267 (Walpole to Mann, March 25 and July 11, 1743).

[32] *Ibid.*, 366 (Walpole to Mann, December 26, 1743).

to pieces. The Affair is over with me; that it may be short Dear Ranby, is all I desire.

"Give me more Opium; knock me down. I expect nothing but to have ease. Dear Horace if one must die, 'tis hard to die in pain.

"Why do you all stand round me! are ye all waiting there, because this is the last night.

"Insisted on Ranby's telling him if he should die before morning: and Ranby gave him no hopes: he then talk'd in private with Ranby; then a quarter of an hour just before three with Ld Walpole. Afterwards again with Ranby. To Ranby, ' 'Tis impossible not to be a little disturb'd at going out of the world, but you see I am not afraid.' "[33]

Lord Orford died in Arlington Street on March 18th 1745, in his sixty-ninth year. Horace Walpole, who noted down the progress of his illness and these melancholy details of his last night, may also be allowed to write his epitaph.

"He had lived to stand the rudest trials with honour, to see his character universally cleared, his enemies brought to infamy for their ignorance or villainy, and the world allowing him to be the only man in England fit to be what he had been; and he died at a time when his age and infirmities prevented his again undertaking the support of a government which engrossed his whole care, and which he foresaw was falling into the last confusion."[34]

[33] MS. at Farmington, unpublished. I cannot reconcile this document with the statement of Walpole's letter to Mann of April 15, 1745, that "his fortune attended him to the last; for he died of the most painful of all distempers with little or no pain."

[34] *Lewis,* xix. 32 (Walpole to Mann, April 15, 1745).

VI

London (1745-7)

I

LORD ORFORD left to Horace Walpole the remainder of the lease of the house in Arlington Street in which he died, five thousand pounds in money, and a thousand pounds a year from the place of Collector of the Customs. The surplus income from the Collectorship of the Customs was to be shared between Horace and his brother Edward, and produced for each of them a further four hundred pounds a year. The surplus of Lord Orford's personal estate was also to be divided between Edward and Horace.[1] But actually there was no surplus for them to divide, as their father was found to have left between forty and fifty thousand pounds in debts.[2] The second Lord Orford was obliged to close Houghton while the estate recovered from the burdens laid upon it. It was the nemesis of long years of splendid hospitality, and the reckless adornment of a great house. It was also an effective retort to the charges of habitual peculation which had been so often levelled at the dead Minister. Houghton indeed, with its pictures, its furniture, its park and plantations, remained a monument of vast expanse. But Lord Orford's enemies had to moderate their accusations when they

[1] *Lewis,* xiii. 15 *(Short Notes of My Life).* The most detailed description by Horace Walpole of his inheritance and his general financial position is given in *Works,* ii. 364–92, *(Account of my Conduct relative to the Places I hold under Government, and towards Ministers).* He states there that he received, at his father's dying wish, an additional £2,000 from his eldest brother; but that of the £5,000 which should have come to him out of his father's estate, he only obtained £1,000.

[2] *Works,* ii. 365. *Lewis,* xix. 32 (Walpole to Mann, April 15, 1745).

realized that he had left to his children a pile of debts instead of his fabled hoards of treasure.

He had, however, provided nobly for his sons, by obtaining for them various patent offices under the Crown. These were either complete sinecures, or offices whose duties were carried out by deputies who received a modest salary for their services; and nothing but death could dislodge their fortunate occupants. Of the three brothers, Robert, second Earl of Orford, held the office of Auditor of the Exchequer, which was valued at £7,000 a year: and Edward Walpole was Clerk of the Pells, for which he received £3,000 a year. They already held other offices which added substantially to these far from contemptible incomes. Horace Walpole had received, several years before, the offices of Clerk of the Estreats and Comptroller of the Pipe, which together produced about £300 a year, and that of Usher of the Exchequer, which at first brought in £900 a year, but increased greatly in value in subsequent years. We have seen that in 1744, a few months before Lord Orford's death, he had told Conway that his places were bringing him in nearly two thousand pounds a year.[3] With the addition of the income from the Collectorship of the Customs, which came to him after the death of his father, it would appear that his places were worth at this time approximately three thousand four hundred pounds a year.[4]

It was natural enough that Horace Walpole, in the course of his long life, should be attacked now and then as an idle placeman drawing a large and undeserved income out of the public funds. His own conscience was always perfectly clear in the matter. Had not his father rendered inestimable services to the British nation? Had he not been the faithful and trusted Minister of two kings? Was he not absolutely justified in securing, as a reward for these services, the financial independence of his children by an ancient and honourable means? In 1782, when a particularly violent attack was in progress and the word "bloodsucker" had been freely used, Walpole drew up an *Account of my Conduct relative to the Places I hold under Government, and towards Ministers,* in which he defended his right to hold these offices, using his antiquarian knowledge to reinforce his argu-

[3] *Ante,* p. 92. [4] *Works,* ii. 364–6. *Sedgwick,* xxxviii–ix.

ments. "I presume boldly to say that my father had a legal right of making the provision for me he did in the places I hold. Patent places for life have existed from time immemorial, by law, and under all changes of Government. He who holds an ancient patent place enjoys it as much by law as any gentleman holds his estate, and by more ancient tenure than most gentlemen hold theirs, and from the same fountain, only of ancienter date, than many of the nobility and gentry hold their estates, who possess them only by grants from the Crown, as I possess my places, which were not wrung from the Church, and in violation of the intention of the donors, as a vast number of estates were; nor can I think myself as a patent placeman a more useless or a less legal engrosser of part of the wealth of the nation than deans and prebendaries. While there are distinctions of ranks, and unequal divisions of property, not acquired by personal merit, but by birth or favour, some will be more fortunate than others."[5]

Secure in the enjoyment of his offices, and justified in his occupation of them by such comfortable doctrines as these, Horace Walpole was at twenty-eight a reasonably wealthy man. A substantial unearned income, a house in Arlington Street, and presumably a certain amount of private capital formed a very satisfactory inheritance for a youngest son. Abstemious and celibate, with the pursuit of *virtù* as his single mild extravagance, he was perfectly content with his fortune. He was now quite independent of any family ties, and indeed of any personal ties whatever. His eldest brother, unable to maintain Houghton, usually lived in London with his mistress, Miss Norsa, a handsome Jewess; while his wife racketed about Europe or paid an occasional unwelcome visit to England. The second brother Edward, with whom Horace was on bad terms at this time owing to a dispute about one of the family boroughs, dwelt at Englefield Green with his children, three daughters and a son, by a pretty milliner's apprentice named Dorothy Clement, who had lived with him as his mistress until her death in 1738:[6] he represented Great Yarmouth in Parliament, but his main interest was in music; he played exquisitely on the violoncello, and had invented an instrument which he called the pentachord, from

[5] *Works,* ii. 365. [6] *Last Journals,* i. 93

the number of its strings.[7] Their half-sister, Lady Mary, married Charles Churchill, the son of Sir Robert's old friend General Churchill by Mrs. Oldfield, the actress, a few months after her father's death. So Horace was completely free to live where he chose and as he chose. He gave a sigh of thankfulness that he was no longer obliged to spend all his summers in Norfolk, but was at liberty to stay at the country houses of his friends, with Rigby at Mistley, where he "rode about and sailed," and with the Edgcumbes at far-away Mount Edgcumbe. A projected visit to The Hague was prevented by the danger from the French ships which were besieging Ostend. And he began to look about for a small house at a convenient distance from town.

II

Towards the end of 1745 Walpole and Gray were reconciled after four and a half years of complete estrangement. The renewal of their friendship was brought about by "a lady, who wished well to them both."[8] The lady was a Mrs. Kerr, who has not otherwise been identified. As a result of her efforts Walpole wrote a friendly letter to Gray, who came up from Cambridge to see him at the beginning of November. A complicated series of interviews followed, which were not made easier by Gray's natural stiffness and pride, and the jaunty *insouciance* which Walpole appears to have displayed, at any rate at their first meeting. Ashton hovered in the background, and his mysterious part in the quarrel was now made clear to Gray; it is clear no longer, but evidently he had been guilty of some sort of treachery, and Gray no longer cared about him sufficiently to be surprised or particularly resentful.

Gray wrote a detailed and amusing narrative of the reconciliation in a letter to his friend Wharton, which is worth quoting in full. "I wrote a Note the Night I came, and immediately received a very civil Answer. I went the following Evening to see *the Party* (as Mrs. Foible says), was something abash'd at his Confidence: he came to meet me, kiss'd me on both Sides with all the Ease of one, who receives an Acquaintance just come out of the Country, squatted me into a Fauteuil, begun to talk of the Town and this

[7] *Ibid.*, 102. [8] *Lewis,* xviii. 69 (Walpole to Mason, March 2, 1773).

and that and t'other, and continued with little Interruption for three Hours, when I took my leave very indifferently pleased, but treated with wondrous Good-breeding. I supped with him next night (as he desired) Ashton was there, whose Formalities tickled me inwardly, for he I found was to be angry about the Letter I had wrote him. However in going home together our Hackney-Coach jumbled us into a Sort of Reconciliation: he hammer'd out somewhat like an Excuse; and I received it very readily, because I cared not two pence, whether it were true or not. So we grew the best Acquaintance imaginable, and I set with him on Sunday some Hours alone, when he inform'd me of abundance of Anecdotes much to my Satisfaction, and in short open'd (I really believe) his Heart to me with that Sincerity, that I found I had still less Reason to have a good Opinion of him, than (if possible) I ever had before. Next morning I breakfasted alone with Mr. W: when we had all the Eclaircissement I ever expected, and I left him far better satisfied, than I had been hitherto. When I return, I shall see him again. Such is the Epitome of my four Days."[9]

Once these preliminaries had been successfully concluded, the friendship between Walpole and Gray was soon firmly re-established, and continued without interruption until Gray's death in 1771. Their correspondence was resumed, and Gray spent much of his time with Walpole whenever he came to London. When Chute returned to England in 1746, Gray wrote informing him, in shy and faintly apologetic terms, of the happy ending of the storm which he had seen gathering long ago at Florence. "I find Mr. Walpole made some mention of me to you. Yes, we are together again. It is about a Year, I believe, since he wrote to me to offer it, and there has been (particularly of late) in Appearance the same Kindness and Confidence almost as of old. What were his motives I cannot yet guess: what were mine, you will imagine, and perhaps blame me. However as yet I neither repent, nor rejoice overmuch: but I am pleased."[10] Of course Gray was pleased: but caution and understatement were still to replace, for a year or two yet, the old affectionate tones in which he used to speak of his friend.

[9] *Gray*, i. 226–7 (Gray to Wharton, November 14, 1745).
[10] *Gray* i. 248 (Gray to Chute, October 2, 1746).

III

At the time of these delicate negotiations between Walpole and Gray, the "Forty-Five" was at its height. While their broken friendship was being pieced together in Arlington Street, Prince Charles was advancing steadily into England. Walpole's whole scheme of existence was gravely threatened, and he was well aware of it. "Now comes the Pretender's boy, and promises all my comfortable apartments in the Exchequer and Custom House to some forlorn Irish peer, who chooses to remove his pride and poverty out of some large old unfurnished gallery at St. Germain's. Why really, Mr. Montagu, this is not pleasant! I shall wonderfully dislike being a loyal sufferer in a threadbare coat, and shivering in an antechamber at Hanover, or reduced to teach Latin and English to the young princes at Copenhagen."[11] Certainly, if Prince Charles had succeeded, the position of these rich young Walpoles, whose rank and fortunes were wholly founded on their father's success in maintaining the Hanoverian dynasty, would not have been an easy one. However, Horace Walpole faced bravely enough the threat of poverty and possible exile. His letters to Mann were cheerful and optimistic even in the darkest moments.[12] By Christmas the tide had turned, and the invaders were in flight for Scotland. In the following April the battle of Culloden ended the rebellion.

The great event of the summer of 1746 was the trial and execution of the captured Scottish lords. London had known nothing so sensational for many years. The stately ceremonial of a trial for high treason by the House of Lords, Kilmarnock's good looks and Balmerino's gallant bearing, the various efforts for their reprieve, the unfamiliar and almost mediaeval spectacle of their execution, stirred the imagination of the whole country. The episode interested and moved Walpole very deeply; and the accounts in his letters to Mann of the trial, which he witnessed,

[11] *Lewis,* i. 24 (Walpole to Montagu, September 17, 1745).

[12] Leonard Whibley pointed out to me the curious fact that Walpole, while sending Mann the fullest possible details of the "Forty-Five," says nothing whatever of his reconciliation with Gray, which would have been a subject of great interest to Mann; while Gray, when describing the progress of the reconciliation very fully in his letters to Wharton, completely ignores the fact that an invading army was marching towards London.

and the executions, for which he relied on other observers, are the earliest of those elaborate descriptive passages which are his supreme achievement as a letter-writer. In none of the great set-pieces in his later letters did he excel these accounts, with their perfect ease of narrative, their exquisite selection and presentation of detail, their masterly balance between the solemnity and the triviality of which he was always so vividly conscious on these great occasions. "I am this moment come from the conclusion of the greatest and most melancholy scene I ever yet saw!" he began one of his letters to Mann. But while he described with deep feeling the demeanour of the doomed men, he was equally interested in the conduct and remarks of the most futile of the spectators—of Lady Townshend with her sudden passion for Kilmarnock, or of old Norsa, the Jewish tavern-keeper who was the father of his brother's mistress.[13]

Before the memories of the rebellion began to fade, Walpole made effective use of them in an Epilogue which he wrote for certain performances of Rowe's *Tamerlane* at Covent Garden. It was customary to act *Tamerlane* every year on the 4th of November, the birthday of King William III, and on the 5th, the anniversary of his landing at Torbay in 1688. In 1746 the nation was acclaiming another William, the Duke of Cumberland, who had triumphed at Culloden over the forces of Jacobitism and Popery, and had thus reaffirmed the political and religious principles which his great namesake had established in England. Who could be more appropriately invited to write the Epilogue to *Tamerlane* than that enthusiastic young Whig, Horace Walpole? And certainly he turned out a first-rate piece of work. The Epilogue was spoken by Mrs. Pritchard in the character of the Comic Muse, and the audience were delighted at the outset by its ingenious allusions to their recent dangers, and in particular to the risk they had of having the stage supervised by a censorship of bigoted priests.

> "Chains, real chains, our heroes had in view,
> And scenes of mimic dungeons chang'd to true.
> An equal fate the Stage and Britain dreaded,
> Had Rome's young missionary spark succeeded.

[13] *Lewis*, xix. 280–7 (Walpole to Mann, August 1, 1746).

> But laws and liberties are trifling treasures;
> He threaten'd that grave property, your pleasures."

The Epilogue rose to its climax in a series of elaborate compliments to the young hero.

> "What youth is he with comeliest conquest crown'd,
> His warlike brow with full-blown laurels bound?
> What wreaths are these that vict'ry dares to join,
> And blend with trophies of my fav'rite Boyne?
> Oh! if the Muse can happy aught presage,
> Of new deliv'rance to the state and stage;
> If not untaught the characters to spell
> Of all who bravely fight or conquer well;
> Thou shalt be WILLIAM—like the last design'd
> The tyrant's scourge, and blessing of mankind;
> Born civil tumult and blind zeal to quell,
> That teaches happy subjects to rebel."[14]

These were exactly the sentiments and the tone which the audience wished to hear. The Epilogue was received at both performances with great applause, and was printed immediately afterwards. Walpole did not allow his authorship to be publicly disclosed, but he was amused and flattered by his success as a popular author.

IV

Earlier in the same year Walpole had written another poem, *The Beauties,* his longest and most elaborate performance since the *Epistle to Ashton from Florence.* This was also in the form of an epistle, and was addressed to John Giles Eckhardt, a German portrait-painter whom he was employing a good deal at this time. But it was really written to amuse Lady Caroline Fox, the wife of his friend Henry Fox. Walpole had dashed it off in less than three hours, while on a summer visit to Rigby at Mistley. "When I left London," he explained to her husband, "I piqued myself upon paying my court to Lady Caroline by some present that should make her think me a reasonable creature, and capable of entertaining myself without music, which I don't love, and

[14] *Works,* i. 25–7.

without seeing a thousand people for whom I don't care a straw....As a fit of poetry is a distemper which I am never troubled with but in the country, you will have no reason to apprehend much trouble of this sort: the trees at Vauxhall and purling basons of goldfish never inspire one."[15]

Lady Caroline Lennox was the eldest daughter of the Duke of Richmond, and had made a runaway marriage with Henry Fox two years before. The Duke and Duchess of Richmond had decided that a great-grand-daughter of Charles II was an unsuitable wife for an ambitious politician nearly eighteen years her elder; and Fox and his wife, though their marriage was an entirely happy one, were still under their displeasure. Lady Caroline was rivalled in beauty and charm by her sister Lady Emily Lennox; and Walpole, in writing *The Beauties* to amuse Lady Caroline, was careful to bestow the largest share of compliments upon Lady Emily. But his compliments in this odd little catalogue of beautiful women were scattered broadcast among a score or so of the girls and younger married women of his acquaintance; and it was only in the last lines that his own personal preference for one of them, a certain Elizabeth Evelyn, was announced.

The Beauties seems to have been suggested, both in subject and in manner, by Addison's lines *To Sir Godfrey Kneller on his Picture of the King*. Eckhardt is invited to stop thinking of the beauties of ancient Greece, and of the women who sat as models to Correggio and Carlo Dolci, and turn his attention to the Fair who were the glory of contemporary Britain. He might form the whole galaxy of Olympus out of the company assembled in a London ballroom. Miss Hervey should be Juno; Lady Caroline Fitzroy would make an admirable Pallas; Lady Emily Lennox, of course, should be Venus; and so on.

> In smiling CAPEL's bounteous look
> Rich autumn's goddess is mistook.
> With poppies and with spiky corn,
> Eckhardt, her nut-brown curls adorn;
> And by her side, in decent line,
> Place charming BERKELEY, Proserpine.

[15] *Lewis,* xxx. 99–100 (Walpole to Henry Fox, July 19, 1746).

Mild as a summer sea, serene,
In dimpled beauty next be seen
AYLESB'RY, like hoary Neptune's queen[16]

The poem flows on in this engaging fashion, without a trace of sensuality, without the least suggestion of strong feeling, until the concluding lines are reached. Then comes a reference to his old friend Lady Sophia Fermor, who had recently died, eighteen months after her marriage to Lord Granville; her beautiful sister Juliana weeps over her. The poem then ends with a description of another afflicted family—two sisters, Mrs. Boone and Miss Elizabeth Evelyn, bewailing the death of a third sister, Miss Mary Evelyn.

Two beauteous nymphs here, painter, place,
Lamenting o'er their sister grace,
One, matron-like, with sober grief,
Scarce gives her pious sighs relief;
While t'other lovely maid appears
In all the melting pow'r of tears;
The softest form, the gentlest grace,
The sweetest harmony of face;
Her snowy limbs and artless move
Contending with the queen of love,
While bashful beauty shuns the prize,
Which EMILY might yield to EVELYN's eyes.[17]

Walpole was apologetic about giving Miss Evelyn the preference over Lady Emily Lennox, and insisted that "Lady Caroline must forgive any private partialities in the last line."[18] When Fox suggested publication, he replied that "the conclusion of the poem is more particular than I would choose publicly to subscribe to."[19] It would seem that Walpole was, for once, feeling an emotion akin to love; but his love was tempered with his usual caution. He had written to Mann a few years before: "I own, I cannot much felicitate anybody that marries for love. It is bad enough to marry; but to marry where one loves, ten times worse. It is so charming at first, that the decay of inclination renders it

[16] *Works,* i. 21. *Ibid.,* 23–4.
[18] *Lewis,* xxx. 101 (Walpole to Henry Fox, July 19, 1746).
[19] *Ibid.,* 105 (Walpole to Henry Fox, July 24, 1746).

infinitely more disagreeable afterwards."[20] We do not know whether the gentle and modest charms of Elizabeth Evelyn ever inclined him to think of altering these views. She remains a shadowy figure, scarcely mentioned in the whole range of his letters; though her portrait by Eckhardt hung at Strawberry Hill to the end of his life.[21] She married a Mr. Peter Bathurst, and vanished from Walpole's sight. Many years afterwards, as late as 1777, Walpole's niece, the Duchess of Gloucester, read of the death of a Mrs. Bathurst in the newspaper, and wrote to ask her bachelor uncle, "Is it your old love?"[22]

The Beauties got into print before the end of the year, somewhat to Walpole's annoyance; but at least he was not displeased at the popularity of the poem, and made no objection when Dodsley wished to reprint it two years later in his *Collection of Poems*. It was no doubt a valuable advertisement for Eckhardt; but so much did Walpole employ this "modest worthy man,"[23] who had begun his career by painting draperies for the portraits of Jean-Baptiste Vanloo, that for months at a time he can scarcely have needed other patrons. He was commissioned to paint almost the whole circle of Walpole's relations and friends—the Conways, the Churchills, Miss Evelyn, Hanbury Williams, Rigby, Bentley, George Montagu, Conyers Middleton, and many more. He also painted Walpole and Gray in the attitudes and, more or less, in the costumes of certain well-known portraits by Van Dyck.[24]

V

Later in the summer of 1746 Walpole rented a small house within the precincts of Windsor Castle. George Montagu was living two doors away; Ashton had recently become a Fellow of Eton, and was in residence there; Gray was spending the summer with his mother and aunts at Stoke Poges. It was, in fact, a reunion of his Eton friends, with the Triumvirate and the Quad-

[20] *Ibid.*, xviii. 367 (Walpole to Mann, December 26, 1743).

[21] *Sale Catalogue of Strawberry Hill*, 221.

[22] Duchess of Gloucester to Horace Walpole, September 14, 1777 (MS. at Chewton Priory, unpublished).

[23] *Works*, iii. 448–9 (note).

[24] Eckhardt's portraits of Walpole and Gray are in the National Portrait Gallery.

ruple Alliance both represented; and Gray marked the occasion by disclosing his *Ode on a Distant Prospect of Eton College,* which he had written during the unhappy summer of 1742. The poem delighted Walpole so much that he immediately sent copies to Conway and Fox, and was probably instrumental in persuading Gray to publish it in the following year.

Windsor was pleasantly accessible from London, and Walpole retired to his "little tub of forty pounds a year" at intervals throughout the winter. In London he saw a great deal of Chute and Whithed, who had lately returned to England. They had been in Rome during the Forty-Five, and had been conspicuous for their optimism and confidence during the darkest days of the rebellion, when most of the English in the city were exultant Jacobites.[25] "Mr. Whithed is infinitely improved; and Mr. Chute has absolutely more wit, knowledge, and good nature, than, to their great surprise, ever met together in one man."[26] Such was Walpole's verdict on the returned travellers; and Chute remained his close friend, unfailingly sympathetic and congenial, to the end of his life.

The house at Windsor was not, however, exactly what Walpole required, in spite of the proximity of his friends. He wanted to live in the country and near the river, and to look out on his own lawns and meadows. And suddenly, in the spring of 1747, he discovered a house which fulfilled all his wishes. It was situated close to the river, on the reach which runs northward from Hampton Court to Twickenham; and the holder of the lease was Mrs. Chenevix, a woman who kept a famous toy-shop and china-shop at Charing Cross. It was an unattractive little dwelling, perched on some rising ground which commanded exquisite views of the river and the meadows beyond. Walpole fell in love with it at once, and bought the remainder of the lease from Mrs. Chenevix. In a few years it had developed into one of the most celebrated houses in England.

The acquisition of this house, presently to be known as Strawberry Hill, was a turning-point in Walpole's life. Hitherto his

[25] *Lewis,* xix. 136, 141 (Mann to Walpole, October 26 and November 9, 1745). The Jacobites retaliated by "telling everybody they were of the meanest extraction and that Mr. Chute was Mr. Whithed's governor."

[26] *Ibid.,* 329 (Walpole to Mann, November 4, 1746).

existence had been agreeable, cultivated, urbane, but slightly aimless; now at last he struck root. His life began to assume a pattern. His interests—as politician, historian, letter-writer, author, antiquary, *virtuoso*—continued to radiate in all directions; but now they were all anchored to the main interest, the central passion of his life, Strawberry Hill.

VII

Preparations for a Career (1747)

I

THE visitor to Strawberry Hill now drives from London to Twickenham for the greater part of the way through crowded and noisy streets. He will scarcely pass along any road which is not lined with houses or shops. In the whole of his drive he will not see a green field or an untrimmed hedge. He will pass through Twickenham without noticing anything to suggest that it was at one time a prosperous and self-contained little town, clustering round its church, with the elegant and fanciful villas of the wealthy scattered on its outskirts and along the banks of the Thames.

But in 1747 Twickenham was one of the most agreeable places of residence in England. Situated on a long curving reach of the clear and unpolluted Thames, looking across rich meadows and rushy eyots to the woods and parkland of Richmond and Ham, a pleasant drive from London through charming country landscapes, it had been for the last hundred years a favoured place of residence for people of wealth and condition. Its many large and comfortable houses, sometimes adorned by their owners with unrestrained whimsicality, were occupied by a variety of dowagers, *dilettanti,* retired generals, opulent merchants, and other well-to-do members of society. In recent years Pope and Kneller had given the neighbourhood a flavour of literature and the arts; indeed Pope's villa, with its garden and grotto and the parties of eminent people who used to assemble there, had greatly added to the fame of Twickenham. Pope had died two years before Walpole went to Strawberry Hill; but his villa, only a few hundred yards away, was unaltered, and his memory was still green. All round Twickenham, on both sides of the river, lay palaces and mansions and parks—Hampton Court, Kew, Richmond, Ham, Chiswick, Gunnersbury, Sion. It was a neighbourhood of great variety, in which Walpole could find retirement or social life, country simplicities or elaborate hospitality, according to his mood.

Strawberry Hill stood some distance south-west of the main town of Twickenham, close to the road which ran from Twickenham to Hampton Court. The little house was almost adjacent to this road, which bounded the property on the northern side. To the east lay a meadow, the road from Twickenham to Teddington, another meadow which extended to the river-bank, a couple of small eyots, and then the main stream of the Thames. The "hill," on which the house was placed, was little more than a slight rise of ground; but it was enough to add considerably to the beauty and distance of the views up and down the river, and across to Richmond Hill and the great trees of the Park. From the meadow east of the house, presently to become the lawn, one looked down the Thames to the town of Twickenham, "exactly like a seaport in miniature,"[1] and saw Pope's Villa, the Church, the pleasant groups of red houses, and the long narrow eyot that lay in front of them, until the river curved out of sight in the direction of Richmond. If one looked up the river, there was an equally charming view of the suburbs of Kingston.

The original builder of Strawberry Hill was a nobleman's coachman, and the house had been nicknamed Chopped-Straw Hall, as a suggestion that the coachman had got the money to build it by selling his master's hay and feeding his horses on chopped straw. Afterwards the house had had a number of tenants, including a duke, a bishop, and Colley Cibber; Mrs. Chenevix was the last of this series. The owners of the property, when Walpole took over the remainder of her lease, were "three minors of the name of Mortimer." As soon as he could manage it, Walpole bought the property from these minors by a special Act of Parliament.

The only surviving pictures of this original Strawberry Hill are

[1] *Lewis*, xx. 380 (Walpole to Mann, June 12, 1753).

some very rough sketches by Walpole.[2] They show a shapeless unsymmetrical building without any architectural interest. It was certainly the surrounding landscape, and not the house itself, that inspired his first rapturous descriptions of his new possession. "It is a little plaything-house that I got out of Mrs. Chenevix's shop," he wrote to Conway, "and is the prettiest bauble you ever saw. It is set in enamelled meadows, with filigree hedges:

> A small Euphrates through the piece is rolled,
> And little finches wave their wings in gold.

Two delightful roads, that you would call dusty, supply me continually with coaches and chaises: barges as solemn as Barons of the Exchequer move under my window; Richmond Hill and Ham Walks bound my prospect; but, thank God! the Thames is between me and the Duchess of Queensberry. Dowagers as plenty as flounders inhabit all around, and Pope's ghost is just now skimming under my window by a most poetical moonlight."[3]

Walpole did not immediately set himself to improve or alter the house, except for a few necessary domestic adjustments. He certainly did not begin to contemplate, until at least two years had passed, the complete reconstruction in the Gothic style which he afterwards carried out; and it was quite five years before the first Gothic ornaments appeared, and pinnacles and battlements cut the Middlesex sky. His first activities were planting and gardening. About five acres of land went with the house, and he set to work to adorn this area with flowers and shrubs and trees. Next year he bought some small meadows, and his territory swelled to fourteen acres. Mounds were levelled, terraces were planned; cows and ornamental sheep grazed in the meadows; and Walpole settled down to enjoy, summer after summer, the growth and blossoming of his lilacs and his syringas, his honeysuckle and his acacias.

II

In 1747 Walpole completed his thirtieth year. The acquisition

[2] *Genesis of Strawberry Hill,* 58. Besides the sketch reproduced here, there is another in a copy of the 1774 *Description of Strawberry Hill* in the New York Public Library; and others are in the Huntington Library.

[3] *Toynbee,* ii. 279 (Walpole to Conway, June 8, 1747).

of Strawberry Hill gave him a fixed background; he had half a century still to live, and henceforth his life was to be based upon that house and upon the things he assembled within it. But already, in 1747, his activities and interests seem to have resolved themselves into three main groups. First and foremost, he was a letter-writer, a man of position and of the world, and the self-appointed chronicler, through his letters, of contemporary life and events. Secondly, he was a *virtuoso,* a collector, an antiquary, and the author of a considerable and varied body of literary work. Thirdly, he was a politician and a writer of political memoirs. His political interests flagged in his last years; otherwise he pursued the various activities, which have been roughly grouped in these three categories, with unabated enthusiasm and enjoyment to the end of his long life.

He had already determined to become the chronicler of his century; and his only hesitation was as to the most suitable form in which to cast his chronicle. It was a novel undertaking to write the history of an age in the guise of a series of familiar letters to private friends, and for a long time while he considered the compilation of a more formal type of historical memoir, for which his letters could serve as the rough material. It has already been pointed out that Mann was a particularly suitable recipient for a historical chronicle in letter form, placed as he was in a foreign country and deeply interested in political developments at home; but Walpole did not envisage these letters reaching posterity in the precise form in which they reached Mann. Nor, indeed, have they done so. Mann, as well as Montagu, was expected to preserve Walpole's letters; and he was also required to return them periodically to their writer by the hands of some trustworthy person travelling from Italy. Walpole's excuse for this procedure was his intention to use them as rough material for his *Memoirs;* but in actual fact he subjected them to an elaborate process of editing, annotation, and (in many cases) alteration, and left them to his executors in the shape of a historical and social chronicle in letter form, carefully prepared for the benefit of posterity.

Walpole's first request to Mann to return his letters was made in his letter of September 18, 1748; in the revised form in which his letter now exists, he has rather significantly omitted the passage containing his request. Mann replied on October 25: "I shall be vastly glad to contribute anything that is in my power to the work you have in hand, and would encourage you by all means to go on with it. How could you doubt of my having kept your letters? not one of them is wanting, you will believe that I set the highest value upon them when I assure you that I frequently highly entertain myself with the perusal of them. Therefore if you have no objection to my keeping them, I will beg to have them returned whenever you may have no further use for them. I will not pretend to judge which of them you may want but will send them all together by the first safe opportunity by land, though it is very uncertain when such a one may offer."[4] The letters were sent to England in the care of a Mr. Schutz in the following January; and Walpole acknowledged their receipt in his letter of March 23, in another passage omitted when he was re-copying the correspondence. Mann never had them back again, though five years later he was still making plaintive requests for their return. "May I urge a right to the restitution of the many inestimable [letters] you borrowed of me some years ago, of which I made an exact list before I parted with them, and I keep your letter that demanded them as a note of hand for the debt."[5] In 1754 he had to send back another consignment of letters in the care of Walpole's friend Thomas Brand; and at intervals throughout his life he returned further instalments of letters, none of which he ever saw again.

Mann's reference to "the work you have in hand" was not the earliest mention of some kind of historical work on which Walpole was engaged. On December 22, 1746 Gray had written to inquire about Walpole's various literary enterprises. "Among the little folks, my godsons and daughters, I can not choose but enquire more particularly after the health of one: I mean (without a figure) the Memoires: Do they grow? Do they unite, and hold up their heads, and dress themselves? Do they begin to think of making their appearance in the world, that is to say, fifty years hence, to make posterity stare, and all good people cross themselves?"[6] In his next letter he mentioned the same topic

[4] *Lewis,* xix. 508 (Mann to Walpole, October 25, 1748).
[5] *Ibid.,* xx. 397 (Mann to Walpole, November 9, 1753).
[6] *Gray,* i. 257–8 (Gray to Walpole, December 22, 1746).

again. "You need not fear but posterity will be ever glad to know the absurdity of their ancestors: the foolish will be glad to know they were as foolish as they, and the wise will be glad to find themselves wiser. You will please all the world then; and if you recount miracles you will be believed so much the sooner."[7]

Walpole, then, was writing a chronicle or record of his own times as early as 1746, and was still engaged upon it in 1748. Yet we have in *Short Notes of my Life* his statement, under the year 1751, that "about this time I began to write my *Memoires.* At first, I only intended to write the history of one year."[8] And this is not one of the many inaccuracies of the *Short Notes.* The first of the annual narratives of political events and intrigues, to which he afterwards gave the collective title of *Memoires of the last ten years of the Reign of George the Second,* does cover the year 1751. What, then, was the earlier historical work which Gray described as "the Memoires" and for whose preparation the letters to Mann were requisitioned by their writer?

Among the papers at Farmington is an unpublished manuscript entitled *Memoires, From the Declaration of the War with Spain.* The document runs to some twenty closely written pages, and is presumably Walpole's earliest attempt at a history of his own times. It opens with an introductory passage of the type familiar in his published *Memoirs,* in which he addresses Posterity, and proclaims to that unborn audience his disinterested motives and the accuracy of his statements of fact. He also explains in some detail his religious standpoint. He was concerned lest his readers should assume, from the violence of his attacks on Papists and Popery, that he was strongly prejudiced in favour of orthodox Protestant doctrines; he therefore takes the opportunity of expounding his deistic opinions, his disbelief in the doctrine of the Trinity, and his faith in "one only Supreme Being." The date of this document is uncertain, but it obviously forms a part of the early *Memoirs* in which Gray was interested. Possibly further portions of this work may still exist in manuscript. At any rate Walpole had reorganized his entire project by 1751, when he began the series of narratives of contemporary events which he

[7] *Ibid.*, 263–4 (Gray to Walpole, January 1747).

[8] *Lewis,* xiii. 23 *(Short Notes of my Life).*

was to carry on, with varying degrees of assiduity, for the next forty years.

As time went on, Mann ceased to be in certain respects the ideal correspondent for all the ground which Walpole wished to cover. His interest in political developments, and in the doings of people whom he had known as visitors to Florence or in the distant days of his English life, remained as strong as ever; but there were other aspects of contemporary England which could not possibly interest him. Walpole wished to record the current gossip about men and women who had been at school or in the nursery when Mann left England; he wished to discuss changes of fashion and of convention which would have been meaningless to his friend. Clothes altered; people played different card-games and used different slang; the gallantries of Lady Townshend were eclipsed by those of Miss Chudleigh, and Miss Chudleigh's glamorous absurdity was outshone by the beauty and novelty of the Gunnings. Walpole might have written copiously on all these topics to Mann, regardless of his friend's feelings; he did, indeed, keep him reasonably well-informed about every change of fashion and *personnel* in England. But he knew that a letter loses in conviction and in sincerity if an immediate response is not assured in the correspondent: and therefore he looked about for a more suitable corespondent to whom he might impart the more intimate and eclectic details of contemporary social life. His choice fell upon George Montagu; and Montagu, with whom he had carried on an occasional correspondence since their school days, began to receive letters of an ever-increasing brilliance and elaboration, devoted almost entirely to social anecdote and description, with a flavouring of antiquarianism and *virtù*.

"As I am so much in town and in the world, I flatter myself with having generally something to tell you that may make my letters agreeable in the country."[9] So Walpole wrote in May 1745 to Montagu, in one of the earliest letters of the series which was to develop into so memorable a correspondence. And indeed Montagu was as appropriate a choice for Walpole's social gossip as Mann had been for the political intelligence of the day. Mann was exiled by duty in a foreign capital; Montagu was exiled by his

[9] *Ibid.*, ix. 13 (Walpole to Montagu, May 18, 1745).

own choice in the depths of the country. But while obstinately confining himself for long periods to his country retreats, and giving himself up to "ports and parsons," Montagu was always delighted to receive the latest news from London. He knew all the people in Walpole's world; as a member of the great clan of Montagu, he was related to half of them: and he was peculiarly well fitted, alike by position and by temperament, to enjoy the floods of anecdote and gossip which Walpole lavished upon him. He had grown into a whimsical and ease-loving bachelor, somewhat troubled by gout and his increasing girth, living in a series of hired country-houses far from London, where he passed the time with wine and cards, a little hunting, and a good deal of miscellaneous reading and mild antiquarian study. He usually had an unmarried sister or brother living with him; occasionally an influential relative gave him a temporary or sinecure office; he spent an eventful year in Ireland as Usher of the Black Rod when his cousin Lord Halifax was Viceroy, and he was private secretary to Lord North when the latter was Chancellor of the Exchequer. A more appropriate office than either of these was the Deputy Rangership of Rockingham Forest, which carried with it a number of pleasant privileges, green coats and the disposal of unlimited venison, which were greatly to his taste. Along with his indolence went a great deal of wit and ability. He was admirable company; Walpole made constant attempts to persuade him to settle at Twickenham, and was always quoting his sayings and queer expressions, which were backed up by an explosive delivery and often by shouts and whoops of laughter. His laziness was reflected in his letters; Walpole's longest and most brilliant epistles often drew an appreciative but wholly perfunctory reply of less than a dozen lines. But when occasionally he took the trouble to write a proper letter, he struck out phrases and epigrams worthy of a correspondent of Walpole.[10]

As Walpole's life advances, one realizes ever more clearly with what intelligence and skill he selected his principal correspondents. Each correspondent was in a somewhat different walk of life: each was particularly connected with one of Walpole's interests, or with one of the subjects about which he wished to

[10] The letters between Walpole and Montagu form volumes ix. and x. of the Yale Edition of Walpole's *Correspondence*.

enlighten and inform posterity. We have seen the particular appropriateness of Mann as the correspondent with whom political matters could be discussed, and Montagu's similar appropriateness with regard to social anecdote. In Gray, he had a perfect foil for the discussion of literary matters; in Cole, an eager and well qualified recipient of his letters on antiquarian topics. Each correspondence, in fact, became an encyclopædia of what Walpole had to say on one particular subject. Some correspondents, such as Gray, sent back first-rate letters in reply; some, like Cole, sent back valuable information to assist Walpole in his books and collections; some, like Montagu, gave little or no epistolary return. And if for any reason a correspondence terminated, another correspondent was soon selected to carry on that subject. When Gray died, his position as Walpole's chief correspondent on literary matters was presently filled by Mason; when Walpole's friendship with Montagu came to its sudden and inexplicable close, the Countess of Upper Ossory was chosen to receive those records of social occurrences which Montagu had enjoyed for the past twenty-five years, and was now to enjoy no longer. In several of Walpole's other correspondences the same peculiarity can be traced.[11] Perhaps it was slightly cold-blooded, this careful selection and substitution of correspondents: but Walpole was convinced of its necessity. He was genuinely fond of the friends to whom his letters were addressed; he lamented their deaths deeply and sincerely; he was unhappy over his permanent estrangements from Montagu and Bentley, and his temporary coolness with Mason. But the enlightenment of posterity was a matter of still greater importance. While bewailing the departed friend, he lost no time in finding a suitable correspondent to take his place.

III

Walpole's letters have always met with the appreciation they deserve. Innumerable critics and moralists have had their fling at his character, and have gone on to extol the grace, ease, wit and unfailing readableness of his correspondence. Historians have

[11] Cf. *Lewis,* i. xxxv. It was Mr. Lewis himself who first drew my attention, some years ago, to this habit of Walpole's.

sneered at the writer and made unsparing use of his work. Indeed, it has been observed that some of them have made use of little else.

There had been good letters before in the English language. The correspondence of Pope and Swift and their circle had been published; Richardson's novels were revealing the unexplored possibilities of expression through the epistolary form. But Walpole had no predecessor in his attempt to depict by means of private letters the whole vast scene of contemporary English life. His enterprise was as original as it was successful.

There was one model only whom he imitated, Madame de Sévigné. He read her letters constantly, he knew a great deal about seventeenth-century France, he discussed her with fellow-enthusiasts such as Selwyn and Montagu, and in certain particulars he came to imitate her style. Quite unconsciously, and only to a limited extent, she had done for the France of her own day what Walpole proposed to do for eighteenth-century England: and for her own private circle, what Walpole wished to do for his own particular friends. Here was a woman, long since laid in her grave, whose life remained more vivid and more real to him than the lives of the people he knew. With his craving for immortality, how could Walpole not wish to do the same? His friends, his house, the whole of contemporary England from King George II down to his own servants, interested him passionately. Why should not Strawberry Hill be known as intimately to posterity as Les Rochers, and George Selwyn, let us say, as M. de Coulanges? Why should not the London of George II be as familiar to coming generations as the Paris of *Le Roi Soleil*?

To this extent Madame de Sévigné influenced him; and she was the only influence. His letters have the same naturalness and ease as hers, admitting of negligence yet seldom losing elegance; the same consummate ability in relating an anecdote or describing a scene; the same power to enthral and charm. But here the resemblance ends. The deeply personal note, which sounds in Madame de Sévigné's letters, is rarely echoed in Walpole's. He was politely anxious to please his correspondents; he would not allow his vivacity to flag, his courtesies to seem perfunctory; but he had not the urgent desire to win a response of affection and gratitude that inspired Madame de Sévigné's letters to Madame de Grignan. She was living in the moment, summoning all her forces to obtain response, reciprocal warmth, some expression of love from her exalted daughter: he was looking, beyond the country solitude of Montagu or the even more distant figure of Mann, to the detached approval of posterity. At the most, Madame de Sévigné only expected that copies of her letters would be perhaps handed round a small and intimate, if highly critical, circle. Before Walpole's eyes was the vast and ever-widening audience of the generations to come.

IV

Walpole's letters are the main foundation of his posthumous fame. He was known as a matchless letter writer to a small circle of his friends; but to the majority of his contemporaries he was famous as an antiquary and *virtuoso*. Almost all his writings were concerned directly or indirectly with antiquarian subjects; and in all England there was no more striking example of the results of antiquarian enthusiasm than his celebrated house.

At his return from Italy his taste was very much that of other rich and travelled young men of his day. He appreciated and had a critical knowledge of classical sculpture and architecture, and of the more recent schools of Italian painting. He was living in one of the supreme eras of English architecture, and watched with approval the rise of some of the noblest classical buildings that this country had seen. But by the time he settled at Strawberry Hill his own personal interests in art and architecture were moving very decidedly towards mediævalism. He admired the work of Burlington and Kent: but his own little house, he determined two years later, should be uncompromisingly Gothic. He had for some time been investigating the earlier history of his own family, and the fascination of antiquarian research had seized him. The Robsarts, the Gestingthorpes, the FitzOsberts—it was romantic to be descended from the bearers of such names. And even more romantic possibilities opened up as his researches proceeded—an elusive descent from the de Veres, a hopeful but finally unverified relationship with Chaucer.[12] His cousins the Phillipses of Picton Castle had compiled a tremendous pedigree in which he, Horace Walpole, and King George II were found

[12] *Ibid.*, ix. 68–9 (Walpole to Montagu, August 11, 1748).

equally descended from Cadwallader.[13] Genealogy became for him the most delightful of hobbies; and the study of his remoter ancestors soon extended itself to the buildings in which they had lived and worshipped.

The antiquary of the seventeen-forties was of necessity something of an explorer. He had a remarkably open field; he was enthusiastic, ignorant, full of amateurish and improbable theories: vistas of exciting discovery stretched out before him. All over England stood the ruined monasteries and castles, neglected, crumbling, turned into cottages and cowsheds and quarries for building. One pushed through the nettles and skirted the duck-ponds, thrust aside a hurdle and entered the chapel or the refectory of a great monastic house. One rode or drove through almost impassable lanes, and came upon historic mansions tumbling in ruin, with paint still visible on their carvings, painted glass in their windows, and perhaps a farm labourer's family shivering in one of the towers. One traced forgotten cloisters, detected the site of kitchens and high altars, stood in great undercrofts whose forests of pillars glistened with water; one found the castle well and the castle privies, and made unlikely speculations about the tiltyard and the ladye's bower; and returned to the inn inspired with the romance of the past. And the parish churches were equally fruitful of interest and romance. In disused chancels, in recesses behind the squire's smart pew with its cushioned armchairs, were hidden the dusty and crumbling effigies of the Mowbrays and the de Veres—the gilding thin upon the alabaster, the rusted helms hanging above, paint flaking from the coats which perhaps one was entitled to quarter with one's own. In the windows might be unbroken figures of saints, portraits of kings and queens; the sexton would often be glad to sell a few armorial quarries or some carving or a brass, the patron might give away whole windows of painted glass to an antiquarian friend.[14] So Walpole, on his way to stay with

[13] This document is now in the possession of Mr. W. S. Lewis.

[14] Walpole often made additions to Strawberry Hill in this way. For instance, the China-room was paved with some glazed tiles sold to him by a verger of Gloucester Cathedral. The most flagrant example was the painted glass window in the Chapel in the garden, representing Henry III and his Queen, which was taken out of Bexhill Church and given to him by Lord Ashburnham. This has recently been restored to Bexhill Church.

Nugent at Gosfield or with Rigby at Mistley, would turn aside his chaise to explore some dilapidated castle or forgotten church. From those small beginnings came the elaborate tours with Chute, the "Gothic pilgrimages" which he described so brilliantly in his letters. His passion for Gothic, the passion which influenced the taste of a century, began in this quiet way, with genealogies, with visits to a few churches and castles: then, fed by Ashmole, Dugdale, county histories, the deeper knowledge of Chute and Gray, but above all by the beauties of spire and arch and tracery which he now began to observe and appreciate, it increased day by day, until his house and his writings were irrevocably destined to follow Gothic forms.

V

Walpole is not much remembered as a politician, and the readers of his historical memoirs cannot be numerous. But his political activities were incessant during the greater part of his life, and they were a good deal more serious and more effective than some of his critics have admitted. Walpole took his position as a Member of Parliament very seriously indeed; his *Memoirs* are a serious and successful attempt to record the inner history of his time: and Macaulay's strictures on the frivolity of this light-hearted senator, this *dilettante,* this lover of art and leisure who dared to call himself a Whig, had remarkably little justification.

Walpole had always confessed to a strong taste for political intrigue. The more involved and chaotic the political scene became, the better he was pleased. "You perhaps recollect that I have another Gothic passion, which is for squabbles in the Wittenagemot," he wrote to Montagu in 1753:[15] and again a few years later, "I never had an aversion to living in a Fronde."[16] He had aided party warfare with some vigorous pamphleteering, and his love of faction was a joke among his more phlegmatic friends. But it is difficult to squabble effectively in the Wittenagemot if you are handicapped by a fragile and unimpressive physique, a weak voice, and a shy and hesitating delivery. Although

[15] *Lewis,* ix. 149 (Walpole to Montagu, June 11, 1753).
[16] *Ibid.,* 195 (Walpole to Montagu, August 28, 1756).

he spoke occasionally in debate, he soon found that he could do more work behind the scenes, directing the actions of other men, giving advice, dropping hints, evolving complicated schemes of action. And he seldom wanted friends, themselves prominent in the House, through whom he could act, and who gladly availed themselves of his quick intelligence and ready advice. Fox and Rigby, men generously endowed with the qualities of pugnacity and vociferation which he lacked, were for years in constant touch with him; and some of the results of their association are set out in great detail in their earlier *Memoirs*. Both Fox and Rigby were ambitious political careerists, and in years to come their paths diverged from Walpole's; but by that time Conway was beginning to achieve distinction in the House, and Walpole duly became his political mentor. His personal affection for Conway caused him to work with especial assiduity for his cousin's advancement, and for the success of the group of politicians to which he belonged: only to be rewarded, when that party eventually came into power, with heart-breaking ingratitude.

It is probable that Walpole eventually came to regard his letters to Mann and others as his bequest to the general audience of posterity, and the *Memoirs* as his testament to the comparatively small number who would trouble to examine closely the political conduct of their forefathers. The *Memoirs* were addressed to an audience of specialists, and are a record of details which would otherwise have been lost. In an age when Parliamentary reporting was of the vaguest description, when Doctor Johnson could compose imaginary speeches in the privacy of his study and publish them as veracious records of what had been said in debate, such reports as Walpole's, taken from notes carefully made as the speeches proceeded, were of particular value and authenticity.[17] Sir Walter Scott, discussing with a friend the publication of the *Memoirs* in 1822, observed that "it is comical that Lord Orford should have delayed trusting the public with his reminiscences, until so many years had destroyed all our interest in the Parliamentary and Court intrigues which he tells

[17] Professor Basil Williams (*Life of Chatham*, i. 270 n. 3; ii. 336) stated that wherever Walpole's reports of speeches can be checked, they are remarkable for their accuracy.

with so much vivacity. It is like a man who should brick up a hogshead of cider, to be drunk half a century afterwards, when it could contain little but acidity and vapidity."[18] This was an objection that Walpole must have foreseen perfectly clearly. But he had planned that his narrative of the closing years of George II should be accessible to the scholars and historians of all future ages; and in directing his executors not to publish them until a quarter of a century after his death, he had never supposed that they would meet with an immediate popular success. If the multitudes of posterity found them vapid, he did not care; they would find the small but eager audience for which he had composed them.

It is instructive to read Walpole's postscript to the *Memoirs of the Year* 1751, and the many similar passages throughout the *Memoirs* in which he turns aside from his main narrative in order to address the reader directly. The theme of those digressions is always the same—his truthfulness and his impartiality. Posterity should have a narrative as impartial as the natural prejudices of a human being would allow, from one who was after all, in spite of strong party feelings, more of a spectator than a partisan. "As personal enmity undoubtedly operates on every man's mind more or less, I have, in a subsequent portion of these Memoires, specified the persons whom I did not love, that so much may be abated in the characters I have given of them, as are not corroborated by facts."[19] "Some of my nearest friends are often mentioned in those Memoires, and their failings I think as little concealed as those of any other persons. Some whom I have little reason to love, are the fairest characters in the book."[20] "I would as soon wish to be rejected for flattering one party, as for blaming another. . . . If I write, I must write facts."[21] Walpole sincerely believed in his own disinterestedness as an historian. But it is quite impossible to accept his estimate of his own impartiality. Against certain individuals and families he nourished a blind prejudice that nothing could shake, a prejudice that was personal rather than political. He was absolutely implacable towards any man whom he suspected of treachery against his father. His hatred

[18] Lockhart, *Life of Scott* (Scott to Lord Montagu, March 15, 1822).
[19] *Memoirs of George II,* i. xxxv n.
[20] *Ibid.,* xl. [21] *Ibid.,* 208.

of Lord Hardwicke and the Duke of Newcastle arose mainly from this cause. Politically he was to be numbered among their supporters; yet he never mentions them in the *Memoirs* or in his letters without contempt. His dislike of Pelham was also based on personal grounds. In 1751, and again in 1752, he asked Pelham that the Collectorship of the Customs, from which he drew an income of £1,400 a year, but which would lapse to the Crown after the deaths of his two brothers, should be granted to him for the period of his own life if he happened to survive them both. His application failed; he was angry and mortified, and the acerbity of his references to Pelham in the *Memoirs* was intensified.[22] His family quarrels with his uncle Horace similarly account for the vindictiveness displayed whenever he is mentioned. But what the younger Horace himself described as "the faithful attendant of wit, ill-nature,"[23] is often strongly in evidence in his accounts of people who had done no injury to him or to his father.

In the *Memoirs* he was partial, he was ill-natured, he was capricious and changeable in his judgments. But as historical records these writings remain invaluable. They contain accounts of transactions which would otherwise be hopelessly obscure, reports of debates which would otherwise be lost, facts and details otherwise unrecorded. They throw their light on an extremely intricate period of English political history. When the *Memoirs* open, there were no public issues of overwhelming importance before the nation: Pelham had "composed a system of lethargic acquiescence, in which the spirit of Britain, agitated for so many centuries, seemed willing to repose."[24] But below this stagnant surface, there was a chaos of minor intrigues and constantly shifting factions. The Bedfords, the Grenvilles, Pitt, Lyttelton, Fox, Hardwicke, the Townshends, were all manœuvering for posi-

[22] Mr. Romney Sedgwick in his introduction to the *Letters from George III to Lord Bute* (xxxviii–xliii) has given a detailed account of Walpole's behaviour in this matter, and of the anonymous memorial by which he sought to embarrass the Government shortly after the failure of his second application to Pelham. Walpole does not emerge with credit from the searching analysis to which Mr. Sedgwick has subjected his motives and conduct on this occasion. See also *Works,* ii. 366–7, and *Toynbee,* iii. 132–4 (Walpole to Pelham, November 25, 1752).

[23] *Memoirs of George II,* i. 28. [24] *Ibid.,* 323.

tion, forming secret alliances and oppositions; and when Pelham died and was succeeded in power by the Duke of Newcastle, and the nation plunged into war in Europe and America, the same intricate manœuvres continue to fill Walpole's pages. The incidents in which he himself took a prominent part are usually described in particular detail; and perhaps the most effective portion of the entire work is the account of the trial of Admiral Byng, and of his own fruitless efforts to save him from an unjust and politically engineered sentence. This is almost the only passage, at any rate in the earlier *Memoirs,* that displays the strong personal emotion which Hervey so often infused into his own *Memoirs.* Some comparison between Hervey and Walpole, the greatest memoir-writers of their century, is inevitable; and Hervey has the advantage in every respect. He was an actor, and an important one, in the events he describes; his narrative acquires unity from its setting in the small circle of the court, and drama from the memorable and dominant figure of Queen Caroline. His writing exceeds Walpole's in force and eloquence; his characters are more powerfully drawn, he is savage and passionate where Walpole is peevish and ill-natured. His *Memoirs* are his masterpiece, the work by which, after a lifetime of ephemeral pamphleteering, he wished to be remembered. Walpole certainly did not underestimate his own *Memoirs;* but in the end he regarded his letters as an even more important bequest to posterity.

Walpole's earlier *Memoirs* are, finally, remarkable for their clear statements of his own political principles. They contain too much of the facile Whig claptrap which occurs now and then in his letters, which found expression in the hanging up of a copy of the warrant for Charles I's execution with the inscription "Major Charta,"[25] and in vapourings about "the least bad of all murders, that of a King."[26] But they do show that he was seriously perturbed at certain signs of the increase of the royal prerogative, and that he began to feel under George II anxieties which were justified under George III. "I am sensible," he wrote in 1756, "that from the prostitution of patriotism, from the art of ministers who have had the address to exalt the semblance while they

[25] *Lewis,* ix. 197 (Walpole to Montagu, October 14, 1756).

[26] *Ibid.,* xxi. 79 (Walpole to Mann, April 20, 1757).

depressed the reality of royalty, and from the bent of the education of the young nobility, which verges to French maxims and to a military spirit, nay, from the ascendant which the nobility itself acquires each day in this country, from all these reflections, I am sensible, that prerogative and power have been exceedingly fortified of late within the circle of the palace; and though fluctuating ministers by turns exercise the deposit, yet there it is; and whenever a prince of design and spirit shall sit in the regal chair, he will find a bank, a hoard of power, which he may play off most fatally against this constitution." He regarded himself as "a quiet republican, who does not dislike to see the shadow of monarchy, like Banquo's ghost, fill the empty chair of state, that the ambitious, the murderer, the tyrant, may not aspire to it; in short, who approves the name of a King, when it excludes the essence." If the Whiggish postures of his letters seem unduly ridiculous, it should be remembered that he was the son of Sir Robert Walpole, that he had seen the Young Pretender marching far into England, and that he was watching the increasing influence of Bute over the Princess of Wales and her son, the future king. Tories, Jacobites, Scotchmen—while the Whigs squabbled and intrigued, they were gaining power and might gain ascendancy: and England would be delivered to unlimited monarchy, "that authority, that torrent which I should in vain extend a feeble arm to stem."[27]

[27] *Memoirs of George II,* i. 326–7.

VIII

The First Decade at Strawberry Hill (1747-57)

I

THE series of digressions in the foregoing chapter, designed to illustrate as far as possible the three main lines of activity in Walpole's career, has at some points taken us too far forward in time; and it is now necessary to return to a more detailed narrative of his life.

The two or three years which followed the acquisition of Strawberry Hill were comparatively uneventful. The borough of Callington re-elected him to Parliament in 1747. He published a few political pamphlets, and in 1749 was embroiled in a quarrel with the Speaker, Arthur Onslow. Had he begun to write the *Memoirs* as early as 1748, we should have had an elaborate and circumstantial account of this affair; but our only record of it is a passage in the *Short Notes of my Life*.

An Act of Parliament had been obtained by which the assizes were to be transferred from Aylesbury to Buckingham. In some way this Act was a demonstration of enmity by the Grenville faction against Lord Chief Justice Willis, an old friend of Sir Robert Walpole's; and when it was returned from the House of Lords with amendments, the friends of the Lord Chief Justice, who had opposed it before, decided to oppose it again. Horace Walpole was asked to second Mr. Potter, who proposed its rejection; but when Mr. Potter began to discuss the merits of the bill, Thomas Townshend and old Horace Walpole insisted that only the amendments were to be discussed. Horace Walpole briefly states that this was done "to prevent me"; and when the Speaker agreed that only the amendments should be considered, he said that "I had intended to second Mr. Potter, but shall submit to his *oracular* decision, though I would not to the complaisant peevishness of anybody else." This was really very rude; and "the Speaker was in a great rage, and complained to the House." Walpole then became conciliatory, and "begged his pardon, but had not thought that submitting to him was the way to offend him." He then adapted the speech he had proposed to make into one more fitting for Sir William Stanhope, who had been similarly thwarted in speaking against the Grenvilles; and published it in Sir William's name. This pamphlet "made a great noise"; it was answered, and Walpole wrote another squib, *The Speech of Richard Whiteliver,* in support of the first. "All these things," he wrote later, "were only excusable by the lengths to which party had been carried against my father: or rather, were not excusable even then."[1] Any attack on the memory of his father, or on any friend of his father, was the signal for vigorous action on Walpole's part. He was equally ready to oppose, even at this comparatively early date, any assumption of prerogative on the part of the Crown. In 1749 he wrote a pamphlet called *Delenda est Oxonia,* "to assert the liberties of that University, which the ministry had a plan of attacking, by vesting in the Crown the nomination of the Chancellor." This pamphlet, which he regarded as one of the best, was seized at the printer's and suppressed.[2]

Walpole's vigorous political activity was diversified by literary and antiquarian pursuits. In 1748 Dodsley published the first three volumes of his *Collection of Poems,* in which many of the younger poets of the day made their appearance before the general public. Walpole was represented by the *Epistle to Thomas Ashton from Florence, The Beauties,* and the *Epilogue to Tamerlane.* In the summer of 1749 he undertook, in company

[1] *Lewis,* xiii. 20–1 *(Short Notes of my Life).* All three performances—*The Original Speech of Sir William Stanhope,* the pamphlet in which it was answered, and *The Speech of Richard Whiteliver*—were reprinted in *The Foundling Hospital for Wit,* Number VI (1749).

[2] *Lewis,* xiii. 22 *(Short Notes of my Life).* It was thought for a long while that no copy of this pamphlet had survived; but Dr. Paget Toynbee discovered a copy and printed it in *The English Historical Review* (January 1927), 95–108.

with Chute, the first of those antiquarian tours in which he delighted for many years to come. They went no further afield than Sussex, but found that county more than sufficiently Gothic for their taste. "We thought ourselves in the northest part of England; the whole country has a Saxon air, and the inhabitants are as savage, as if King George the Second was the first monarch of the East Angles." Their chaise was overturned three times; they crossed "Alpine mountains, drenched in clouds"; and Arundel, Petworth and Cowdray can seldom have been visited under circumstances of greater discomfort and exhaustion.[3]

Towards the end of 1749 he narrowly escaped death at the hands of the celebrated highwayman James Maclean. He was returning from Holland House to Arlington Street about ten o'clock on a moonlight night, when his chariot was stopped in Hyde Park by two highwaymen. One of them presented a blunderbuss at the coachman, while the other threatened Walpole with a pistol, and required him to give up his money and watch. While he was doing so the pistol went off accidentally; he was knocked backwards, his face blackened with powder and his cheek grazed by the ball, which went through the roof of the chariot just above his head. The highwayman then decamped, taking Walpole's purse, watch and sword, the coachman's watch, and some silver from the footman.[4]

Walpole advertised in the newspapers his willingness to pay twenty guineas to recover his watch and seals, and at once received a letter from his assailants, signed "A:B: & C:D:" offering to return these articles, together with his sword and the coachman's watch, for forty guineas. "Sir," this remarkable letter began, "seeing an advertisement in the papers of to Day giving an account of your being Rob'd by two Highway men on wednsday night last in Hyde Park and during the time a Pistol being fired whether Intended or Accidentally was Doubtfull Oblidges Us to take this Method of assuring you that it was the latter and by no means Design'd Either to hurt or frighten you for tho' we are Reduced by the misfortunes of the world and obliged to have Recourse to this method of getting money Yet we have Humanity

[3] *Lewis*, ix. 96–9 (Walpole to Montagu, August 26, 1749).

[4] *Ibid.*, xiii. 23 *(Short Notes of my Life)*. *London Magazine* (November 1749), 526.

Enough not to take any bodys Life where there is Not a Nessecety for it." The writers then gave careful directions about the transference of the money and the goods, which was to be done through one of Walpole's servants—"the same footman that was behind the Chariot when Rob'd will be Most Agreeable to Us as we Intend Repaying him a trifle we took from him." Finally Walpole was warned that "Now S^r if by any Means we find that you endeavour to betray Us (which we shall goe prepaird against) and in the attempt should even succeed we should leave such friends behind us who has a personall knowledge of you as would for ever seek your Destruction if you occasion ours but if you agree to the above be assured you nor none belownging to you shall Receive any or the least Injury further as we depend upon your Honour for the punctual paym^t of the Cash if you shall in that Decieve us the Concaquence may be fattall to you."[5] It is recorded that Walpole adhered to his original offer of twenty guineas, and that Maclean and his comrade eventually accepted that sum.[6]

In the following summer, Maclean was captured after robbing the Salisbury coach, and was condemned to death and eventually hanged at Tyburn. It turned out that he was the son of a Scottish minister of ancient family who had settled in Ireland, and that his brother was a distinguished dissenting clergyman living at The Hague; he had lost his wife, failed in trade, and had taken to the road to repair his misfortunes. These romantic circumstances, together with his good looks and gay attire, made his trial and condemnation events of immense public interest. Ladies wept, crowds flocked to visit him, women of fashion—and in particular Walpole's friends Lady Caroline Petersham and Miss Ashe—could hardly bear to be out of his cell. He confessed that, among his many other misdemeanours, he had been the man who robbed and nearly shot Walpole, and he stated dramatically that if his pistol had slain Walpole, he had another ready for himself. Walpole, for his part, refused to give evidence against him, and was "honourably mentioned in a Grub ballad for not having

[5] *Toynbee,* Supplement, vol. iii. 132–5 (A: B: and C: D: to Walpole, November 10, 1749).

[6] *Gentleman's Magazine* (November 1749), 522.

contributed to his sentence."[7] As he observed a few years later when describing his misadventure with Maclean in one of his papers in *The World,* "the whole affair was conducted with the greatest good-breeding on both sides."[8]

In 1750 occurred a complete breach with Ashton—"a clergyman," Walpole complained to Mann, "who in one word, has great preferments, and owes everything upon earth to me. I have long had reason to complain of his behavior; in short, my father is dead, and I can make no bishops. He has at last quite thrown off the mask, and in the most direct manner, against my will, has written against my friend Dr. Middleton."[9] Ashton knew perfectly well than an attack on Middleton was the most certain method of antagonizing Walpole; and the result of his action was that Walpole instantly forbade him his house, and inscribed on his picture the lines

> Nullius addictus munus meminisse patroni,
> Quid vacat et qui dat, curo et rogo, et omnis in hoc sum,

an apt paraphrase of the motto on the title-page of his pamphlet against Middleton. A few months later it became evident that Ashton had attacked Middleton in order to ingratiate himself with Walpole's brother Edward. The latter hated Middleton, and was then on particularly bad terms with Horace: so Ashton's opposition to them both was highly acceptable to him. But Edward Walpole's patronage proved to be no more efficacious than Horace's; and Ashton, though he continued to obtain comfortable preferments, never achieved the bishopric on which his heart was set. He died in 1775. His portrait by Reynolds, revealing pomposity and self-satisfaction in every stroke of the brush, hangs in the Hall of King's.

In July of the same year, Middleton died rather suddenly. It was not supposed, even by his most virulent enemies among the orthodox, that the death of this doughty controversialist was brought about by Ashton's *Dissertation on 2 Peter i.* 19. At the end of March 1751 two more deaths occurred in Walpole's circle,

[7] *Lewis,* xx. 168, 184, 188 (Walpole to Mann, August 2, September 1 and September 20, 1750). *London Magazine* (August 1750), 377–9.

[8] *Works,* i. 177.

[9] *Lewis,* xx. 164–5 (Walpole to Mann, July 25, 1750).

those of his eldest brother, the second Earl of Orford, and of Chute's nephew and *protégé* Francis Whithed. Walpole had never seen much of his eldest brother, though they had always been on reasonably friendly terms. His main concern on his death was for his only son, George, who now became the third Earl, and for the destinies of Houghton under his management. The late Earl's enormous sinecures reverted to the Crown at his death; and Walpole had reason to write "indeed I think his son the most ruined young man in Europe." He liked his nephew, and thought that the promise of considerable talents accompanied his good looks and pleasant manners. He decided to do his best for him, and an opportunity at once occurred. Chute had recently arranged a marriage between Whithed and a young girl of great wealth, Miss Margaret Nicoll. After Whithed's death, although he was almost prostrated with grief, Chute suggested that Miss Nicoll should marry young Lord Orford instead, and offered to make every effort to bring about the match. Walpole naturally leapt at this simple method of saving his nephew and Houghton. An indescribable complication of intrigue followed. Walpole, in an unlucky moment, mentioned the scheme to his uncle, old Horace of Wolterton, supposing that he would gladly assist "the re-establishment of his brother's family by so considerable an alliance." Old Horace had other views, and promptly decided that Miss Nicoll should become the wife of one of his own sons. Chute tried to persuade Miss Nicoll, who was apparently kept a close prisoner by some highly disagreeable people who acted as her guardians—"in three years and a half they had given her but fourteen guineas and many blows"—to escape from them and live with a sister-in-law of his own. Old Horace managed to block this scheme: and she was then sent to live with some other people who were under his own influence, and who prejudiced her against Chute and his party. Finally Lord Orford wrecked the entire project by refusing to contemplate marriage with Miss Nicoll, as he had heard that she was ill-tempered and plain. The affair ended in a series of violent quarrels, between Chute and most of his relatives, and between Horace Walpole and his uncle. Young Horace had a stormy interview with old Horace; he then wrote him a furious letter which concluded "I am Sir for the last time of my life Your Humble Servant Horace Walpole": nor was there any sort of reconciliation between them before the older man died six years later.[10] The episode was a complete disappointment to all the parties concerned; its only result was to make almost inevitable the ruin of Houghton, and to confirm Walpole in his high opinion of Chute's friendship and loyalty, and in his view of the odiousness of his uncle Horace. Miss Nicoll was married two years later to the Marquess of Carnarvon; and as Lord Orford was soon to show the earliest symptoms of the lunacy which descended upon him at intervals throughout his life, she may be accounted fortunate.

II

Walpole has recorded that Etheldreda, Lady Townshend, on her first visit to Strawberry Hill, was moved to profane outcries. "Lord God! Jesus! what a house!" she had exclaimed as she climbed the narrow stairs. "It is just such a house as the parson's, where the children lie at the foot of the bed!" A long time was to elapse before Strawberry Hill ceased to be a remarkably small house; but it began to assume some measure of elegance and adornment within three years of its acquisition by Walpole. The shapeless little box presented no feature that needed to be retained; any alteration was an improvement: it was a blank canvas on which its owner could paint any design that his fancy dictated. We have already seen that his recent genealogical and antiquarian studies had led his fancy into Gothic paths; and the plain walls and mean proportions of the house suggested a general reconstruction and an elaborate masking of Gothic adornment.

He first announced his Gothic intentions to Montagu in a letter of September 28, 1749. "Did I tell you that I have found a text in Deuteronomy to authorize my future battlements? *When thou buildest a new house, then shalt thou make a battlement for thy roof, that thou bring not blood upon thy house, if any man fall from thence.*"[11] A few months later he told Mann, "I am going to build a little Gothic castle at Strawberry Hill. If you can pick me up any fragments of old painted glass, arms, or anything, I

[10] The documents in this affair are printed in *Lewis,* xiv. 193–233.
[11] *Ibid.,* ix. 102 (Walpole to Montagu, September 28, 1749).

shall be excessively obliged to you."[12] Mann was surprised and rather shocked. "I will use my utmost endeavours to execute your commission though I am totally at a loss where to search for the fragments you want for your little Gothic castle. Why will you make it Gothic? I know that it is the taste at present but I really am sorry for it—*Basta,* I may be mistaken—*mi pare però un gusto gotico.*"[13]

Mann's observation would have been echoed by many of Walpole's friends: not, however, because they regarded Gothic as an unprecedented and barbarous innovation, but because it had become so prevalent a craze as to be already unfashionable and middle-class.[14] At no time since the Reformation had the Gothic tradition been wholly dormant; all the great classical architects—Wren, Vanbrugh, Hawksmoor, Gibbs—had worked in Gothic when need arose, usually in ecclesiastical and collegiate buildings, and with very varying results. And before the eighteenth century was very old, lesser men had begun to re-adapt Gothic ideas to domestic architecture, and from those dormant seeds of Gothic tradition strange and unlovely flowers had begun to spring. By 1750 a variety of Gothic designs was accessible to every ambitious citizen, and to every pretentious country squire, in the books of Batty Langley and others. Designs for every possible building, from mansions and castles to summer-houses and artificial ruins, were laid before those who desired to build; and many of these designs—the majority of which were really deplorable, far worse than anything that Walpole ever achieved—had duly been put into execution, Apart from the house designed by Kent for Henry Pelham at Esher, there were, as yet, few Gothic mansions of considerable size; but minor buildings in that style were going up on all sides and in the most incongruous settings. There was likewise a rage for Gothic themes in every branch of interior decoration—furniture, wallpapers, window-frames, fireplaces; and the smallest gardens boasted their

[12] *Ibid.,* ix. 111 (Walpole to Mann, January 10, 1750).

[13] *Ibid.,* 119 (Mann to Walpole, February 13, 1750).

[14] This point is well brought out in Sir Kenneth Clark's *The Gothic Revival,* a book to which I am greatly indebted throughout this chapter. I have also made use, both here and elsewhere, of Mr. John Steegmann's delightful book *The Rule of Taste from George I to George IV.*

Gothic hermitages and grottoes. Early in 1753 *The World,* that most up-to-date of periodicals, describes the Gothic craze as virtually dead. Fashionable people, says the writer, William Whitehead, have long since adopted the Chinese taste: and even there the *bourgeois* herd was fast following them. "A few years ago everything was Gothic; our houses, our beds, our book-cases, and our couches were all copied from some parts or other of our old cathedrals. . . . This, however odd it might seem, and however unworthy of the name of TASTE, was cultivated, was admired, and still has its professors in different parts of England. There is something, they say, in it congenial to our old Gothic constitution; I should rather think to our modern idea of liberty, which allows every one the privilege of playing the fool, and of making himself ridiculous in whatever way he pleases. According to the present prevailing whim everything is Chinese, or in the Chinese taste. . . . Chairs, tables, chimney pieces, frames for looking-glasses, and even our most vulgar utensils are all reduced to this newfangled standard: and without doors so universally has it spread, that every gate to a cow-yard is in T's and Z's, and every hovel for the cows has bells hanging at its corners. The good people in the city are, I perceive, struck with this novelty; and though some of them still retain the last fashion, the Gothic, yet others have begun to ornament the doors and windows of their shops with the more modern improvements."[15]

Walpole was almost entirely unaffected by the vogue for Chinese decoration which attacked England in the seventeen-fifties.[16] But he very soon rescued Gothic from the hands of "the good people in the city." He brought it into fashion. He was already a well-known *connoisseur,* an acknowledged arbiter of taste and a man of rank and influence; when he adopted Gothic, talked and wrote about Gothic, built a small but spectacular Gothic house and crammed it with exquisite and precious things, it soon ceased to be regarded as a rather paltry middle-class craze. And apart from the social acceptance which his advocacy gained for the style, the Gothic which he introduced was very much

[15] *The World,* March 22, 1753.

[16] His sole effort in this direction was to cause Bentley to design a most peculiar Chinese building for a corner of the garden; but the scheme was never carried out. *(Genesis of Strawberry Hill,* 68, 72.)

purer and more correct than the designs of the Betty Langley school. That is, perhaps, not saying much; it is impossible to deny that Strawberry Hill contained some atrocities of the first water: but at least Walpole almost always went to original Gothic work for his designs, and never dreamt of inventing Gothic "orders" in the light-hearted manner of Langley.[17] His Gothic was that of an antiquarian; and of the two designers who principally helped him at Strawberry Hill, Chute was particularly strict in his fidelity to ancient models, and Bentley's divagations from them were usually held in check. And Walpole's conception of Gothic recommended itself further to his contemporaries by its modest and unambitious scale. He never advocated the style for public buildings, or for large buildings of any description. The chapters on architecture in the *Anecdotes of Painting* are filled with just appreciations of the great classical architects of England, and with judicious praise of their buildings. He did not live quite long enough to see Wyatt, a *protégé* of his own, rear the astonishing tower of Fonthill into the Wiltshire sky. If he was ever told that the owner of Fonthill was accustomed to speak of Strawberry Hill as "a Gothic mousetrap," he would have received the gibe with perfect equanimity. "I do not mean to defend by argument a small capricious house," he had written in the preface to his *Description of Strawberry Hill*. "It was built to please my own taste, and in some degree to realize my own visions."[18] He could have had no sympathy with people who built private mansions in the style and on the scale of Fonthill; he would have dismissed with a smile the cathedral proportions of those halls and dining-rooms, as worthy of the son of Alderman Beckford. The classical orders were the only permissible architecture for buildings of such a size. It is ironical that incautious historians have sometimes traced the Gothic Revival of the nineteenth century straight back to Walpole, and that his "small capricious house" has been hailed or execrated as the direct ancestor of the Law Courts and the Albert Memorial, Keble College and the St. Pancras Hotel. There was little real connection between the productions of Butterfield and Waterhouse,

[17] *Clark*, 68–72. *Steegmann*, 78–82.

[18] *Works*, ii. 398 *(Description of Strawberry Hill)*.

Street and Scott, and the designs for a little Gothic mansion which were evolved by a group of amateurs a century before them.

III

The earlier Gothicisms at Strawberry Hill emerged from the deliberations and researches of a "Committee of Taste," consisting of Walpole, Chute and Bentley. Every detail was carefully discussed and planned by this trio, and the whole of the eastern half of the house—comprising the dining-parlour, library, staircase, armoury, and many of the smaller rooms—was the outcome of their close collaboration. In later years Chute's sounder Gothic taste gained the mastery over Bentley's fantastic conceptions; and eventually, for reasons unconnected with architecture, Bentley's association with Walpole came to an abrupt close. But for a decade the three men worked and wrangled amicably enough over the construction and adornment of Strawberry Hill.

It is curious to find Chute, who a few years before had hardly been able to tear himself away from his beloved Italy, suddenly emerging as a Gothic architect of exceptional skill. It may be that his love of genealogy, to which science he was more devoted even than Walpole, had wrought the same conversion in both men; it may be that The Vyne, which he was one day to inherit, had implanted Gothic instincts in him at an early age. At all events his feeling for Gothic architecture was extraordinarily pure and true.

Richard Bentley, the third member of the Committee of Taste, had first entered Walpole's circle, apparently through the introduction of Montagu, in the summer of 1750. He was the only son of the great Master of Trinity, who had no appreciation whatever of the graceful and wholly unscholarly talents of his offspring. "Tully had his Marcus," the old man had been heard to sigh; and certainly his overwhelming scholarship and formidable administrative powers had not been transmitted to the younger Richard Bentley. But Walpole looked for other qualities in his friends. "He has more sense, judgment, and wit, more taste and more misfortunes than sure ever met in any man," he wrote at an early stage of their acquaintance.[19] Prominent among these mis-

[19] *Lewis,* ix. 105 (Walpole to Montagu, June 23, 1750).

fortunes was the possession of an ill-tempered and expensive wife, whom Walpole used to call by such unflattering names as Tisiphone and Hecate. Bentley was himself extravagant and unpractical, and the demands of his wife and family reduced him at times almost to penury. Walpole encouraged him to settle close by at Teddington, and for several years he was constantly at Strawberry Hill, supervising the architectural progress of the house, designing chimney-pieces and ceilings and chairs, executing landscapes and drawings to hang on its walls. He was excellent company, and Walpole valued his wit and intelligence as highly as the products of his brush and pencil: indeed if Bentley had lived at Strawberry Hill merely as an architect and draughtsman, their association would have soon come to an end, for he was extremely indolent and would do nothing for weeks on end. But apart from his work on the house, many of the fruits of his association with Walpole have survived; drawings to illustrate Walpole's fugitive poems, title-pages to his prose works[20] and above all the enchanting illustrations to Gray's *Six Poems.*

Sir Kenneth Clark has given the name of Gothic Rococo to Walpole's Gothic achievements at Strawberry Hill, and in particular to Bentley's share in them. "Bentley employed Gothic," he writes, "because its name licensed any extravagant invention."[21] This is, I think, perfectly true; and in his designs for Gray's poems, which Sir Kenneth has described as "the most graceful monument to Gothic Rococo," the Rococo has completely submerged the Gothic except where the subject-matter of the poem, as for example the *Elegy written in a Country Churchyard,* demands the ancient style. Even under the sobering censorship of Chute, Bentley's designs at Strawberry Hill have a gay exuberance which is singularly remote from strict Gothic. Such features as the fragile staircase with its whimsical balustrade, and the

[20] His picture of Walpole conversing with Democritus and Heraclitus, with Strawberry Hill in the distance, was drawn as a frontispiece to the *Memoirs of George II,* and was published as such in 1822. His allegorical backgrounds to the portraits of various statesmen were drawn as title-pages to the different years covered by the *Memoirs,* and were likewise published in the first edition of that work. A title-page for Walpole's *Fugitive Pieces,* and delightful head- and tail-pieces for *The Entail,* are in private collections in England, and were privately reproduced in 1936 by Mr. W. S. Lewis.

[21] *Clark,* 68.

chimney-pieces of the Great Parlour and Yellow Bedchamber, are creations of sheer fantasy raised on the slightest Gothic foundations.

Walpole would not have admitted at this time that there was anything rococo or "frippery" about these earlier attempts at Gothic, although in his later years he acknowledged it readily enough. When he first walked through those diminutive rooms and up that brittle staircase, he felt that he had achieved a triumphant illusion of barbarism and gloom. In public he admitted that "I did not mean to make my house so Gothic as to exclude convenience, and modern refinements in luxury";[22] and he stressed the artificiality of his whole conception when taking Mann to task for innocently wondering if the garden was likewise to be Gothic. "Indeed, my dear Sir, kind as you are about it, I perceive you have no idea what Gothic is; you have lived too long amidst true taste, to understand venerable barbarism. You say, 'You suppose my garden is to be Gothic too.' That can't be; Gothic is merely architecture; and as one has a satisfaction in imprinting the gloomth of abbeys and cathedrals on one's house, so one's garden, on the contrary, is to be nothing but *riant,* and the gaiety of nature."[23] But at times his house would lose for him this air of studied artificiality. In hours of reverie, in solitary musings late at night, and especially in dreams, the flimsy materials which surrounded him—the fretted wood, the moulded plaster, the painted wallpaper—assumed the solidity of ponderous stone: and his narrow passage-ways and snug chambers began to swell into the echoing vaults and sombre galleries of Otranto.

IV

The transformation of the nondescript building called Strawberry Hill into a compact little Gothic villa was completed by 1753. The long gallery with the Cloister below, the big Round Tower and the slender Beauclerk Tower, which doubled the size of the house and imparted to it a certain irregular grace of line, were additions of later years. The works completed in 1753 did not add appreciably to the area of the house or alter its general

[22] *Works,* ii. 397 (Preface to *Description of Strawberry Hill).*

[23] *Lewis,* xx. 372 (Walpole to Mann, April 27, 1753).

dimensions. The exterior was adorned with battlements, pinnacles, arched or quatrefoil windows, and a not very imposing tower; and a more or less Gothic character was imparted to the chimney-pieces and window-frames of the set of little rooms that made up the interior. The only structural addition was an entirely new hall and staircase, designed by Bentley, and perhaps the finest flower of his Gothic invention.

These first adventures in Gothic now appear insignificant in the light of Walpole's more ambitious performances; but they probably gave him more pleasure in the planning and execution than any of his later work. The early seventeen-fifties were halcyon days at Strawberry Hill. The Committee of Taste worked together harmoniously and with enjoyment; expert visitors, like Gray and Montagu, and the inexpert throngs of the world of fashion were equally enraptured; in cathedrals and castles and ancient folios lay unexplored treasures of Gothic ready to be plundered. It was all gay and exciting; and Walpole was a happy man as he watched the rise of his battlements and the ever-increasing beauty of the trees and shrubs he had planted, while the sun glittered on the Thames and splashed the colours of his painted glass about the rooms. It is impossible not to quote, although it has been quoted so many times before, the famous letter to Mann in which he described his house, and the beauty and romance which he found in every detail of it. He had sent Mann a sketch by Bentley of the house as seen from the garden; and after describing the delightful landscapes on every hand, he proceeds: "Now you shall walk into the house. The bow-window below leads into a little parlour hung with a stone-colour Gothic paper and Jackson's Venetian prints, which I could never endure while they pretended, infamous as they are, to be after Titian, &c., but when I gave them this air of barbarous bas-reliefs, they succeeded to a miracle: it is impossible at first sight not to conclude that they contain the history of Attila or Tottila, done about the very æra. From hence, under two gloomy arches, you come to the hall and staircase, which it is impossible to describe to you, as it is the most particular and chief beauty of the castle. Imagine the walls covered with (I call it paper, but it is really paper painted in perspective to represent) Gothic fretwork: the lightest Gothic balustrade to the staircase, adorned with antelopes (our supporters) bearing shields; lean windows fattened with rich saints in painted glass, and a vestibule open with three arches on the landing-place, and niches full of trophies of old coats of mail, Indian shields made of rhinoceros's hides, broad-swords, quivers, long bows, arrows, and spears—all *suppposed* to be taken by Sir Terry Robsart in the holy wars. But as none of this regards the enclosed drawing, I will pass to that. The room on the ground-floor nearest to you is a bedchamber, hung with yellow paper and prints, framed in a new manner, invented by Lord Cardigan; that is, with black and white borders printed. Over this is Mr. Chute's bedchamber, hung with red in the same manner. The bow-window room one pair of stairs is not yet finished; but in the tower beyond it is the charming closet where I am now writing to you. It is hung with green paper and water-colour pictures; has two windows; the one in the drawing looks to the garden, the other to the beautiful prospect; and the top of each glutted with the richest painted glass of the arms of England, crimson roses, and twenty other pieces of green, purple, and historic bits. I must tell you, by the way, that the castle, when finished, will have two-and-thirty windows enriched with painted glass. In this closet, which is Mr. Chute's College of Arms, are two presses with books of heraldry and antiquities, Madame Sévigné's *Letters,* and any French books that relate to her and her acquaintance. Out of this closet is the room where we always live, hung with a blue and white paper in stripes adorned with festoons, and a thousand plump chairs, couches and luxurious settees covered with linen of the same pattern, and with a bow-window commanding the prospect, and gloomed with limes that shade half each window, already darkened with painted glass in chiaroscuro, set in deep blue glass. Under this room is a cool little hall where we generally dine, hung with paper to imitate Dutch tiles."[24]

It was indeed a strange and delightful amalgam—Gothic gloom and luxurious settees, Attila and Madame de Sévigné—that Walpole and his friends had evolved from Mrs. Chenevix's little country retreat. But the rooms remained almost uncomfortably small, and later on in this same letter Walpole mentioned that "the only two good chambers I shall have are not yet built: they

[24] *Ibid.,* 379–82 (Walpole to Mann, June 12, 1753).

will be an eating-room and a library, each twenty by thirty, and the latter fifteen feet high." These rooms were built in the following year. The "eating-room," afterwards known as the Refectory or Great Parlour, was not a particularly striking apartment. It contained a sensational chimney-piece designed by Bentley, and there was some agreeable stained-glass in the large bow-window. Walpole hung in it the portraits of his family and intimate friends. His father, mother and step-mother, his brothers and sisters, Horace and Galfridus Mann, gazed down upon his guests. In later years they were joined by two splendid conversation-pieces by Reynolds: the famous group of his friends George Selwyn, Gilly Williams and Richard Lord Edgcumbe; and the lovely picture of his great-nieces, the three Ladies Waldegrave. The Great Parlour, except for its window and chimney-piece, was just such a comfortable dining-room, adorned with the family portraits, as existed in every country-house in the land. But the Library, immediately above it, was decorated by the Committee of Taste in a vein of mediæval and heraldic fantasy which made it unquestionably the most remarkable room yet built at Strawberry Hill.

The whole approach to the Library prepared the visitor for its exuberant mediævalism. The staircase, with the carved antelopes and the rich colours thrown from the lantern of painted glass, led into the Armoury, that little vestibule with its three deep alcoves, in which Walpole placed trophies of weapons and impressive suits of ancient mail, among them some gorgeous gold-inlaid armour supposed to have been worn by Francis I.[25] From a corner of the Armoury a door opened into the Library. At the further end of the room a large window, its arches filled with fine painted glass, opened on to the lawns and the Thames beyond; round the other walls extended a continuous range of Gothic book-cases of the highest elaboration; above the book-cases were portraits, with two small quatrefoil windows balancing the portraits at the eastern end of the room; and above the portraits was a

[25] The contents of the Armoury were mainly collected in later years. The armour of Francis I, to which experts now assign a later date, was acquired in 1772. Walpole was constantly adding to his treasures, and it is impossible to observe strict chronological order in describing the furnishing and contents of his house.

painted ceiling of astonishing complexity. The whole room—the book-cases, the binding of the books, the windows, the portraits, the ceiling—glowed with colour. Even now, when almost two centuries have elapsed, one is surprised at the turbulent brightness of the ceiling, the vivid blues and reds that still glow on the woodwork of the shelves. Walpole rejected Bentley's design for the book-cases partly because certain of its features were deficient in "a conventional look,"[26] which he perceived in Chute's more successful design. But at the time of its completion the Library must have been a very gay and cheerful apartment, with little suggestion of conventional gloom in any of its features.

The design of the book-cases was the subject of much debate. The Committee of Taste knew all about the construction of chimney-pieces out of the details of mediæval tombs; but they now proposed to utilize ancient ecclesiastical designs for a range of book-cases, and the adaptation was not an easy process. Bentley produced a whimsical design in which the book-shelves were surmounted by double arches and double pinnacles. Walpole promptly rejected it.[27] By this time Bentley had retired to Jersey, for reasons which will be explained later; and Walpole and Chute decided to proceed without consulting him further. "For this time," Walpole told him with exquisite politeness, "we shall put your genius in commission, and, like some other regents, execute our own plan without minding our sovereign." Chute set to work, with his customary regard for established Gothic forms, and found a suitable design for the book-cases in the arched side-doors into the choir of Old Saint Paul's, as they appeared in Hollar's engraving reproduced by Dugdale. Bentley had the same doors in mind in his rejected design; indeed he used them as recesses at either end of his specimen range of shelves: but in designing the actual book-cases, he could not resist the characteristic variation into double arches and double pinnacles of which Walpole so rightly disapproved. Chute took the doors from Hollar's engraving practically without alteration. He depressed the arches slightly, making them somewhat wider and shallower than their prototypes: and he added more detail to the background of the

[26] *Toynbee,* iii. 201 (Walpole to Bentley, December 19, 1753).

[27] Bentley's rejected design is in the possession of Mr. W. S. Lewis and is reproduced in his *Genesis of Strawberry Hill* (fig. 10).

arches, and ran a frieze of cross-crosslets and Catherine-wheels[28] along the top of the shelves. Otherwise the form of each section of the book-cases was a precise copy of the Gothic original. The arches, constructed of light wood, could be swung on hinges away from the shelves; and this had to be done when anyone wanted to reach such books as were hidden behind the elaborate carving of the upper part of the cases. The whole range of book-cases is quite intact at the present day. So is the chimney-piece, which blends the features of two mediæval tombs, one in Westminster Abbey and the other at Canterbury. It framed a painting of the marriage of Henry VI with Margaret of Anjou.

Walpole himself designed the ceiling. Bentley drew it out, and it was executed by a French painter, Jean-François Clermont. In the middle of its expanse glowed the Walpole arms, the golden shield bearing the two black chevronels and the black fess with its gold cross-crosslets, surrounded by a wide ring of shields displaying the arms of families with whom the Walpoles had been allied by marriage—FitzOsberts, Calthorpes, Gestingthorpes, Robsarts, Calibuts, Bacons, and many more. There was the crest of the Walpoles, the Saracen's Head with its curious tasselled cap; their ancient motto, *Fari Quae Sentiat,* was inscribed on Gothic scrolls; armoured knights charged on horseback across the intricately diapered background, and at the corners were helms and mantling and yet more shields. It was Walpole's supreme expression of his pride of ancestry. It still glows with something of its original fire, and the arrogant colours have not yet wholly faded.

V

In June 1750 Walpole had received a letter from Gray, enclosing a poem. "Having put an end to a thing, whose beginning you have seen long ago, I immediately send it to you."[29] The poem thus casually introduced to Walpole's notice was the *Elegy written in a Country Churchyard.* Somewhat to Gray's annoyance, Walpole showed the astonishing production to all his friends. Copies were taken, and early in the following year one of them reached

[28] The cross-crosslets figure on the Walpole coat-of-arms, and the Catherine-wheel forms a part of the crest.

[29] *Gray,* i. 326–7 (Gray to Walpole, June 12, 1750).

the proprietors of a dingy periodical called *The Magazine of Magazines,* who informed Gray that they proposed to print it in their next issue. Gray then asked Walpole, as the person responsible for his embarrassment, to make amends by arranging with Dodsley for the immediate publication of the poem. Walpole duly saw the poem through the press, and added at Gray's request an unsigned note explaining how it had come into the printer's hands. Its success was immediate and overwhelming.

Some months before this, in the summer of 1750, the poem had been read and greatly admired by the Dowager Viscountess Cobham, who lived at the Manor House at Stoke Poges. She discovered that Gray's mother and aunt were living in the same parish as herself, and that he was even then staying with them. She did not know Mrs. Gray and Mrs. Rogers, but was determined to meet the author of the *Elegy;* and the problem of an introduction was solved by her niece, Miss Henrietta Jane Speed, and a guest, Lady Schaub, who paid a somewhat unconventional call on the poet. Gray hid in an inviolable spot in the garden till they had gone: but he returned their visit, liked Lady Cobham, and fell mildly in love with Miss Speed. He celebrated the circumstances of their introduction in his charming mock-heroic poem *A Long Story*. This was also handed about in manuscript, and was much discussed by the fashionable world.[30]

The success of the *Elegy* and the *Long Story* revived Walpole's determination that a book of Gray's poems should be published. He had previously suggested the printing of a joint collection of the poems of Gray and West; but now, with the pencil of Bentley at his command, he formed the project of an illustrated edition of the few poems that Gray was able to muster. These turned out to be six in number—the *Ode on the Spring,* the *Ode on the Death of a Favourite Cat,* and the *Ode on a Distant Prospect of Eton College,* which were already well known from their appearance in Dodsley's *Collection*; the *Elegy,* which was passing through edition after edition; and the *Long Story* and the *Hymn to Adversity,* which had not yet appeared in print. As might have been expected, from start to finish Gray was full of scruples about the scheme. He was embarrassed at the notion of publishing with such *éclat* no more than six poems, four of which had been

[30] *Ibid.,* 335 (Gray to Wharton, December 18, 1750).

reprinted again and again; and he had certainly never intended the intimacies of the *Long Story* to be made public. But his admiration for Bentley's talents overcame his reluctance to appear so openly before the world. He had addressed to Bentley some stanzas of surprising eulogy, in which he went so far as to attribute to Bentley's genius an inspiriting effect on his own reluctant Muse.

> The tardy Rhymes that us'd to linger on,
>   To Censure cold, and negligent of Fame,
> In swifter measures animated run,
>   And catch a lustre from his genuine flame....

In the same vein he justified his consent to the printing of his poems by insisting to Dodsley, the publisher of the volume, that they were "only subordinate, and explanatory to the Drawings, and suffer'd by me to come out thus only for that reason," and stipulating further that the book was to be entitled *Designs by Mr. R. Bentley, for Six Poems by Mr. T. Gray*.[31]

Bentley was working on the illustrations as early as June 1751. In the June of the next year he was finishing them, and the book was published at the end of March 1753. The last stage of its preparation was enlivened by an outburst from Gray, who discovered that Dodsley was arranging to have his portrait by Eckhardt engraved as a frontispiece. His wrath descended on the head of Walpole, who had tried to discourage Dodsley from this scheme, but who as the owner of the portrait had obviously made no very strong objection to it. "Sure you are not out of your Wits!" the indignant author protested to Walpole. "This I know, if you suffer my Head to be printed, you infallibly will put me out of mine....The thing, I know, will make me ridiculous enough; but to appear in proper Person at the head of my works, consisting of half a dozen Ballads in 30 Pages, would be worse than the Pillory. I do assure you, if I had received such a Book with such a frontispiece without any warning, I believe, it would have given me a Palsy."[32] Walpole pacified him with profuse apologies; the engraving of the portrait was stopped; and Dodsley was able to publish the volume without any further crisis.

[31] *Ibid.*, 371 (Gray to Dodsley, February 12, 1753).
[32] *Ibid.*, 372 (Gray to Walpole, February 13, 1753).

It was one of the most charming books imaginable. The poems were spaciously and beautifully printed, the drawings were reasonably well engraved, there was an air of modish intimacy about the whole production. To each poem Bentley had drawn a full-page illustration (usually a scene within an elaborate rococo border), an initial letter, a head-piece and a tail-piece. He was not invariably successful with Gray's more sombre poems; he did not quite know how to deal with "distainful Anger, pallid Fear, and Shame that sculks behind," and the other forbidding abstractions that throng the *Hymn to Adversity* and the *Eton Ode*. Of Gray's many illustrators only one has ever done justice to these conceptions, and he was William Blake. But the calm pathos of the *Elegy* was perfectly suited to Bentley's genuine feeling for pastoral melancholy and beauty of landscape; while such highly contemporary poems as the *Long Story* and the *Ode on the Death of a Favourite Cat* formed even more appropriate material for his wild fancy and fertile invention of detail. The full-page illustration to the *Elegy* is undoubtedly the most beautiful piece of work, of any description, that Bentley has left behind; but his most characteristic performances, and the most in harmony with Walpole and the general spirit of Strawberry Hill, are the decorations to the two latter poems. The picture of Gray being conveyed to his hiding-place by the Muses, with Lady Schaub and Miss Speed and Mr. Purt sweeping through the air, within a riotous border of garlands and urns and Sir Christopher Hatton dancing and Queen Elizabeth confronting the Pope, is in perfect harmony with the engaging poem which it illustrates. And the decorations of the ode on the death of Walpole's cat—cats dressed as mandarins, cats mourning poor Selima in hatbands and scarves, Destiny cutting the nine threads of her life, mice rejoicing at her death, the brilliant *cul de lampe* of the final scene in Charon's boat, where she arches her back and spits at the angry heads of Cerberus—are a triumphant exaltation of a *bagatelle* into the realms of art.

The production of this book was a great amusement to Walpole, and probably gave him the idea of setting up a private press of his own, which he carried out four years later. He had learnt to enjoy dabbling in the details of book-production, and at the same time he had the pleasure of presenting in a worthy manner work which he admired. But he was not able to give any more of Bentley's work to the world. In the autumn of 1753 that unfortunate man had been driven, partly by his creditors and partly by his wife, into a complication of distresses which obliged him to retire to Jersey. Walpole was much upset, and embarked on various schemes to stabilize his friend's affairs. He wrote him a series of admirable letters, and continually urged him to send drawings and landscapes. He had found it hard enough to get Bentley to do any work at Strawberry Hill; and now, instead of doing as his patron wished, Bentley annoyed him by setting on foot a series of absurd schemes, such as the working of a quarry of granite, and the importing of French wine. Walpole was extremely patient over Bentley's projects; but he only fell in with one of them, the sending to Strawberry Hill of a German painter named Müntz, whom he had met in Jersey. Müntz duly arrived, and was taken into Walpole's service, and set to painting and decorating and a variety of other tasks. His work had considerable merit; and his employer at first got on with him well enough. "He is very modest, humble and reasonable; and has seen so much, and knows so much, of countries and languages that I am not likely to be soon tired of him."[33] As a humble substitute for Bentley he kept his place at Strawberry Hill for several years.

VI

Apart from the incessant stream of his letters, Walpole was not writing much during these years. His period of genuine literary activity had not yet begun. But when, early in 1753, Dodsley set on foot a new periodical called *The World,* Walpole became one of its first and most welcome contributors. *The World* was edited by Edward Moore, a *protégé* of Lord Lyttelton's: and the audience to which it was intended mainly to appeal was the London world of fashion, rather than the world in any wider sense. The sober middle-classes had perused the stately moralizings of *The Rambler,* and were now being regaled with the same type of fare in *The Adventurer;* while the more frivolous middle-classes, the young lawyers and coffee-house wits and men about town, were presently to enjoy the able papers of Colman and Thornton in

[33] *Toynbee,* iii. 316 (Walpole to Bentley, July 5, 1755).

The Connoisseur. But *The World* was eminently intended for the amusement of the *beau monde.* Moore, a very agreeable writer, was responsible for a large number of the papers; the others were almost all contributed by the most aristocratic pens of the day. In this galaxy of distinguished amateurs three writers were outstanding: Walpole's neighbour at Twickenham, Richard Owen Cambridge; Lord Chesterfield, whose papers are masterpieces of humour and urbanity; and Horace Walpole himself.

Walpole was not one of the more diligent contributors; he was only responsible for nine papers during the four years' run of *The World,* whereas Cambridge gave twenty-one papers and Chesterfield twenty-three. But those nine papers were very good indeed. The conventions of eighteenth-century periodical literature suited his style. He could assume the character of Adam FitzAdam, the supposititious editor of *The World;* or he could assume some other disguise and address a letter to Mr. FitzAdam: either method gave him opportunities of which he made excellent use. His papers are distinguished not only by his usual subtlety and wit, but by the ability to present learned and antiquarian matter in such a way as to make it most entertaining reading. He exercised this power constantly in his late works; but it appeared for the first time in these essays. They contain all sorts of allusions, anecdotes, references to obscure books, long quotations from unknown writers. Never was learning worn so lightly. No one else could have introduced in *The World,* without utter incongruity, a long letter from the Emperor Maximilian to his daughter, written in a barbarous Germanic French, or a detailed account of the legacies bequeathed by the mother of King Richard II.

His papers are on all sorts of subjects: the theatre, the reformation of the calendar, the composition of letters, on old women being the most satisfactory objects for love (a theme ironically treated, of course, but not without relevance to Walpole's actual experience), on the politeness of highwaymen (with reminiscences of his encounter with Maclean). At the very end of *The World's* career, a "*World* Extraordinary" was issued, consisting of his character of Henry Fox written eight years before, and now published in spite of their increasing differences in politics. But the most interesting of all Walpole's papers was the one which dealt with Theodore, King of Corsica. This potentate, after a gallant and eventful career, was at the moment confined in the King's Bench for debt. Walpole explained his unhappy predicament; invited Garrick to stage a special performance for his benefit, preferably of *King Lear,* that classic portrayal of royalty in distress; and advertised the immediate opening of a subscription at Dodsley's shop, in aid of the distressed monarch. The subscription only raised fifty pounds, a sum which did not satisfy King Theodore, who, after accepting the money, sent a lawyer to threaten Dodsley for having taken such a liberty with his name. Dodsley ignored his threats, which of course came to nothing; but Walpole was rather disconcerted at his *protégé's* "dirty knavery," and told Mann that "I have done with countenancing kings!"[34] Nevertheless, his interest in Theodore did not end here. The King of Corsica died in December 1756, immediately after leaving the liberties of the Fleet under the Act of Insolvency, having first registered his kingdom among his assets for the benefit of his creditors. He was buried in the churchyard of St. Anne's, Soho, where Walpole erected a tombstone, which still survives, to his memory, with an inscription of which the following epitaph was a part:

> The GRAVE, great Teacher, to a Level brings
> Heroes and Beggars, Galley-slaves and Kings.
> But THEODORE this Moral learn'd, ere dead;
> FATE pour'd its Lessons on his living Head,
> Bestow'd a KINGDOM, and deny'd him BREAD.[35]

VII

These were pleasant and carefree years for Walpole. There were unhappy periods ahead—the shock of Conway's neglect after his rise to power in 1765, the embarrassing and unprovoked controversy over Chatterton's death—but throughout the seventeen-fifties his star was prosperous. In London, at Strawberry Hill, in his antiquarian tours and summer visits to country-houses, he passed a contented life, always surrounded by amusing and agreeable people.

At Strawberry Hill his immediate neighbours were pleasantly

[34] *Lewis,* xx. 373–4 (Walpole to Mann, April 27, 1753).
[35] *Ibid.,* xxi. 140.

varied. There were the "dowagers as plenty as flounders." There was an attorney's wife who was always drunk by night-fall, and who would then order her servants to drive away imaginary thieves by firing guns out of the windows.[36] Just across the road lived Lord Radnor, whose domain the Committee of Taste christened "Mabland," in allusion to the odd and faintly nightmarish improvements which its owner was constantly making there. (A singular Chinese summer-house in his grounds appears in several of the views of Twickenham which various artists drew from Walpole's garden.) Another neighbour and frequent visitor was Richard Owen Cambridge, Walpole's contemporary at Eton, the author of the *Scribleriad* and other works; a versatile and amiable man, an inveterate gossip and something of a bore. But Walpole's principal friends at Twickenham were two women, different from one another in every imaginable way, but extremely distinguished in their respective spheres, Lady Suffolk and Mrs. Clive.

Lady Suffolk was living quietly at Marble Hill, her villa near Twickenham, in the afterglow of her career as the favourite mistress of George II. The daughter of a Norfolk baronet, Sir Henry Hobart of Blickling, she had married Lord Suffolk, then Mr. Howard, just before the accession of George I. She soon became a leading figure in the opposition court of the Prince and Princess of Wales—that memorable circle which had included Pope and Gay, Hervey and Chesterfield, and the brilliant group of maids of honour headed by Miss Bellenden and Miss Lepell. The Prince became Mrs. Howard's lover: when he succeeded to the throne, he installed her at St. James's Palace; Mr. Howard, with whom she had seldom been on particularly good terms, accepted a pension, and a formal separation was arranged. She now found herself in a position of obvious importance but little actual power; she had to encounter the jealousy of the Queen and the caprices and ill-temper of the King; and although she maintained her position at Court for seven years, her intrigues on behalf of the politicians opposing Sir Robert Walpole met with consistent failure. Her ambition, allied to a cold and placid temperament, enabled her to put up with what must have been an extremely dis-

[36] *Ibid.*, ix. 74 (Walpole to Montagu, September 3, 1748).

agreeable situation, in which, as Hervey put it, "she was forced to live in the constant subjection of a wife with all the reproach of a mistress":[37] but with all her cleverness and patience she was no match for Queen Caroline, had no real influence over the unattractive monarch who loved her, and never scored a political success of the slightest importance. Some honours for her relations, and an adequate fortune for herself, were all she gained from her years of royal favour. She was liked and respected by every one; her character as drawn by Hervey, a member of the opposite faction at Court, is almost as cordially worded as Walpole's glowing tribute to her after many years of friendship. She had retired from Court in 1735, and had since lived mainly at Marble Hill. Lord Suffolk had died two years before her retirement, and her second and happier marriage with the Hon. George Berkeley came to an end with his death early in 1747. When Horace Walpole, later in that year, came to live at Twickenham, she soon learnt to value the company of the young man whose father she had so perseveringly opposed at Court. She had always been deaf, an affliction on which Pope had based one of the most engaging of his compliments;[38] even as, in one of his more bitter moods, he had based the character of Chloe on her rather heartless detachment and placidity.[39] This deafness rendered her conversation something of a monologue, and it was a monologue of the sort that Walpole enjoyed—scandal of old courts, gossip and reminiscence about the great people of former days. Whenever they were both at their country villas, he used to spend some evenings with her every week, listening to the tranquil flow of her recollections, or piecing together with her assistance, and the assistance of his own memories of his father's talk, some long-forgotten transaction of politics or intrigue. These conversations formed the ground-work for a great part of the *Reminiscences* which he wrote for the Berrys towards the close of his own life: and he paid a grateful and affectionate tribute to his old friend in the course of that work. In her lifetime he could give her little repayment; but it may be mentioned that he and Chute did at least design her a Gothic barn at Marble Hill.

[37] *Hervey,* 43. [38] The poem *On a certain Lady at Court.*
[39] *Moral Essays,* Epistle II. 157–80.

Catherine Clive was the most famous comic actress of the day. She was eight years older than Walpole, and almost from childhood had delighted London audiences in boisterous comic parts. She had a charming voice, and used to sing Purcell to George Montagu when he stayed with Walpole; but her ambition to play serious and stately *rôles* was seldom gratified by the managers. Only the affection of her public saved her from disaster when she tried to play Portia, and she returned with resignation to Mistress Quickly and Lady Wishfort. Her marriage to a barrister named George Clive soon ended in a separation by mutual agreement, and she retired with her brother, James Raftor, to a house in the Twickenham neighbourhood, where she was living when Horace Walpole settled there. He soon became fast friends with the jovial and rubicund Kitty, and when he bought Little Strawberry Hill, a small house almost adjoining his property in the direction of Teddington, he gave it to her for her life. Her installation in this house, presently to be known as Cliveden, was a most successful arangement. The blowsy, witty, downright actress, with her flaming face and uproarious laughter, proved a perfect neighbour. She got on admirably with his friends, men and women alike; she was excellent company when he happened to be alone; she worked carpets and screens for his house, and he gave her goldfish and advice about her garden. "Tho I am now," she wrote to him, "representing women of qualitty and coblers wives &c &c to crowded houeses, and flattering applause; the characture I am most desirous to act well is a good sort of a countrey gentlewoman at twickenham."[40] Their incongruous friendship naturally provoked a good deal of ridicule, not all so good-natured as Lady Townshend's observation that Strawberry Hill "would be a very pleasant place, if Mrs. Clive's face did not rise upon it and make it so hot."[41] But only the most ill-informed of newspaper lampooners failed to perceive the extreme improbability of a love-affair between Horace Walpole and Kitty Clive.

A constant succession of people stayed at Strawberry Hill: Walpole's sister Lady Mary Churchill and her husband, Conway and Lady Ailesbury, Lord March—the "old Q." of half a century later—and his Florentine mistress the celebrated Contessa Rena.

[40] *Toynbee,* Supplement, iii. 139 (Mrs. Clive to Walpole, December 3 [1755]).
[41] *Ibid.,* iii. 260 (Walpole to Bentley, November 3, 1754).

Chute was a regular visitor; Gray came every summer; Montagu was often persuaded to leave his rural retreats for a few days' stay at Twickenham. But Walpole's most faithful guests, who came more or less regularly every Christmas and Easter, were George Selwyn, George James Williams and Richard Edgcumbe, the triumvirate whose portrait by Reynolds hung in the Great Parlour.

George Selwyn was one of the oddest of the celebrities of his day. He was a noted wit, and Walpole has recorded any number of his *bons mots*, most of which, detached from their immediate background and from the irresistible sleepy drawl in which they were delivered, sound rather feeble. He had influence in a couple of boroughs, Gloucester and Ludgershall, and always sat in Parliament for one of them, but worried very little about politics; his interests were exclusively social and personal. For many years he was an assiduous and usually an unlucky gambler; but in time he eschewed the gaming-tables, and passed his life as a leisured wit and man of fashion, and as the admiring mentor of two of the most promising young men of the time, Lord March and Lord Carlisle. His affection for Lord March led him into several extravagances, especially in the devotion he conceived towards the little girl Mie Mie, his friend's daughter by the Marchesa Fagniani, whom he practically brought up as his own child. He was remarkable also for his macabre interest in corpses and executions, of which endless stories were told. Many aspects of his character would provide first-class material for a psycho-analyst's case-book; but the impression he made on his contemporaries, and the impression he makes on any reader of his letters and of the voluminous correspondence addressed to him, remains that of a very kindly, agreeable and amusing man.[42]

If Selwyn was liable to be erratic in his actions and inclinations, "Gilly" Williams was the embodiment of normality and common-sense. He was the son of a well-known lawyer, and was related to the Guilford family, receiving the office of Receiver-General of Excise from his nephew Lord North in 1774; he led a pleasant

[42] *Jesse, passim.* Lady Louisa Stuart's *Notes* on Jesse's book, edited by W. S. Lewis (Oxford University Press, 1928), form an invaluable pendant and corrective to it. See also Selwyn's letters to Lord Carlisle, printed in *H.M.C., Carlisle MSS.*, 15, vi.

idle existence between a large circle of friends in London and a large number of hospitable houses in the country, but not much is known either of his public or his private life. He is remembered only through his friendship with Walpole and a few scattered references in other contemporary records, but principally because of the brilliant series of his letters to Selwyn.[43] These letters are full of insight, intelligence and a very agreeable wit; and they contain some of the most penetrating criticisms of Walpole, both sympathetic and malicious, that were made by any of his contemporaries. He really understood Walpole, and Walpole's relations to his own time and to posterity. His remark that *"monstrari digito praetereuntium* has been his whole aim" has already been quoted. In less amiable moods, his comments were equally perceptive. "Horry is gone a progress into Northamptonshire to Lady Betty Germaine's. Is it not surprising how he moves from old Suffolk on the Thames to another old goody on the Tyne; and does not see the ridicule which he would so strongly paint in any other character?"[44]

The third member of Walpole's "out of town party" was Richard Edgcumbe, the son of the first Lord Edgcumbe, whom he succeeded in the title in 1758. He had been a friend of Walpole's for many years past, and had habitually confided to "dear Hory" the involved love-affairs of his youth. "I do not choose you before the rest of my acquaintance," he had written in 1744, "only because I had rather talk with you than any body else, and upon a subject I love most, but because I think you have more Feeling, and will be more sensible of my present uneasiness."[45] He retained his confidence in Walpole's sympathy to the end of his life, and when he died in 1761 he made him trustee for his mistress and his four children by her. He was an artist of some ability, and at least one example of his talent, the amusing coat-of-arms designed for the Club at White's, became a permanent adornment of Strawberry Hill.

Such, during the seventeen-fifties, were Walpole's principal

[43] *Jesse,* i. and ii. *passim.* See also *Glenbervie,* where he makes his appearance in extreme old age, but with his wit and conversational powers apparently undiminished.

[44] *Jesse,* i. 252 (Williams to Selwyn, July 18, 1763).

[45] *Lewis,* xxx. 65–7 (Edgcumbe to Walpole, August 10, 1744).

resident and visiting friends at Twickenham, where he lived in comparative retirement. In London he passed his time in a round of social and political activity, and it would be impossible to enumerate or describe the people with whom he was in frequent contact. He knew every one, went everywhere, gradually became one of the best-known and most ubiquitous personalities of the day. Certain congenial figures always stand out in the unending procession which moves through his London letters; Lady Townshend, with her downright wit and constant flow of startling remarks; Lady Hervey, the incomparable Molly Lepell of three decades before, with her beauty scarcely impaired, her gaiety and charm undiminished; Miss Anne Pitt, William Pitt's sister, whose wit and originality were greatly to his taste, and with whom he corresponded for many years. These were his friends; he could linger when describing them; but the general atmosphere of contemporary London is best preserved in those of his letters which describe some typical occasion, a ball or a masquerade, thronged with people whom he regarded with interest but also with indifference. The letter about Lady Caroline Petersham's party to Vauxhall is one of his accepted masterpieces: he was indifferent to most of the people concerned, and slightly hostile to one or two of them; its virtue lies in the astonishing way in which he manages to reproduce the rhythm of a midsummer night's amusement in London, the movement and laughter, good manners and ill-temper, casual encounters and attractions and antagonisms. Once again George Montagu acts almost as a representative of posterity, in spite of the careful implications to the contrary in Walpole's opening sentence. "I shall relate it to you to show you the manners of the age, which are always as entertaining to a person fifty miles off, as to one born an hundred and fifty years after the time. I had a card from Lady Caroline Petersham to go with her to Vauxhall. I went accordingly to her house, and found her and the little Ashe, or the pollard Ashe, as they call her; they had just finished their last layer of red, and looked as handsome as crimson could make them. On the cabinet stood a pair of Dresden candlesticks, a present from the virgin hands of Sir John Bland: the branches of each formed a little bower over a cock and hen treading, yet literally! We issued into the Mall to assemble our company, which was all the town if we could get it; for just so many had been summoned, except Harry Vane, whom we met by *chance*. We mustered the Duke of Kingston whom Lady Caroline says she has been trying for these seven years; but alas! his beauty is at the fall of the leaf; Lord March, Mr. Whithed, a pretty Miss Beauclerc and a very foolish Miss Sparre. These two damsels were trusted by their mothers for the first time of their lives to the matronly conduct of Lady Caroline. As we sailed up the Mall with all our colours flying, Lord Petersham, with his nose and legs twisted to every point of crossness, strode by us on the outside, and repassed again on the return. At the end of the Mall she called to him, he would not answer; she gave a familiar spring, and between laugh and confusion ran up to him, 'My Lord, my Lord! why, you don't see us!' We advanced at a little distance, not a little awkward in expectation how all this would end, for my Lord never stirred his hat or took the least notice of anybody: she said, 'Do you go with us, or are you going anywhere else?'—'I don't go with you, I am going somewhere else'; and away he stalked, as sulky as a ghost that nobody will speak to first. We got into the best order we could, and marched to our barge, with a boat of French horns attending and little Ashe singing. We paraded some time up the river, and at last debarked at Vauxhall. There, if we had so pleased, we might have had the vivacity of our party increased by a quarrel, for a Mrs. Loyd, who is supposed to be married to Lord Haddington, seeing the two girls following Lady Caroline and Miss Ashe, said aloud, 'Poor girls, I am sorry to see them in such bad company!' Miss Sparre, who desired nothing so much as the fun of seeing a duel, a thing which, though she is fifteen, she has never been so lucky to see, took due pains to make Lord March resent this; but he, who is very lively and agreeable, laughed her out of this charming frolic with a great deal of humour. Here we picked up Lord Granby, arrived very drunk from Jenny's Whim; where, instead of going to old Strafford's catacombs to make honourable love, he had dined with Lady Fitzroy, and left her and eight other women and four other men playing at brag. He would fain have made over his honourable love upon any terms to poor Miss Beauclerc, who is very modest, and did not know at all what to do with his whispers or his hands. He then addressed himself to the Sparre, who was very well disposed to receive both; but the tide of champagne turned, he hiccupped at the reflection of his marriage, of which he is wondrous sick, and only proposed to the girl to shut themselves up and rail at the world for three weeks. If all the adventures don't conclude as you expect at the beginning of a paragraph, you must not wonder, for I am not making a history, but relating one strictly as it happened, and I think with full entertainment enough to content you. At last, we assembled in our booth, Lady Caroline in the front with the vizor of her hat erect, and looking gloriously jolly and handsome. She had fetched my brother Orford from the next box, where he was enjoying himself with his Norsa and his *petite partie,* to help us mince chickens. We minced seven chickens into a china dish, which Lady Caroline stewed over a lamp with three pats of butter and a flagon of water, stirring, and rattling, and laughing, and we every minute expecting to have the dish fly about our ears. She had brought Betty, the fruit-girl, with hampers of strawberries and cherries from Roger's, and made her wait upon us, and then made her sup by us at a little table. The conversation was no less lively than the whole transaction. There is a Mr. O'Brien arrived from Ireland, who would get the Duchess of Manchester from Mr. Hussey, if she were still at liberty. I took up the biggest hautboy in the dish, and said to Lady Caroline, 'Madam, Miss Ashe desires you would eat this O'Brien strawberry'; she replied immediately, 'I won't, you Hussey!' You may imagine the laugh this reply occasioned. After the tempest was a little calmed, the Pollard said, 'Now, how anybody would spoil this story that was to repeat it, and say, I won't, you jade!' In short, the whole air of our party was sufficient, as you will easily imagine, to take up the whole attention of the garden; so much so, that from eleven o'clock till half an hour after one we had the whole concourse round our booth: at last, they came into the little gardens of each booth on the sides of ours, till Harry Vane took up a bumper, and drank their healths, and was proceeding to treat them with still greater freedom. It was three o'clock before we got home."[46]

This party took place in 1750. Ten years later—and indeed for many years after that—he was still describing parties with the same enjoyment and the same easy mastery. On just such another

[46] *Ibid.,* ix. 105–11 (Walpole to Montagu, June 23, 1750).

June night, in 1760, his old acquaintance Miss Chudleigh—who was then kept by the Duke of Kingston, whom she subsequently married, in spite of her previous secret marriage to Augustus Hervey—gave a ball in honour of the birthday of the Prince of Wales. Walpole was present at the ball, and his description of it may be quoted as a further (and final) illustration of the inexhaustible amusement and enjoyment which he got out of his London life.

"You had heard, before you left London, of Miss Chudleigh's intended loyalty on the Prince's birthday. Poor thing, I fear she has thrown away above a quarter's salary! It was magnificent and well understood—no crowd—and though a sultry night, one was not a moment incommoded. The court was illuminated on the whole summit of the wall with a battlement of lamps; smaller ones on every step, and a figure of lanterns on the outside of the house. The virgin-mistress began the ball with the Duke of York, who was dressed in a pale blue watered tabby, which, as I told him, if he danced much, would soon be *tabby all over,* like the man's advertisement; but nobody did dance much. There was a new Miss Bishop from Sir Cecil's endless hoard of beauty daughters, who is still prettier than her sisters. The new Spanish embassy was there—alas! Sir Cecil Bishop has never been in Spain! Monsieur de Fuentes is a halfpenny print of my Lord Huntingdon. His wife homely, but seems good-humoured and civil. The son does not degenerate from such highborn ugliness—the daughter-in-law was sick, and they say is not ugly, and has as good a set of teeth as one can have, when one has but two and those black. They seem to have no curiosity, sit where they are placed, and ask no questions about so strange a country. Indeed, the ambassadress could see nothing; for Dodington stood before her the whole time, sweating Spanish at her, of which it was evident, by her civil nods without answers, she did not understand a word. She speaks bad French, danced a bad minuet, and went away—though there was a miraculous draught of fishes for their supper, as it was a fast—but being the octave of their *Fête-Dieu,* they dared not even fast plentifully. Miss Chudleigh desired the gamblers would go up into the garrets—'Nay, they are not garrets—it is only the roof of the house hollowed for upper servants—but I have no upper servants.' Everybody ran up: there is a low gallery with book-cases, and four chambers practised under the pent of the roof, each hung with the finest Indian pictures on different colours, and with Chinese chairs of the same colours. Vases of flowers in each for nosegays, and in one retired nook a most critical couch!

"The lord of the festival [the Duke of Kingston] was there, and seemed neither ashamed nor vain of the expense of his pleasures. At supper she offered him Tokay, and told him she believed he would find it good. The supper was in two rooms and very fine, and on all the sideboards, and even on the chairs, were pyramids and troughs of strawberries and cherries; you would have thought she was kept by Vertumnus. . . ."[47]

VIII

There remains one person who deserves more than a passing mention among the members of his Twickenham or London cliques. In the middle seventeen-fifties the figure, absurd yet imposing, of Lady Mary Coke begins to appear in his correspondence; and before the end of the decade he is addressing to her letters which conclude "Your absolute Slave Horace Walpole."

The lady with whom he now began to exchange these high-flown gallantries was the youngest of the four daughters of the second Duke of Argyll. She and her sisters were all remarkable for their striking appearance, and likewise for their loud discordant voices, which caused them to be known collectively as "the screaming sisterhood" and "the bawling Campbells." They all had mild idiosyncrasies of various kinds, but Lady Mary's eccentricities were more pronounced, and increased to a startling extent with the years. In 1747 she had married Walpole's old acquaintance at Florence, Edward Coke, who became Viscount Coke upon his father's being created Earl of Leicester. She had disliked Lord Coke and made no secret of it, yet allowed the marriage to take place; whereupon her husband retaliated by leaving her immediately after the ceremony. When Lord Coke, repenting of his behaviour, presently claimed his marital rights and his bride's dowry, both were obstinately withheld, although Lady Mary was carried off to Holkham by her father-in-law and literally

[47] *Toynbee,* iv. 393–4 (Walpole to the Earl of Strafford, June 7, 1760).

kept a prisoner there for several months. After much commotion and legal argument, a separation was arranged; and eventually Lord Coke died while his wife was still a young woman. She had always been quick-tempered, resentful, and abnormally sensitive to any slight, and the humiliating circumstances of her marriage increased these characteristics to the point of mania. A wealthy and attractive widow, she came to the decision that no suitor was worthy of her hand unless he was of the royal blood of England; and in due course she fixed her regard on the Prince of Wales's second brother, Edward Duke of York, a loquacious and empty-headed youth twelve years younger than herself. The Duke, with his "little mean figure, and a pale face, with white eyelashes and eyebrows, and a certain tremulous motion of the eye that was far from adding to its beauty,"[48] was slightly flattered by the admiration of a mature and fastidious woman of fashion: but he was also very much amused. Lady Mary made it plain that she would consent only to marriage with the royal youth; and her attitude of "awful reserve maintained and distant encouragement held out" caused endless amusement to the other members of his family.[49] Although there was not the remotest suggestion of a secret marriage or even of a secret understanding between them, she adopted, after his early death in 1767, the woes and almost the weeds of widowhood.

At the time of which we are treating, however, these troubles lay some years ahead. Mary was still happy in the juvenile attentions of the Duke of York; and she was able at the same time to appreciate the equally insubstantial gallantries of Horace Walpole. He had always been acquainted with her and her sisters—Lady Dalkeith (who afterwards married Charles Townshend), Lady Strafford and Lady Betty Mackenzie—and was a regular correspondent of Lady Strafford and her husband. He admired Lady Mary—her striking if somewhat forbidding beauty, her stately demeanour, her pride of ancestry: he realized the more human qualities beneath her enormous assumption of dignity. He was prepared to bear with her absurdities, her wrong-headedness, the submission which she exacted from her friends. And she was grateful in return. She was flattered by Walpole's mocking

[48] *Coke,* i. lxxxviii (the introductory memoir by Lady Louisa Stuart).
[49] *Ibid.,* lxxxix–xc.

intimacy, his letters of ludicrous compliment, his references to her "absolute sovereignty" over him, his claims to be "one who pretends to the honour of your hand."[50] "Shall Wolfe and Boscawen and Amherst be the talk of future ages, and the name of Mary Coke be not known? 'Tis the height of disgrace! When was there a nation that excelled the rest of the world whose beauties were not as celebrated as its heroes and its orators? Thais, Aspasia, Livia, Octavia—I beg pardon for mentioning any but the last when I am alluding to you. . . ."[51] It was flattering and delightful to be addressed in such terms. And she could hardly have been perturbed when the Duke of York asked his middle-aged rival, one night at the opera, when he intended to marry her; to which Walpole replied that he proposed to do so directly he was given the command of a regiment.[52]

IX

In later years Walpole must often have looked back to this tranquil decade as the happiest period of his life. There were few storms, either political or personal, to disturb his serene passage into middle-age. His circle of friends was yet unbroken by death or estrangement: Conway, Selwyn, Montagu, Chute, Gray, Bentley, Lady Suffolk, Mrs. Clive, Lady Hervey, Lady Mary Coke... he was fated to quarrel with some of them, and save for Lady Mary, he would outlive them all; but these sorrows were still on the far horizon. His house was increasing in charm and in celebrity, his garden grew ever more beautiful, pictures and porcelain and armour and books crowded his rooms. Years of undiminished activity and happiness seemed to lie ahead.

He accepted serenely enough the harbingers of middle-age, even though they included an attack from an unexpected enemy, the gout. Approaching baldness had been disguised by a "tour" so effective that Montagu, unexpectedly appointed to a post in Ireland, lost no time in adopting a similar device. Trouble with his eyes was remedied by green spectacles; and when the shopkeeper was solicitous to choose a pair which would not ruffle his

[50] *Lewis,* xxxi. 14 (Walpole to Lady Mary Coke, December 27, 1759).
[51] *Ibid.,* 20–1 (Walpole to Lady Mary Coke, February 12, 1761).
[52] *Ibid.,* ix. 264 (Walpole to Montagu, December 23, 1759).

hair, he replied "Lord! Sir, when one is come to wear spectacles, what signifies how one looks?"[53] But Walpole's way of life might well have led him to expect immunity from the gout: and it was with a strong sense of injustice that he wrote to Lord Strafford that "virtue and leanness are no preservatives"[54] against this malady. He had not even the consolation of its being a hereditary complaint, for his father, whose habits were eminently designed to provoke the gout, was never touched by it. His own first attack of gout occurred in 1755; a more severe attack followed five years later: and thereafter it was a constant misery to him. Medical science has now analysed the conditions which the eighteenth century grouped under the general name of "gout." Some of Walpole's earlier attacks were probably a form of acute rheumatism; although later in life his complaint turned to gout in its most genuine and painful form. In neither case can he have derived any benefit from the daring *régime* of exposure to cold, indifference to wet feet, and insufficient clothing in which he took such pride and which some of his friends described in terms of such unrestrained horror.[55] But Walpole's fundamental toughness for many years surmounted both his gout and the methods with which he tried to suppress it. He grew ever leaner, his eyes shone ever more brilliantly in a paler face: but in his worst fits of pain he was still "Ariel the Sprite in a slit shoe,"[56] and his vivacity remained undiminished. He had not yet wholly given up dancing in favour of loo, and the embarrassments and ill-tempered exchanges of Princess Emily's card-table were still a few years away.

He continued to set down for the benefit of posterity, in his letters and his memoirs, the records of his time. These were his monument; through them he would be known to future ages. But Strawberry Hill, the house for which his love grew from day to day, could be certain of no such survival. The happy months he spent there were his own; the cutting and carting of his hay, the nightingales in the undergrowth, the squirrels coming to be fed under the windows—these were personal and perishable delights. But was there no way of preserving the house and the exquisite

[53] *Lewis,* xxi. 131 (Walpole to Mann, September 3, 1757).
[54] *Toynbee,* iv. 414 (Walpole to the Earl of Strafford, August 7, 1760).
[55] e.g. *Cole,* 53–5.
[56] *Lewis,* ix. 292 (Walpole to Montagu, August 12, 1760).

things within it? Were they to be as evanescent as the scent of his honeysuckles, as the sunlight glittering on the Thames? He had known Houghton in its glory, and was now watching its decline; he had seen the same process in family after family, and in house after house; and he could not suppose that Strawberry Hill, the selfish creation of a childless man, would suffer a different fate. Later on, perhaps, he would take what measures he could to save Strawberry Hill from the doom that was approaching Houghton. But at present he could only smile a little sadly as he composed *The Entail,* the fable of the butterfly which lived in a rose, and could not endure the thought of its lovely dwelling becoming the abode of meaner creatures.

A CATERPILLAR grovel'd near,
A subtle slow conveyancer,
Who summon'd waddles with his quill
To draw the haughty insect's will.
None but his heirs must own the spot,
Begotten, or to be begot:
Each leaf he binds, each bud he ties
To eggs of eggs of BUTTERFLIES

When lo! how Fortune loves to tease
Those who would dictate her decrees!
A wanton BOY was passing by;
The wanton child beheld the FLY,
And eager ran to seize the prey;
But, too impetuous in his play
Crush'd the proud tenant of an hour,
And swept away the MANSION-FLOW'R.[57]

[57] *Works,* i. 28–9.

IX

The Middle Years: Literary and Social Life (1757-65)

I

IT was hardly to be expected that Walpole would always address his writings to posterity, without revealing his literary talent to his contemporaries. He did indeed manage to reach the age of forty without making any public appearance as an author, except in a few pamphlets and *pièces d'occasion*. But the preparation of the *Designs for Six Poems* had shown him that book-production can be an amusing and interesting occupation; and by 1757 he had decided to set up a private press at Strawberry Hill. An interest in printing was by no means incongruous with his Gothic surroundings. Was he not following the precedent set by Tiptoft, Earl of Worcester, and Widville, Earl Rivers, the patrons of Caxton, the most learned and accomplished noblemen of their age?[1] Had not Archbishop Parker maintained in his household a painter, an engraver and a printer,[2] and might not a printer with equal propriety join Bentley and Müntz at Strawberry Hill? So the printing-press was set up; and since it is difficult to own a private press without succumbing to the temptations of authorship, Walpole's literary ambitions were immediately stimulated. The bulk of his most important and most original literary work belongs to the ten or twelve years which followed its establishment.

The press was erected in June 1757 in a little building in the garden, so close to the house that it had to be removed when the cloister and gallery were added a few years later. The printer was William Robinson, an erratic Irishman whose theatrical appear-

[1] *Works*, i. 281–91. [2] *Printing-Office*, 1.

ance won the admiration of Garrick. He was the first of a succession of printers who caused Walpole endless trouble until one Thomas Kirgate arrived in 1765, and proved so satisfactory that he remained at Strawberry Hill, with one considerable interval, until his employer's death. Walpole had intended that the first fruits of his press should be the description by a German named Paul Hentzner of his journey into England in 1598. Hentzner's account of England was a work of considerable antiquarian interest, and contained an excellent first-hand description of Queen Elizabeth at prayers and at dinner in Greenwich Palace. It was duly published later in 1757, with a translation by Bentley opposite the Latin text; but in the end a work of very much greater importance was chosen to be the opening production of the press. Gray had brought to London the manuscript of his two great odes, *The Progress of Poesy* and *The Bard,* which he had at last completed after years of anxious effort. He had intended that the odes should be published by Dodsley; but Walpole insisted on acting as Dodsley's printer on this occasion, and the *Officina Arbuteana* was thus assured of the first and the most remarkable of its productions. There was an opening ceremony of some sort, to which Dodsley and other booksellers and printers were invited; and on July 16 Robinson began his single-handed task of turning out two thousand copies of the handsome quarto pamphlet, with its dignified pages and noble type.[3]

Gray had entered into the whole scheme rather unwillingly. For one thing, he had never much cared for the publicity that was usually attached to Walpole's enterprises. (Indeed the press had already become the subject of gossip, and people were saying that it was going to be used for mysterious political ends.)[4] Then Walpole, foreseeing that the odes would be criticized for their obscurity, urged him to add some illustrative notes; this also went

[3] I have accepted Walpole's statements in his *Journal of the Printing-Office at Strawberry Hill* as to the number of copies that were printed of each book, the dates of publication, and so forth. There can be no doubt, however, that some of his statements were inaccurate and confused, the result of his habit of making entries in the *Journal* long after the event. Mr. A. T. Hazen's admirable *Bibliography of the Strawberry Hill Press* (1942) has cleared up many difficulties, and is indispensable to any student or collector of the productions of Walpole's press.

[4] *Lewis,* ix. 214 (Walpole to Montagu, July 16, 1757).

against the grain, and he curtly rejected the suggestion.[5] In fact these odes meant more to him than Walpole, who remembered his indifference about the *Elegy* and his deprecatory attitude towards others of his poems, can have ever realized. Walpole admired them, was awed by them, smilingly excused their obscurity to his more critical friends. They were a heaven-sent opportunity for the worthy inauguration of his press. But Gray regarded them as masterpieces, and was pathetically anxious that they should be appreciated and understood. The fuss about their printing and publication was wholly distasteful to him; and although he never allowed Walpole to suspect the extent of his distaste, he confided it to other friends.[6] The intensity of his feeling about the poems, his anxiety for their favourable reception and his bitter disappointment when their reception was cold and unsympathetic, can best be explained by the supposition that he intended the public verdict to be a test of his own poetic powers. He proposed to abide by the judgment passed by his contemporaries on these odes, which he regarded as the summit of his achievement. And it is significant that he never wrote any work of sustained passion or power after the failure of these two magnificent poems to please the general opinion of his age.

In one letter after another he repeated to his friends the charges of obscurity and incomprehensibility that were levelled against him. Lord Barrington believed that the last stanza of *The Bard* related to Charles I and Oliver Cromwell. Mr. Fox did not wonder that King Edward could not understand what the Bard was saying to him. A writer in the *Critical Review* mistook the Æolian lyre for the harp of Æolus. A lady of quality wished that titles had been prefixed to tell her what the poems were about. Mr. Wood, the author of the *Ruins of Palmyra,* owned himself disappointed in his expectations. Poor Gray, who laboured under a

[5] *Gray,* ii. 508 (Gray to Walpole, July 11, 1757).

[6] *Ibid.,* 508–9 (Gray to Brown, July 25, 1757); 512 (Gray to Mason, August 1, 1757). There is a passage in *Glenbervie* (i. 135), where Gilly Williams describes an occasion at Strawberry Hill when Gray read the manuscript of *The Progress of Poesy* to an audience consisting of Walpole, Selwyn, Edgcumbe, Mason, and Williams himself. It sounds very unlike Gray; and Mason was certainly not intimate with Walpole before the publication of the *Odes.* Williams was an old man when he told this story, and I cannot help thinking that his memory may have played him false.

cloud of illness and depression throughout this summer, was deeply wounded by every inept criticism and inane observation that drifted to his ears; he ignored the fact that in some quarters his odes were meeting with a great deal of applause, and that all the people whom he liked and whose opinion he respected—Walpole, Miss Speed, Mason, Hurd—were enthusiastic in their praise. He spent the summer as usual in the seclusion of his aunt's house at Stoke Poges, where his melancholy was somewhat alleviated by the smiles of Miss Speed, who "seems to understand"; and by a visit which the Garricks paid to her and Lady Cobham. Garrick was full of fun and good stories, and warm in his praises of the odes: he did his best to cheer Gray while he remained at Stoke, and afterwards addressed to him a charming poem of condolence, six stanzas of engaging flattery, which Walpole printed forthwith at Strawberry Hill. It was among the earliest of the leaflets which, for many years to come, the press was to send forth upon particular occasions.

II

Meanwhile Walpole was also preparing to undergo the pains and pleasures of authorship. During the year 1757 he spent five months in compiling *A Catalogue of the Royal and Noble Authors of England, with Lists of their Works:* and this performance, elegantly printed in two octavo volumes, and dedicated to his cousin Lord Hertford, was issued from the Strawberry Hill press in April 1758, in a private edition of three hundred copies.

As the motto of the book Walpole chose a sentence from a letter of Cardinal d'Este to Ariosto—"Dove, diavolo! Messer Ludovico, avete pigliato tante coglionerie?" And he repeatedly claimed that his work was nothing more than a collection of amusing trifles. "This is intended as a *treatise of curiosity.*" "These sheets are calculated for the closets of the *idle* and *inquisitive.*"[7] He did not pretend to have been exhaustive or scholarly or impartial; he only wished to be readable and entertaining. The style was conversational, with all the violence of opinion and exaggeration of epithet that conversation allows and careful writing does not. Out of the tomes of Bale and Anthony à Wood

[7] *Works,* i. 301, 315.

and Thomas Tanner, and from more remote and sometimes almost inaccessible sources, he extracted much that was interesting and curious in the lives and writings of our royal and noble authors, and offered it to his readers. His work had entailed a great deal of study and research; libraries had been searched for him in Florence and Rome, scholars and *literati* had assisted in the work: but the result was light and gay enough to be acceptable to the idlest of his readers. Nobody could detect pedantry in the tones of polite admiration in which he spoke of Tiptoft and Rivers, or condemn as unentertaining his conjectures about the Earl of Surrey and the Fair Geraldine, and about the Earl of Essex and Queen Elizabeth. Of all Walpole's works, the *Royal and Noble Authors* best bears out Macaulay's brilliant critical metaphor—"He rejects all but the attractive parts of his subject. He keeps only what is in itself amusing or what can be made so by the artifice of his diction. The coarser morsels of antiquarian learning he abandons to others, and sets out an entertainment worthy of a Roman epicure, an entertainment consisting of nothing but delicacies, the brains of singing birds, the roe of mullets, the sunny halves of peaches."[8]

In short, the book was extremely readable and entertaining; and so long as it remained in the "closets of the idle and inquisitive," and was read only by the friends and acquaintances to whom he had presented it, all was well. But he sold the copyright for two years to two London booksellers, Dodsley and Graham; and when they published an edition of two thousand copies at the end of 1758, the book had to take its chance in a pedantic and in some cases a hostile world. For the two years' copyright he received two hundred pounds, the whole of which sum he immediately made over to Bentley,[9] who had returned from Jersey as impecunious and irresponsible as ever. It was an act of generosity for which he had to pay dearly. The book attracted more notice, and more unfavourable criticism, than he had thought possible; and from beginning to end it involved him in a great deal of miscellaneous irritation. The peculiarity of its subject, the casual and negligent style, the feeble arguments and hasty conclusions, the violent Whig sentiments and scornful allusions to the Stuarts

[8] *Edinburgh Review* (October 1833).

[9] *Printing-Office,* 7, 31. The imprint of this edition was 1759.

and the Pope, annoyed a variety of people. Tories, Jacobites, satirical journalists searching for easy copy, and learned clergymen in the country, all voiced their objections to it. The *Critical Review* was extremely rude; the *Gentleman's Magazine* was hardly more polite; Walpole was attacked in pamphlets by offensive scribblers, and was defended in other pamphlets by writers whom he regarded as equally objectionable. And, incidentally, his unexpected tribute to the Scotch, whom he characterized as "the most accomplished nation in Europe; the Nation to which, if any one country is endowed with a superior partition of sense, I should be inclined to give the preference in that particular,"[10] was to bring him into trouble when that accomplished nation achieved its zenith of unpopularity in the days of Wilkes and Bute.

Walpole by no means enjoyed his initiation into the amenities of the literary and learned worlds. But even before the storm broke, he had complained to Montagu at some length about the penalties of authorship: and although he had just entered upon the period of his greatest literary activity, he vowed that he would not write any more. His eyes were giving him trouble; he had written quite enough; he had shown the world that he inherited something of his father's abilities, "having always lived in terror of that oracular saying, *Ηρώων παῖδες λῶβοι*, which Mr. Bentley translated... 'the sons of heroes are loobies.'" Finally, "I find my little stock of reputation very troublesome, both to maintain and to undergo the consequences—it has dipped me in *erudite* correspondences—I receive letters every week that compliment my learning—now, as there is nothing I hold so cheap as a learned man, except an unlearned one, this title is insupportable to me."[11]

This was the attitude which, expressed still more forcibly in a letter to Mann, aroused the indignation of Macaulay. Walpole nourished a deep disdain, not for learning but for the typical exponents of learning, not for letters but for the average practitioner of letters. This brand of snobbery was a part of his mental equipment, just as it was a part, rather more surprisingly, of

[10] *Works,* i. 492. The reference to the merits of the Scots brought him the friendship of Sir David Dalrymple, Dr. Robertson and other northern *savants.*

[11] *Lewis,* ix. 227 (Walpole to Montagu, October 24, 1758).

Gray's. He wished to write books on antiquarian subjects without becoming associated with the pedantry and dinginess of antiquaries; he vaguely thought that his books, the productions of a gentleman's leisure, ought to be exempt from the searching criticisms of professionals.

For all his lamentations over the "erudite correspondences" which arose from the *Royal and Noble Authors,* two at least of these correspondences proved both flattering and agreeable. Lady Hervey sent him some compliments and some courteously worded objections which she had received from Hume, to which he replied in an elaborate and deferential letter to "a man whose works I have so long admired."[12] (His personal acquaintance with Hume did not begin till some years later, and it was not to be a particularly happy one.) He also received a letter of helpful and intelligent criticism from an unknown Yorkshire clergyman, the Rev. Henry Zouch, with whom he corresponded regularly on antiquarian topics for the next three or four years. Later on Zouch was supplanted as Walpole's chief correspondent on antiquarian matters by a more substantial figure in the circle of his friends, the Rev. William Cole.

III

Immediately after the completion of the three hundred copies of *Royal and Noble Authors,* Walpole set the press to work on a small volume of his own *Fugitive Pieces in Verse and Prose.* It was an attractive little book, presenting an agreeable medley of his minor writings: it was dedicated to Conway, and the edition was limited to two hundred copies. The verse consisted of a number of his earlier poems, such as the *Epistle to Ashton* and *The Beauties,* and a few which had not previously been published, among them *The Entail.* The pieces in prose included his papers in *The Museum* and *The World,* with two essays intended for the latter periodical but not printed there; his successful political squib, the *Letter from Xo Ho to his friend Lien Chi,* and a few minor pieces such as the inquiry into the age of the celebrated Countess of Desmond, and the inscriptions which he wrote for his mother's monument and for a picture of the late Pope, Benedict XIV.

[12] *Toynbee,* iv. 158–62 (Walpole to Hume, July 15, 1758).

The year 1758 was a memorable one for the press. Besides the *Royal and Noble Authors* and the *Fugitive Pieces,* two other books were printed, and with Walpole's characteristic generosity the proceeds of both were almost entirely devoted to charitable ends. The first book was *An Account of Russia as it was in the Year* 1710, written by Charles, Lord Whitworth, who was sent on a special embassy to Peter the Great in that year. Richard Owen Cambridge, Walpole's fellow-resident at Twickenham, lent him the manuscript, and six hundred out of the seven hundred copies were sold for the benefit of the poor of Twickenham. The other book was a pamphlet by Joseph Spence, *A Parallel, in the Manner of Plutarch, between a most celebrated Man of Florence, and One, scarce ever heard of, in England.* The celebrated Florentine was the great librarian Magliabechi; the obscure Englishman was Robert Hill, a tailor of Buckingham, whose remarkable knowledge of Latin, Greek, Hebrew and the sacred writings had brought him some celebrity but no money. The edition of seven hundred copies was sold by Dodsley for the benefit of Hill, and a subscription was also opened for him.

If 1758 was a highly successful year at the press, 1759 was disastrous in proportion. Work had already been started on an edition of Lucan, with the notes of the great Richard Bentley, which were in his son's possession. But in March the printer Robinson got into trouble, and ran away. He was succeeded by Benjamin Williams, who stayed less than two months, and he by James Lister, who only remained a week. In July the fourth printer, Thomas Farmer, arrived, and work was resumed. Later in the year Walpole began to write an account of a new method of painting on wax, "supposed to be the Encaustic manner of the Ancients," which Müntz had adapted and improved from an invention of the Comte de Caylus. The edition of Lucan was laid aside, and did not appear until the beginning of 1761. A few pages of the treatise on wax painting were printed; but at this juncture Müntz incurred Walpole's extreme displeasure, and was dismissed. "The story is rather too long for a letter," Walpole told Montagu. "The substance was most extreme impertinence to me, concluded by an abusive letter against Mr. Bentley, who sent him from starving on seven pictures for a guinea, to £100 a year, my house, table and utmost countenance. In short, I turned his head, and was forced to turn him out of doors."[13] Montagu was very sympathetic. "I have long seen the Müntz was filling up the vessel of impertinence and own his airs and insolence have been insupportable to me. I know nobody but Mr. Horace Walpole the younger that would have bore it so long. . . . I fancy Scot has debauched him to set up landscape painter. I am sure you would not have been against any way he wanted to put himself in. Those who do much good and oblige so often must find as many vexations and as much ingratitude as you have done."[14] It is not known whether Samuel Scott, the delightful painter of shipping and the Thames, whose work Walpole greatly admired and who was a Twickenham neighbour, really had anything to do with "debauching" Müntz to become a landscape-painter. That Müntz had debauched one of Walpole's maids appears to be less questionable. Anyhow he departed to London, and published his own account of the new method of painting in the following year. In the four years he spent there, his most memorable contribution to Strawberry Hill was the charming portrait of Walpole sitting with his dog by the library window.

It was not long before Strawberry Hill suffered a greater loss: Bentley followed Müntz into outer darkness. In 1758 and 1759 he was still high in Walpole's favour—designing the surprising Gothic features of the Holbein Chamber, designing a "Gothic columbarium" in Linton Church as a memorial to Mann's brother Galfridus, translating Hentzner, editing his father's Lucan, writing complimentary verses for Walpole to find ready set up in type when he visited the press. "I am so lucky," Walpole had told his new correspondent Mr. Zouch, "as to live in the strictest friendship with Dr. Bentley's only son, who, to all the ornament of learning, has the amiable turn of mind, disposition, and easy wit. Perhaps you may have heard that his drawings and architecture are admirable—perhaps you have not: he is modest—he is poor—he is consequently little known, less valued."[15] But the exasperation at the general behaviour of this humble paragon, to which Walpole had sometimes given expression in the past, increased steadily during 1760; and early in the following year there was

[13] *Lewis,* ix. 259 (Walpole to Montagu, November 17, 1759).
[14] *Ibid.,* 259–60 (Montagu to Walpole, November 25, 1759).
[15] *Ibid.,* xvi. 25 (Walpole to Zouch, January 12, 1759).

a complete breach between them. Walpole told Cole that the main reason of his displeasure was Bentley's "being forward to introduce his wife at his house when people of the first fashion were there, which he thought ill-judged."[16] This was borne out by a letter from Walpole to Montagu,[17] which certainly seems to show that Mrs. Bentley was a principal cause of their quarrel. But undoubtedly there were other reasons: Bentley was shiftless, extravagant and idle; and Walpole, the least exacting of patrons, who had made constant and finally successful attempts to secure him some degree of financial independence, felt himself entitled to more gratitude and consideration than he ever received. By the spring of 1761 Strawberry Hill knew Bentley no more. Until his death in 1782 he lived mainly in London, using his talents as a playwright and pamphleteer with fair success, and acquiring one or two minor places and pensions by this means. He retained till his death the £100 a year that Walpole had obtained for him out of a place in his gift in the Customs.[18] Walpole gave financial help to his children;[19] but he and "our charming Mr. Bentley" were never again on terms of the slightest intimacy.

IV

The second main phase in the development of Strawberry Hill began in 1760. Since the completion of the Great Parlour and the Library, Walpole's additions and improvements had been of a very minor order. The only new room of any importance was the Holbein Chamber, completed in 1759, a bedroom deriving its name from a set of tracings of the Holbeins in the royal collection, which adorned its walls; it had an ecclesiastical chimney-piece and a curious pierced screen, both designed in Bentley's most fanciful Gothic. But for some years Walpole had been looking forward to the day when he could afford to build "a gallery, a round tower, a large cloister, and a cabinet, in the manner of a little chapel."[20] These rooms were entirely new additions to

[16] *Restituta,* iv. 384.

[17] *Lewis,* ix. 301–2 (Walpole to Montagu, October 2, 1760).

[18] *Toynbee,* x. 11–3 (Walpole to Mann, February 6, 1777). *Restituta,* iv. 384–6. *Nichols,* iii. 207.

[19] *Ibid.,* xii. 371–2 (Walpole to Lady Ossory, November 16, 1782).

[20] *Lewis,* xxi. 258 (Walpole to Mann, September 9, 1758).

Strawberry Hill; they almost doubled its size, and changed it from a fairly compact squarish house into a long and rather straggling building running east and west. Work was started on these new rooms in the summer of 1760, and after several delays they were all completed by 1763, with the exception of the Drawing Room in the Round Tower, which was not quite finished until 1771.

The Cloister, with the Gallery above it, stretched westwards from the existing group of buildings; the cottage containing the printing-press had already been moved further away in order to make room for this development. Bentley had made a design for the Cloister, but this was rejected, and a less ornate design by Chute was eventually carried out.[21] The five arches of the Cloister were unglazed, and gave directly upon the lawn; above them were the five windows of the Gallery; buttresses rose between the arches and terminated just below the battlements of the roof. The whole exterior of this new building was Gothic of the simplest type; and within the Cloister the same simplicity prevailed. There was a shallow vaulted roof, a paved floor, and presently an array of hideous and very ancient Welsh chairs which Walpole had long coveted from the collection of his friend Richard Bateman, and which he bought after his death.

While the Cloister was simple in design and furniture, the Gallery above it was ornate to the last degree. Bentley's first design for it, a drawing of uncertain date, had shown a pleasant conventual apartment, with an unadorned barrel ceiling and three deep niches with unostentatious Gothic canopies slightly projecting above them.[22] Bentley's disgrace was perhaps already imminent when he drew this modest design; but it is ironical that Walpole and Chute, who had so often checked the exuberance of his taste, proceeded after his departure to design a gallery which was as flamboyant as anything he had ever imagined. In this they had the assistance of a young man named Thomas Pitt, a nephew of the Great Commoner, who had lately come to live at Twickenham, and who "drew Gothic with taste." Pitt designed a good deal of the ornament of these new rooms, and in many ways proved a pleasant neighbour to Walpole during the next few years.

[21] Both designs are reproduced in *Genesis of Strawberry Hill,* 73.

[22] *Ibid.,* 74.

It must be acknowledged that this revised Committee of Taste —Chute, Pitt and Walpole—remained faithful to their Gothic originals to a degree that would have been impossible to Bentley, in designing the main structural and decorative features of the Gallery. The extreme flamboyance of the room was due to the materials in which those features were executed. It is permissible to adapt the tomb of Archbishop Bourchier at Canterbury into a series of recesses in the gallery of a private house; but gold network over looking-glass is not the happiest medium in which to reproduce stone ribbing over a smooth stone surface. The fan-vaulting of Henry VII's chapel at Westminster may well be copied in the ceiling of the same gallery; but its effect is gravely diminished if the vaulting springs from a wall covered with the brightest crimson Norwich damask. There was something genuinely ridiculous in this combination of carefully-imitated perpendicular with the gold and crimson of eighteenth-century furnishing at its most sumptuous; and one misses the fantasy and beauty with which Bentley redeemed his wildest anachronisms.

Nevertheless, the Gallery must have presented a noble spectacle when it was filled with all its treasures. Though not a remarkably large room (it was fifty-six feet by thirteen) it was the largest room at Strawberry Hill; and in it Walpole assembled many of his finest pictures, his most spectacular pieces of porcelain, his most precious marbles and bronzes. Light streamed through the five large windows, in which Peckitt had depicted all the quarterings of the Walpoles in painted glass. On the other side of the room were five deep canopied recesses, the middle recess containing a chimney-piece designed by Chute and Pitt. The furniture was covered with the same crimson damask as the walls; its woodwork was painted black and gold. The walls were loaded with pictures, the recesses were filled with them—portraits of relations and friends, portraits of the celebrities of the sixteenth and seventeenth centuries, the painting by Mabuse of the marriage of Henry VII, landscapes and subject-pieces by an endless variety of artists. There was work by Cornelius Johnson, Rubens, Lely, Rosalba, Liotard, Reynolds—an extraordinary medley of periods and styles. On an ancient sepulchral altar stood the famous Boccapadugli eagle, which had been dug up in the Baths of Caracalla in 1742, and which Walpole liked to think had inspired

Gray with the line about the "ruffled plumes and flagging wing."[23] And between two of the windows hung Van Somer's portrait of Henry Carey, Lord Falkland, "all in white," a picture which haunted its owner strangely. It became a part of the fantasy which found expression in *The Castle of Otranto,* and was transformed in that story into the portrait of Duke Manfred's grandfather,[24] which sighed so deeply, and descended from its frame, and "marched sedately but dejected" along the gallery of the visionary castle.

The Round Tower was built at the end of the wing formed by the Cloister and Gallery, and was the western termination of the house. It was a sturdy tower of three stories, battlemented and machicolated, with a great bow-window (considerably later in style) overlooking the road to Hampton. Each floor contained one big circular room. The ground floor became the new kitchen; the first floor was called the Round Drawing-Room, and was approached from the Gallery through a small lobby. Its main features were the bow-window, and a chimney-piece "taken from the tomb of Edward the Confessor, improved by Mr. Adam, and beautifully executed in white marble inlaid with scagliuola, by Richter."[25] The Round Drawing-Room was hung, like the Gallery, with crimson Norwich damask; the chairs were of Aubusson tapestry, of flowers on a white ground, with green and gold frames. It contained a few good pictures, and many of Walpole's larger books and volumes of prints.

The Chapel, which later came to be called the Tribune, opened off the Gallery. It was a small room, square with a semi-circular recess in the middle of each wall; the roof, vaulted in imitation of that of the chapter-house of York Minster, rose to an apex formed of a large star of yellow glass. The windows were entirely filled with ecclesiastical stained glass, and the dominant light of the room was the "golden gloom" which filtered down through the great star. In one of the recesses stood an altar of black and gold, copied from a tomb in Westminster Abbey. "The sable mass of the altar," Walpole wrote, "gives it a very sober air, for not-

[23] *Progress of Poesy,* I. 2. Gray, however, noted that this passage was "a weak imitation of some incomparable lines" of Pindar.

[24] *Works,* ii. 466. *Lewis,* i. 88 (Walpole to Cole, March 9, 1765).

[25] *Works,* ii. 468.

withstanding the solemnity of the painted windows, it had a gaudiness that was a little profane."[26] The ecclesiastical atmosphere was, however, so successfully conveyed that the Duc de Nivernais, the French ambassador, pulled off his hat when he entered the room; after which, "perceiving his error, he said, 'Ce n'est pas une chapelle pourtant,' and seemed a little displeased."[27] Walpole, of course, had never intended to distress the faithful by making a frivolous imitation of a chapel; he was growing ever more serious about his buildings, and in the construction of a Gothic castle the chapel held a very special place. Great hall, south tower, armoury, cloister, gallery, round tower, chapel—one after another they were coming into being. His fantasies found concrete form; the little house called Strawberry Hill was fast assuming the splendours of the Castle of Otranto.

It is possible that when Monsieur de Nivernais was shown the Chapel, quite soon after its completion, it still retained a degree of austerity which the ever-increasing pressure of Walpole's collections was soon to dispel. If he had inspected it in 1774, the date of Walpole's printed *Description of Strawberry Hill,* he would have found that its walls and niches were adorned with very secular objects indeed. Walpole never allowed any Gothic prejudices about uncrowded rooms or undecorated surfaces to interfere with his remorseless and incessant accumulation of objects of art. He selected the Chapel as the repository of his smaller and more exquisite treasures; and, with cabinet-pictures and miniatures crowding the walls, and shelves and brackets loaded with trinkets extending in all directions, it must indeed have reverted to the gaudiness which he had originally felt to be "a little profane." In the niches were placed casts or bronzes of the Venus de Medicis, an Antinous, the Apollo Belvedere, the Farnese Flora, and his own mother. Above the altar was a cabinet which contained his marvellous collection of miniatures—the Olivers, the Coopers, the Hoskins—and his superb enamels by Petitot and Zincke. The antiques belonging to Conyers Middleton, which he had bought after the Doctor's death, were placed about the room. In two glass-cases were some of his supreme

[26] *Lewis,* x. 64 (Walpole to Montagu, April 14, 1763).
[27] *Ibid.,* xxii. 136 (Walpole to Mann, April 30, 1763).

treasures—the bust of Caligula in bronze, with silver eyes; the missal "with miniatures by Raphael and his scholars"; and the silver bell carved with miraculous ornament by Benvenuto Cellini. Jostling them were such curiosities as Henry VIII's dagger, a mourning-ring of Charles I, the great seal of Theodore, King of Corsica, and the cravat carved in wood by Grinling Gibbons. The entire room was an indescribable display of pictures, bronzes, carvings, ivories, enamels, faience, pot-pourri jars, snuff-boxes, kettles, tea-pots, cups and saucers, seals and rings. The whole extraordinary array of beauty and of trumpery has long since vanished. Walpole's little sham chapel is now the private chapel of the priests of Saint Mary's College, and Mass is said beneath his golden star.

V

In the summer of 1758 Walpole bought from the widow of George Vertue, the celebrated engraver, who had died two years previously, some forty manuscript notebooks at the cost of £100. During a long and industrious life, Vertue had collected every available scrap of information about painters, engravers, sculptors, and architects, and about their works, from the earliest times. He had hoped some day to compile a History of the Arts in England; but he possessed no literary skill, and his history never advanced beyond the enormous mass of chaotic and often hardly intelligible material which accumulated in his notebooks. Walpole had known him well, and since his death had written prefaces to reprints prepared by him of the catalogues of the collections of Charles I, James II, and Villiers, Duke of Buckingham. From the notebooks which now came into his hands, he compiled his next work, the *Anecdotes of Painting in England.*

It is hardly possible to exaggerate the service that Walpole rendered to the history of art by his rescue of Vertue's manuscripts, and by his extremely competent handling of them in the *Anecdotes of Painting.* If Vertue's notes had perished, our knowledge of painting in England in the sixteenth and seventeenth centuries would be far slighter. And it is only necessary to compare Vertue's original texts, which have been published in full by the Walpole Society, with the well-arranged chapters and elegant little biographies of the *Anecdotes,* to realize the difficulties encountered by Walpole and his highly successful solution of them. He was obliged to make a general index to the whole of the forty-odd notebooks. Some of these were accounts of tours, others contained lists of pictures, others were journals of the artistic information that Vertue picked up from day to day, and only a few contained biographical details arranged below the names of the painters to whom they related. Thus important facts about a particular artist might be buried in half-a-dozen different books; and it is not surprising that at times Walpole found the compilation of the *Anecdotes* a heavy and laborious business.

Nevertheless he carried out the work with remarkable speed, assisted by an attack of gout which debarred him from other occupations. After some preliminary examination of the manuscripts, he began his book on January 1, 1760. He finished the first volume in August, and by the end of October the second volume had also been completed. Printing was begun almost immediately, but owing to the misconduct and eventual flight of Thomas Farmer, the fourth in his ill-fated succession of printers, the book did not appear until early in 1762. In the meantime he had written the third volume of the *Anecdotes*; this was published two years later, together with his *Catalogue of Engravers.*

The first two volumes carried the history of English art to the end of the Commonwealth. They were illustrated wherever possible with portraits of the artists under discussion. Walpole's name was carefully subordinated to Vertue's on the title-page: and the same modesty was observed in his dedication to Lady Hervey, in which he spoke of being "forced to pay my debts to your Ladyship in Mr. Vertue's coin." The dedication was followed by an interesting preface, commenting on the rarity of native genius in the earlier history of the arts in England, and urging that in the years of expansion and splendour which lay ahead, English painting and sculpture and architecture should play a more worthy part. Flushed with the unparalleled victories of 1759, and with all the speculation and excitement of a new reign, Walpole surveyed the future. "Our eloquence and the glory of our arms have been carried to the highest pitch. The more peaceful arts have in other countries generally attended national glory. If there are any talents among us, this seems the crisis for their appearance; the Throne itself is now the altar of the graces; and whoever sacrifices to them becomingly, is sure that his offerings will be smiled upon by a Prince, who is at once the example and patron of accomplishments."[28] Earlier in the preface he had paid his tribute to Hogarth; compliments now followed for Reynolds, Ramsay, Scott, for Adam and Chambers, for a number of sculptors. And however keenly he may have been disappointed by the subsequent fluctuations of English history and the subsequent conduct of George III, his hopes for the future of English art were amply fulfilled. The period of its greatest splendour was close at hand.

The *Anecdotes of Painting* bears a general resemblance, both in form and in manner, to the *Royal and Noble Authors*. Vertue's industry and erudition gave to the *Anecdotes* a more solid foundation; but Walpole's own prejudices and predilections, his passion for anecdotes and his unfailing selection of the best and most entertaining, his usual good sense and his occasional lapses into sheer frivolity, are equally apparent in both works. The opening chapters of the *Anecdotes* are general surveys of art in England during the earlier reigns—extracts from mediæval charters, chronicles, and rolls, with detailed discussion of such works as the Wilton Diptych and his own painting of the marriage of Henry VI. But as soon as the figures of individual painters began to emerge, he adopted Vertue's biographical method, which was in any case particularly suitable to his own style. The book is extraordinarily varied and readable. There are some passages of great importance, among them the chapter entitled "State of Architecture to the End of the Reign of Henry VIII," with its vital clues to his own appreciation of Gothic, and its acknowledgment of the assistance of Gray, "who condescended to correct what he never could have descended to write." There are also passages of engaging nonsense, such as the suggestion, so irritating to Macaulay, that art declined under the Commonwealth owing to the personal unattractiveness of the victorious party. "Had they countenanced any of the softer arts, what could those arts have represented? How picturesque was the figure of an Anabaptist!" And throughout the book there are always digressions and discussions of the most varied interest—extracts from the journals

[28] *Works,* iii. 7–8.

of Nicholas Stone, or a discourse on Jeffrey Hudson the royal dwarf, or the details of the dispersion of the collections of Charles I, or reflections on the splendour of the Van Dycks at Wilton, and on the particular beauty of Lely's portraits of women. It is interesting, also, to note how his own artistic standards had altered since he compiled the *Aedes Walpolianae*. His tastes had shifted from the lavish and spectacular to the small, detailed and exquisite. Houghton had given place to Strawberry Hill; and the critic who was enraptured by Rubens and Salvator Rosa now regarded with equal enthusiasm the miniatures of Oliver and the enamels of Petitot.

Written in intervals snatched from politics and building and a most active social life, the *Anecdotes of Painting* was a really remarkable piece of work. But the unexpected industry and thoroughness with which Walpole grappled with Vertue's manuscripts did not exclude the possibility of inaccuracies and omissions; and some of these were pointed out by the Rev. William Cole in a highly appreciative letter which he addressed to him on May 16, 1762. This letter initiated one of the most interesting of the Walpole correspondences, and brought into the Walpole circle one of its most agreeable figures.

William Cole had been on terms of friendship with Walpole at Eton. The friendship continued at Cambridge: and some sort of acquaintanceship was afterwards kept up, though it was Cole's letter about the *Anecdotes of Painting* that led to the renewal of more active intercourse between them. Cole was a man of substantial middle-class Cambridgeshire stock, and Cambridge and its neighbourhood remained the centre of his interests to the end of his life. From boyhood he had been an ardent antiquary, following in the royalist and conservative tradition of the great nonjurors, Thomas Baker and Thomas Harne. He had taken orders at the age of thirty, and became a Tory country parson of the most rigid High Church views, inclining to Catholicism in doctrine and practice, and looking back with affection to the great days of the Church under King Charles and Archbishop Laud. In 1762 he was residing at his living of Bletchley in Buckinghamshire, a learned but sociable bachelor, looking after his parish and farming his glebe, and continually adding to his already vast collection of antiquarian notes, sketches and extracts. He was altogether without literary ambition. He had no desire for his work to be published during his lifetime, though he contributed most generously to the books of other men. All his writings, even his cherished *Athenæ Cantabrigienses,* were to be bequeathed to the nation to serve as a quarry of material for scholars long after his death. In perfect contentment he went on compiling volumes upon volumes of transcripts in his exquisitely careful hand, flavouring his learned pages with personalities and gossip often scandalous and almost always entertaining; and keeping, by way of relaxation, elaborate diaries about his tea-parties, his servants and the progress of his hay.[29]

Walpole discovered in Cole the ideal recipient for his views on all antiquarian subjects: a correspondent whose letters in return were amusing and intelligent, who was delighted to give help and to undertake laborious research in any antiquarian matter, and whose methodical habits ensured that the entire correspondence would be carefully preserved. From 1762 onwards the letters between them were regular and copious. Walpole came to entertain a warm affection for the bulky, downright, opinionated country clergyman; while Cole found that Walpole's literary and architectural pursuits added greatly to the interest of his own life, and looked upon this friendship as one of its happiest occurrences. His sturdy convictions about Church and State were in profound opposition to Walpole's Whig doctrines; and Walpole's indifference to religion, and his often-expressed hatred of episcopacy and priestcraft, were matters of occasional irritation to him. But their political and religious differences seldom raised more than a passing ripple in the smooth flood of their correspondence; and Cole was speaking in all sincerity when he called Walpole "my worthiest and kindest friend."[30]

VI

Every year Walpole would make at least one long excursion, to see ruins and cathedrals, churches and country houses. Unlike

[29] Two volumes of these delightful diaries have been published, edited by the late F. G. Stokes, and with introductions by Miss Helen Waddell: *A Journal of my Journey to Paris in the Year* 1765 and *The Blecheley Diary,* 1766 (Constable, 1931).

[30] *Lewis,* i. 370 (Cole to Walpole, April 29, 1775).

Gray, who was also in the habit of making a sight-seeing tour every summer, he did not go in search of natural beauty. He never visited Scotland or the Lakes or the valley of the Wye, and his commendations of landscape were almost invariably provoked by a finely situated house or a well laid-out park. In later years, in his essay *On Modern Gardening,* he was to describe how Kent, rejecting old-fashioned formalism, "leaped the fence, and saw that all nature was a garden."[31] Walpole himself considered that all nature, in the widest sense, ought to resemble a garden; and when mountains and forests ceased to present the features of some immense and nobly diversified parkland, and grew rugged and sublime and melancholy, he could not share Gray's admiration of their wild and comfortless expanses. But he would travel any distance, over any sort of road, to examine a ruined castle, or a mansion with a few fine pictures, or a church with painted glass and alabaster monuments; and if the road proved impassable to his postchaise, he was known to bestride one of the horses and flounder onward through seas of mud to the object of his curiosity. Most of all, he loved to visit remote country houses, preferably in the absence of their owners, and explore them from attic to cellar, discovering unknown masterpieces, identifying forgotten portraits, tracing historical associations, and half-killing the housekeeper with exhaustion and boredom. His *Journals of Visits to Country Seats*[32] reveal most clearly the thoroughness of these investigations. The letters which kept Chute or Montagu posted in his travels only described the most remarkable of all the things he saw. In them Burleigh and Chatsworth, Wilton and Bulstrode are memorably depicted, their atmosphere captured and reproduced, their beauties and faults and peculiarities committed to paper in a few consummate sentences. But in the *Journals of Visits to Country Seats* almost every picture, statue, coat of arms, prospect and view-point will be found carefully recorded.

It is tempting to quote Walpole's descriptions of a score of great houses—of Drayton, with its traditions so lovingly maintained by its "divine old mistress" Lady Betty Germaine; of the "beautiful decent simplicity" of the exterior of Knole, and the "ancient magnificence" within of Blenheim, with "all the old

[31] *Works,* ii. 536.

[32] Walpole Society, vol. xvi. (1928), edited by Paget Toynbee.

flock chairs, wainscot tables, and gowns and petticoats of Queen Anne, that old Sarah could crowd among blocks of marble." No less delightful are his sketches of the house-parties of which he was a member. The impact of this inquisitive and lively *virtuoso* on a country household is suggested by his description of a visit to Ragley, the ancient seat of the Conways, then occupied by his cousin Lord Hertford. "You cannot imagine how astonished a Mr. Seward a learned clergyman was, who came to Ragley while I was there. Strolling about the house he saw me first sitting on the pavement of the lumber room with Louis, all over cobwebs and dirt and mortar, then found me in his own room on a ladder writing on a picture, and half an hour afterwards lying on the grass in the court with the dogs and the children in my slippers and without my hat. He had had some doubt whether I was the painter or the factotum of the family; but you would have died at his surprise when he saw me walk into dinner dressed and sit by my Lady Hertford. Lord Lyttelton was there, and the conversation turned on literature: finding me not quite ignorant added to the parson's wonder; but he could not contain himself any longer, when after dinner he saw me go to romps and jumping with the two boys; he broke out to my Lady Hertford, and begged to know who and what sort of man I really was, for he had never met with anything of the kind."[33]

In 1764 Walpole had the privilege of giving to the world, from his own press, that remarkable book *The Life of Edward Lord Herbert of Cherbury, Written by Himself*. Some months before, he had been lent the manuscript of Lord Herbert's singular autobiography, and had carried it home to Strawberry Hill, where he and Gray read it aloud by turns to amuse his widowed niece Lady Waldegrave, and "could not go on for laughing and screaming."[34] Lord Powis, the owner, was at first unwilling to have it printed, feeling that the extravagance of his ancestor's exploits, and still more the manner in which they were recounted, might have a compromising effect on his own personal dignity. But Walpole addressed to him a flattering dedication, and further explained in his preface that "the noble family, which gives these sheets to the world, is above the little prejudices which make many a race

[33] *Lewis*, ix. 225 (Walpole to Montagu, August 20, 1758).
[34] *Ibid.*, x. 130 (Walpole to Montagu, July 16, 1764).

defraud the public of what was designed for it by those who alone had a right to give or to withhold":[35] so Lord Powis allowed the printing to go forward. The publication of this precious manuscript was one of the greatest services that Walpole performed through the Strawberry Hill Press.

VII

The next chapter, which deals with Walpole's activities in the political field between 1754 and 1765, will explain how the closing years of this tranquil and prosperous period were marred for him by a series of political storms which centred round the beloved figure of Conway. It will there be seen that the dismissal of Conway in April 1764 from the King's bedchamber, and from the command of his regiment, for voting in Parliament against the policy of the Court party, roused Walpole to a frenzy of resentment and partisanship. He leapt to his cousin's aid, offered him once again half his own fortune, began to retrench his own expenses in order to make the offer a worthier one, composed an indignant reply to a pamphlet in which Conway was attacked, and quarrelled irrevocably with his neighbor Thomas Pitt. Throughout the spring and early summer he was in a condition of extreme nervous excitement. He spent the greater part of these anxious months at Strawberry Hill; and the atmosphere of his Gothic creation, working on a mind exhausted by political and personal tension, resulted in the strange nightmare of *The Castle of Otranto.*

As Walpole, worried and depressed, wandered about the little mock castle which he had constructed in brick and wood and plaster, Otranto began to rise, in all its gloom and horror, upon those slender foundations. The flamboyant gallery of Strawberry became grim and bare and enormous. The cloister echoed cavernously, and secret passages stretched beneath it. Elegant bedrooms turned into the forbidding chambers, hung with tapestry and carpeted with matting or rushes, of more ancient days. The picture of Lord Falkland, all in white, began to exercise its curious spell. Then one night early in June, just as he was finishing his passionate defence of Conway, he "had a dream, of which

[35] *Works,* i. 231.

all I could recover was that I had thought myself in an ancient castle (a very natural dream for a head filled like mine with Gothic story), and that on the uppermost bannister of a great staircase I saw a gigantic hand in armour. In the evening I sat down, and began to write, without knowing in the least what I intended to say or relate."[36] For the next two months he lived entirely in a world of Gothic fantasy. He put politics out of his mind; his correspondence dwindled almost to nothing; except for one party for the French and Spanish ambassadors, entertaining ceased at Strawberry Hill. Night after night he immersed himself in the ambitions of Manfred, the woes of Hippolyta and Matilda. He wrote blindly on, often into the small hours of the morning, sometimes until he was so exhausted that he broke off the narrative in the middle of a sentence. On August 6 *The Castle of Otranto* was completed.[37]

The scene of the novel was laid in the principality of Otranto, in the kingdom of Naples, at some unspecified time during the period of the Crusades. (Walpole chose the "very sonorous" name of Otranto from the map, and did not even know that there was a castle there until his friend Lady Craven sent him a drawing of it many years after his novel was published.[38]) Manfred is tyrant and usurper of Otranto; Hippolyta is his gentle and patient wife; Matilda is their lovely daughter; and a marriage is about to be celebrated between Conrad, their only son, and Isabella, the daughter of Frederic, Marquis of Vicenza. During the festivities, a colossal helmet, crowned with sable plumes, falls from the skies, and dashes the young prince to pieces. Theodore, a young peasant and a stranger to the neighbourhood, remarks on the resemblance of the helmet to that on the statue of the good Duke Alfonso in the church nearby; whereupon Manfred, in a fury, imprisons him under the helmet. Manfred then proposes to divorce his sterile wife and raise up new heirs to his principality by a marriage with Isabella, a course strongly opposed by Father Jerome, Hippolyta's confessor. Isabella flees from the importunities of Manfred; and

[36] *Lewis,* i. 88 (Walpole to Cole, March 9, 1765).

[37] For a detailed and excellent description of the writing of *The Castle of Otranto,* and the circumstances which led up to it, see Mr. Oswald Doughty's introduction to his edition of the novel (Scholartis Press, 1929).

[38] *Toynbee,* xiii. 419–20 (Walpole to Lady Craven, November 27, 1786).

Theodore, who has emerged from inside the helmet, enables her to escape from the castle. He is recaptured by Manfred, but is assisted to escape in his turn by Matilda, with whom he falls in love. Meanwhile Manfred is continuously harassed by fearful portents, and his woes are increased by the arrival of a silent and mysterious knight, with a sword which is carried by fifty men, who challenges him, as an usurper, to mortal combat. The stranger turns out to be Isabella's father. Terrific developments follow, into which it is impossible to enter in detail. Human passions and superhuman phenomena bring the story to its fearful climax. Manfred accidentally stabs his daughter Matilda to death. Theodore is revealed to be the son of Father Jerome, and the rightful heir, by a highly involved descent from Alfonso the Good, to the principality of Otranto. "The moment Theodore appeared, the walls of the castle behind Manfred were thrown down with a mighty force, and the form of Alfonso, dilated to an immense magnitude, appeared in the centre of the ruins. 'Behold in Theodore, the true heir of Alfonso!' said the vision: and having pronounced those words, accompanied by a clap of thunder, it ascended solemnly towards heaven, where the clouds parting asunder, the form of Saint Nicholas was seen; and receiving Alfonso's shade, they were soon wrapt from mortal eyes in a blaze of glory."[39] After this apotheosis, there is little more to be said. Manfred abdicates, and he and Hippolyta retire into monastic life. Theodore becomes Prince of Otranto: but "it was not till after frequent discourses with Isabella, of his dear Matilda, that he was persuaded he could know no happiness but in the society of one with whom he could forever indulge the melancholy that had taken possession of his soul."[40]

Walpole had plunged into the writing of his novel without premeditation; and he was always rather proud of the artless manner in which he had gone about its composition. But the story which emerged from such fortuitous beginnings was a very deftly constructed piece of work, observing the dramatic unities with almost complete fidelity, and moving towards the close without digression or delay. Walpole explained that the plan of his work, in so far as it had a plan, was "an attempt to blend the

[39] *Works,* ii. 88. [40] *Ibid.,* 90.

two kinds of romance, the ancient and the modern. In the former all was imagination and improbability: in the latter, nature is always intended to be, and sometimes has been, copied with success.... The author of the following pages thought it possible to reconcile the two kinds. Desirous of leaving the powers of fancy at liberty to expatiate through the boundless realms of invention, and thence of creating more interesting situations, he wished to conduct the mortal agents in his drama according to the rules of probability; in short, to make them think, speak, and act, as it might be supposed mere men and women would do in extraordinary positions."[41]

It is impossible to feel that Walpole achieved his aim of blending ancient romance and the contemporary novel. He had passed his life in observing the subtler shades of human character, and recording them in his letters: but he could not create character. His figures speak the language of the novel of his day, and exhibit the contemporary emotions. Matilda and Isabella talk and behave, amid a welter of ghosts and portents, as Clarissa Harlowe or Sophia Western would have done. But the delicate shades of character, given to their heroines by Richardson and Fielding, are lacking in Walpole's novel. All the actors in *The Castle of Otranto* are reduced to the simplest terms—the wicked and ambitious baron, the valiant and high-minded youth, the chaste and amiable maidens. Yet in spite of this simplification, which was perhaps inevitable, the reader is still left with a painful sense of incongruity. For example, Theodore finds Isabella in the forest, whither she has fled after a series of frightful experiences at the castle, and offers to escort her into the deeper recesses of the cavern where she is seeking refuge. The following dialogue then takes place. "'Alas! what mean you, sir?' said she. 'Though all your actions are noble, though your sentiments speak the purity of your soul, is it fitting that I should accompany you alone into those perplexed retreats? Should we be found together, what would a censorious world think of my conduct?'—'I respect your virtuous delicacy,' said Theodore; 'nor do you harbour a suspicion that wounds my honour. I meant to conduct you into the most private cavity of these rocks; and then, at the hazard of my

[41] Preface to the second edition of *The Castle of Otranto* (*Works*, ii. 7, 8). See also *Toynbee*, vi. 198–9 (Walpole to Joseph Warton, March 16, 1765).

STRAWBERRY HILL : THE CHAPEL or TRIBUNE
From a drawing by EDWARD EDWARDS, dated 1781,
at Farmington, Connecticut
By kind permission of Mr. W. S. Lewis

STRAWBERRY HILL : THE SOUTH FRONT
From an aquatint by J. C. STADLER after a drawing by
JOSEPH FARINGTON

life, to guard their entrance against every living thing. Besides, lady,' continued he, drawing a deep sigh, 'beauteous and all perfect as your form is, and though my wishes are not guiltless of aspiring, know, my soul is dedicated to another.'..."[42] Certainly the blending of supernatural events and Gothic savagery with the *beaux sentiments* of his own day was the least successful feature of Walpole's novel.

The purely Gothic parts of the book—the horror, the gloom, the unearthly portents—are infinitely more effective. However ridiculous certain particular occurrences may be, however irrationally the characters may sometimes behave, the reader remains absorbed and impressed, even though the bleeding statue and the skeleton hermit no longer fill him with horror and awe. Perhaps the dream-like inconsequence of the story constitutes its main charm; it arose from a dream, the fantasy of an exhausted brain, and the unearthly impulse of the original dream still lingers. Walpole has been described as "perhaps the first surrealist writer": [43] and the atmosphere of *The Castle of Otranto,* with the unreason and exaggeration of its events, the nightmare juxtaposition of unrelated objects, the vast helmet that descended on the little prince, the gigantic leg in the gallery and the gigantic hand on the banister, is decidedly surrealist. The story sums up all the fantastic possibilities inherent in the Gothic style. The giant helmet falls from the skies, the portrait walks sighing from its frame, unexpected paternities are acknowledged and dreadful injustices are plotted, and finally the Castle of Otranto is burst asunder by Alfonso's enormous spectre, as though it had been as fragile as Strawberry. It is all absurd and nonsensical, and oddly exciting to read.

This strange story, which flared up so suddenly and so inexplicably in his brain, meant a great deal to Walpole. So far it was his only sustained piece of purely creative writing, and was all the more important to him for that reason. He wrote to Madame du Deffand a few years afterwards: "Je vous avoue, ma Petite, et vous m'en trouverez plus fol que jamais, que de tous mes ouvrages c'est l'unique où je me suis plu; j'ai laissé courir mon imagination; les

[42] *Works,* ii. 60.

[43] Bonamy Dobrée, in *From Anne to Victoria* (Introduction, viii).

visions et les passions m'échauffaient. Je l'ai fait en dépit des règles, des critiques, et des philosophes; et il me semble qu'il n'en vaille que mieux."[44] It had nothing to do with his personal relationships, in the sense in which Beckford was to pour out the complications of his own private life in the astonishing fantasy of *Vathek*. One need not look for early memories of Conway in the heroic and virtuous Theodore, or transmute the figure of Isabella, fleeing from Manfred's violence through the gloomy vaults of Otranto, into the majestic form of Lady Mary Coke. But the story was his justification of Strawberry Hill and of all his Gothic dreams. To a great degree, Otranto and Strawberry were identical. Walpole himself said so more than once; and Mr. Lewis has shown how many of the rooms in Walpole's castle—the Gallery, the Chapel, the Blue Bedchamber, the Holbein Chamber, and half a dozen more—occupied precisely the same relative positions in the castle of his imagination.[45] But another Gothic building, whose structure was lying dormant in Walpole's mind, also played a part in the formation of Otranto. The year before he wrote his novel, Walpole visited Cambridge; five years afterwards, he went there again; and on entering one of the colleges, he suddenly found himself in the courtyard of Otranto. He described his experience to Madame du Deffand. "En entrant dans un des collèges que j'avais entièrement oublié, je me trouvais précisément dans la cour de mon château. Les tours, les portes, la chapelle, la grande salle, tout y répondait avec la plus grande exactitude. Enfin l'idée de ce collège m'était restée dans la tête sans y penser, et je m'en étais servi pour le plan de mon château sans m'en apercevoir; de sorte que je croyais entrer tout de bon dans celui d'Otrante."[46] This college, which Dr. Warren Hunting Smith has conclusively identified with Trinity,[47] supplied Otranto with the courtyard, great hall and a few other features which Strawberry Hill lacked. Otranto, the visionary culmination of all Walpole's Gothic dreams, was at the same time a very exact blend of two particular Gothic structures—the

[44] *Lewis,* iii. 260 (Walpole to Madame du Deffand, March 13, 1767).

[45] *Genesis of Strawberry Hill,* 89–90. See also *Architecture in English Fiction* by Warren Hunting Smith (Yale University Press, 1934).

[46] *Lewis,* vi. 145 (Walpole to Madame du Deffand, January 27, 1775).

[47] *Times Literary Supplement,* May 23, 1936.

child of an incongruous marriage between Strawberry Hill and Trinity Great Court.

Walpole's satisfaction at having achieved *The Castle of Otranto* was somewhat clouded by anxiety as to its publication and possible reception. For a man of the world and a Member of Parliament, it really was a very wild performance; and, as he said afterwards, "it is not everybody that may in this country play the fool with impunity."[48] But he showed the story to Gray, and Gray encouraged him to print it. His fear of ridicule and hostile criticism prevented him from bringing out the book under his own name; nor would he venture to print it at his own press. At the very end of 1764 (under the imprint of 1765) a London publisher issued five hundred copies of *The Castle of Otranto, a Story. Translated by William Marshal, Gent. from the Original Italian of Onuphrio Muralto, Canon of the Church of St. Nicholas at Otranto.* This title-page, so reminiscent, in its elaborate deception, of those which Voltaire prefixed to such of his books as were least acceptable to authority, was not enough for Walpole; he added a preface by the supposed translator, stating that "the following work was found in the library of an ancient Catholic family in the north of England," that it was "printed at Naples, in the black letter, in the year 1529," and that "the style is the purest Italian." Suggestions followed that the book was religious propaganda designed by "an artful priest" to turn the minds of the populace away from the Renaissance and its spread of tolerance and enlightenment, back to "their ancient errors and superstitions." The style, construction and conduct of the story were heartily commended; the light relief introduced by the servants was explained and condoned; and it was affirmed that "the piety that reigns throughout, the lessons of virtue that are inculcated, and the rigid purity of the sentiments, exempt this work from the censure to which romances are but too liable."[49]

Walpole must have found great amusement in writing this preface; but his deception turned out to be quite unnecessary. The book was the greatest possible success; it was praised on all

[48] *Lewis,* xxviii. 6–7 (Walpole to Mason, April 17, 1765).
[49] *Works,* ii. 3–5.

sides, and apparently was believed by many people to be the work of Gray.[50] Walpole instantly jettisoned William Marshal, Gent. and Onuphrio Muralto, and issued a second edition in April 1765, in which his authorship was disclosed. He added a new preface, explaining the reasons for his deception and apologizing for it, and proceeding to justify the introduction of the comic servants by a reference to the gravediggers in *Hamlet* and the citizens in *Julius Cæsar*. The rest of the preface consisted of a heated if somewhat irrelevant attack on Voltaire, for his disrespectful treatment of Shakespeare in his commentary on Corneille. He also added in this edition a dedicatory sonnet to Lady Mary Coke, in which he told her that

> "Blest with thy smile, my dauntless sail
> I dare expand to Fancy's gale,
> For sure thy smiles are Fame."

The disclosure of its authorship did not diminish the success of *The Castle of Otranto*. Some of his friends, indeed, were inclined to mock. Gilly Williams wrote to Selwyn, "How do you think Horry Walpole has employed that leisure which his political frenzy has allowed of? In writing a novel, and such a novel, that no boarding-school Miss could get half through without yawning. . . . He says it was a dream, and I fancy one when he had some feverish disposition in him."[51] But most judgments were favourable, and even people like Warburton, who were usually hostile to Walpole, were enthusiastic about his novel. Its kindly reception brought some consolation to him in the dark months which were to follow, when he was suffering the bitter disappointment of Conway's ingratitude and the neglect of the party which he had helped bring into power.

[50] *Toynbee,* vi. 205 (Walpole to Hertford, March 26, 1765).
[51] *Jesse,* i. 372 (Williams to Selwyn, March 19, 1765).

X

The Middle Years: Political Life (1754-65)

I

THE narrative of Walpole's literary and social life has been carried in the preceding chapters up to the earlier months of 1765. It is now necessary to give a survey of his political activities during the period of eleven years which closed with that momentous spring, and which began with the redistribution of power on the death of Pelham in March 1754.

Walpole left behind him, in his series of *Memoirs* and *Journals,* an elaborate history of the political events of his time, with especially detailed and exhaustive accounts of his own share in them. But it is impossible, in a biography of this nature, to follow him through the political labyrinths which he described so minutely. The biographer can only attempt to deal with his conduct on certain important public issues, and to touch on such political events as affected the general course of his life.

II

Directly after Pelham's death, the various sections of his party began to manœuvre for power. The death of the Prince of Wales in 1751 had put an end to any organized Whig opposition. The Tories formed a compact body, but were quite outnumbered in the House. There was, however, no man in the vast Whig majority who could claim Pelham's indisputable pre-eminence; and his death was the signal for an immediate renewal of political activity.

Pelham was succeeded at the head of the Government by his brother the Duke of Newcastle, whose command of numerous boroughs and long-exercised distribution of patronage had made him the most influential man in public life. But the House of Commons contained two men of consummate ability and ambition, Pitt and Fox; and Newcastle's administration could hardly hope to survive without the support of one of them. At first, both accepted office under him: but the degree of power which they obtained did not fulfill their expectations, and by mutual arrangement these lifelong antagonists deliberately set out to hinder and persecute their leader; even going so far, while still nominally serving under him, as to oppose his measures and cover his more faithful followers with scorn and ridicule. It was essential for Newcastle to break up this unofficial coalition between the two most able and dangerous men in Parliament; and in the following year he came to terms with Fox, who was made Secretary of State and leader of the House of Commons.

Horace Walpole was bitterly mortified by this coalition between Fox, whose political career he had assiduously watched and supported, and Newcastle, whom he could never forgive for his treatment of Sir Robert. Fox's earlier association with Newcastle, and still more this whole-hearted coalition, took place against his urgent advice;[1] and although he did not care to come to an open breach with so dangerous a man, he declined to act as his political adviser on any future occasion. Their personal cordiality remained undiminished, but Walpole considered their political association to be entirely at an end. In pursuance of this view, he felt himself at liberty to initiate, in October 1756, a piece of intrigue which operated strongly to Fox's disadvantage, and took no particular pains to conceal from Fox his own part in the affair.[2] Yet, only a few weeks later, he published the highly eulogistic character-sketch of Fox which he had written long ago at the time of their warmest friendship; and wrote to him that "it would be hard if I could not make it better, when I have known the subject years longer!"[3] Fox appears to have welcomed the publication of

[1] *Memoirs of George II,* i. 334; ii. 90–1. *Memoirs of George III,* i. 167. *Holland,* i. 205–6.

[2] *Memoirs of George II,* ii. 102–3. *Holland,* ii. 8–9. *Holland Letters,* 96.

[3] *Holland Letters,* 99.

the sketch with great satisfaction, in spite of the author's recent conduct towards him; and it was at his own suggestion that Dodsley was asked to print it as an extraordinary number of *The World.*

Rigby, for his part, had already ceased to pay much heed to Walpole's "ardour for factious intrigues"; impoverished and ambitious, he had attached himself to the Duke of Bedford's interest, an alliance wholly unacceptable to his friend.[4] At this juncture, therefore, Walpole was left without any political ally and spokesman through whom he could advance his personal views and further his "factious intrigues." But before long the defection of Fox and Rigby was amply compensated. He was able to establish in their place the man to whom of all men he was most devoted, Henry Conway. Conway had sat in Parliament since 1741, but his fairly constant military service had hitherto prevented him from taking any conspicuous part in politics. But from 1754 onwards he began to take some part in debate; and in that year the Duke of Devonshire appointed him his chief secretary when he became Lord Lieutenant of Ireland. Before long, Walpole's personal affection and admiration for Conway, and his solicitude for Conway's career, came to provide his main political impulses; and his activities in public affairs, by the end of the period under discussion in this chapter, developed into a kind of partisan crusade on behalf of his idolized friend.

III

Early in 1757 old Horace Walpole of Wolterton, who had been raised to the peerage in the previous year, died and was succeeded by his son, the member of Parliament for King's Lynn. This borough was by far the largest and the least obsequious of those in which the Walpoles had influence; and the electors made it clear to young Lord Orford that they did not wish to be represented by a stranger. The second seat for the borough was already occupied by Sir John Turner, a nephew of Sir Robert Walpole; but the electors of Lynn preferred that both their representatives should be connected with the well-loved family. Lord Orford

[4] *Memoirs of George II,* ii. 91.

was still eager to maintain the political influence of the Walpoles; the days were yet distant when he was to lose the control of Lynn altogether, and nominate a former waiter at White's as the member for Castle Rising.[5] He now appealed to his uncle Horace to vacate his comfortable seat for Castle Rising, whither he had migrated from Callington three years before, and to stand for Lynn, promising him that there would be no opposition and that he need not go down to Lynn for the election. His friends at Lynn, he wrote, "were all unanimously of opinion that you were the only person who from your near affinity to my grandfather, whose name is still in the greatest veneration, and your own known personal abilities and qualifications, could stand in the gap on this occasion and prevent opposition and expence and perhaps disgrace to the family."[6] This was really asking a great deal from a man of Horace's temperament. A large and thriving town, with a Mayor and Corporation and thousands of inhabitants, was a very different proposition from the decaying villages which he had hitherto represented in Parliament. There would be deputations, petitions, requests for patronage and promotion from his constituents; there was an active Tory element in the place, which in time might venture to oppose even a son of old Sir Robert's; and his keenest supporters were likely to be exacting in the demands they made on their member. An indignant clergyman wrote to his friend: "The intended representative for Lynn is a most delicate Italian fop. And, *inter nos,* will not go to that place to be chosen. Whether the Earl, his nephew, has pressed him enough on this subject I can't say. But I can say that, if I know anything of the spirit of the better and worser sort of people there, it is a slight they will not forget: how little so ever they may talk of it just at the time when it is put upon them."[7] Horace Walpole, with his unfailing family loyalty, agreed to do as his nephew wished; and at a subsequent election, when it had become absolutely necessary, he even appeared in his constituency. Apart from his disinclination to visit the place, he represented Lynn

[5] *Lewis,* xviii. 173 (Walpole to Mason, [October 1774]). *Toynbee* ix. 75 and n. (Walpole to Mann, October 22, 1774).

[6] *Ibid.,* Supplement, ii. 98 (Lord Orford to Horace Walpole, [February 1757]).

[7] *Pyle,* 287 (Rev. Edmund Pyle to Rev. Samuel Kerrich, February 22, 1757).

with reasonable assiduity for eleven years, and remained unopposed until his final retirement from Parliament in 1768.

IV

It was while Walpole was out of Parliament at the beginning of 1757, between his resignation of Castle Rising and his election for Lynn, that he made his spirited though unavailing attempt to save the life of Admiral Byng. Sentence of death had been passed upon Byng by court-martial, in consequence of his failure to join battle with the French fleet which was on the point of attacking Minorca, and which subsequently captured that important island and its British garrison. Walpole had no previous inclination to be a partisan of Byng, had never spoken to him or known any of his family, and indeed from a distance had rather disliked him—"the man I never saw but in the street, or in the House of Commons, and there I thought his carriage haughty and disgusting."[8] He had thought, in common with the rest of the nation, that Byng had been gravely to blame for not having engaged the French fleet in battle, and that the loss of Minorca was entirely due to negligence or cowardice on his part. But his view was altered when he read Byng's pamphlet in his own defence; and when he learnt of the sentence passed upon him, and that there was every prospect of its being carried into execution, he became convinced that the Admiral was "one marked for sacrifice by a set of ministers, who meant to divert on him the vengeance of a betrayed and enraged nation." The verdict of the court-martial was dictated by the positive and unalterable wording of one of the Articles of War; and it was accompanied by an urgent recommendation to mercy. It was in fact rumoured that some members of the court-martial would only agree to Byng's condemnation if their verdict was accompanied by such a recommendation, worded so strongly that it could not possibly be ignored. The charges of cowardice were absolutely disproved; Byng was convicted on the charge of negligence alone; and when it became evident that he was to be sacrificed to popular clamour and the resentment of the City merchants, the Navy was distressed and indignant. Some of the officers of the court-martial, when they realized that New-

[8] *Memoirs of George II,* ii. 120.

castle and Hardwicke were determined on Byng's execution, were filled with remorse; and two of them, Admiral Norris and Captain Keppel, the latter a Member of Parliament, wished to be absolved from their oath of secrecy, as they had something of importance to communicate to Parliament. It was at this point, a few days before the date fixed for the execution, that Walpole, unable himself to speak in the House because he had not yet been elected for King's Lynn, took vigorous action. He describes the scene in his *Memoirs.* "Coming late that day to the House, though not a member, Horace Walpole was told of the application that had been made to Mr. Grenville, and looking for him to try to engage him to undertake the cause, Walpole was told that Mr. Keppel desired to be absolved from his oath as well as Norris. Walpole ran up into the gallery, and asked Keppel if it was true? and being true, why he did not move the House himself? Keppel replied, that he was unused to speak in public, but would willingly authorize anybody to make the application for him. 'Oh! Sir,' said Walpole, 'I will soon find you somebody': and hurried him to Fox, who, Walpole fondly imagined, could not in decency refuse such a request, and who was the more proper from his authority in the House, and as a relation of Mr. Keppel. Fox was much surprized, knew not what to determine, said he was uncertain—and left the house. The time pressed, the Speaker was going to put the question for the orders of the day, after which no new motion can be made; it was Friday too; the house would sit neither on Saturday nor Sunday, and but a possibility of two days remained to intercept the execution, which was to be on Monday; and the whole operation of what Keppel should have to say, its effects, the pardon if procured, the dispatch to Portsmouth, and the reprieve, all to be crowded into so few hours! Walpole was in agony what steps to take—at that instant he saw Sir Francis Dashwood going up to the house; he flew down from the gallery, called Sir Francis, hurried the notification to him, and Sir Francis, with the greatest quickness of tender apprehension (the Speaker had actually read the question and put it while all this was passing) called out from the floor before he had time to take his place, 'Mr. Speaker'—and then informed the house of Mr. Keppel's desire that some method might be found of empowering him and the other members of the court-martial to declare what had been their intention in pronouncing Mr. Byng guilty."[9] A debate followed, a bill was introduced absolving the members of the court-martial from their oath, and the King reprieved Byng for a fortnight while the matter was discussed. After further debates, the bill passed the Commons; but it was rejected by the Lords, after that House had examined all the members of the court-martial. There could now be no further hope of mercy being extended to Byng. He was shot at Portsmouth on March 14, 1757, meeting his death with the serene courage that he had shown throughout the whole miserable affair.

Walpole's precipitate intervention was undertaken from the most humane motives; but he had to admit to Mann that the fate of Byng was a tragedy "in which I have been a most unfortunate actor, having to my infinite grief, which I shall feel till the man is at peace, been instrumental in protracting his misery a fortnight, by what I meant as the kindest thing I could do."[10] It would be unjust to interpret his effort to save Byng as a political manœuvre, or as an endeavour to embarrass certain ministers. His gallant last-minute attempt was wholly unpremeditated—an act of spontaneous and disinterested kindness, on behalf of a man with whom he had not the least acquaintance, but in whom he saw a victim of cruelty and injustice.

A few weeks after Byng's death, Walpole summed up the oddities and contradictions of the political situation in a little pamphlet which he scribbled in a single day, *A Letter from Xo Ho, a Chinese Philosopher at London, to his friend Lien Chi, at Peking*.[11] In terms of grave oriental bewilderment, Xo Ho explains to Lien Chi how confused and how illogical are the politics and institutions of the English nation. He tells how Byng was executed, and how the ministers, who were responsible equally with him for the loss of Minorca, were made ministers again. "If the executed Admiral had lived, he too might be a minister." The monarchy, the politicians, and the climate of England, in the eyes of Xo Ho, are equally odd in their behaviour. "My friend Lien Chi, I tell thee things as they are; I pretend not to account

[9] *Ibid.*, 153–4. [10] *Lewis,* xxi. 65 (Walpole to Mann, March 3, 1757).
[11] Reprinted in *Works,* i. 205–9.

for the conduct of Englishmen: I told thee before, they are *incomprehensible*." Walpole's graceful piece of irreverence had a great success, and five editions of the pamphlet were sold in a fortnight. Kitty Clive was impressed by his audacity; "Lord!" she exclaimed, "you will be sent to the Tower!" "Well," replied Walpole, "my father was there before me."[12]

V

If Walpole had retained any lingering wish to co-operate with Fox, after his alliance with the hated Newcastle, it was dissipated by Fox's conduct in the affair of Byng.[13] His political estrangement from Fox was completed by this episode. Rigby had already sought other alliances. And the outbreak of the Seven Years War involved the return of Conway, his new Parliamentary *protégé*, to active service abroad. Walpole therefore dropped out of active politics for a few years from 1757 onwards; and indeed, until George II's death, the unquestioned supremacy of Pitt brought Parliamentary faction practically to a standstill. The disasters of 1756, the gloomy opening phases of the war, were forgotten in the series of victories with which the old King's reign so astonishingly closed. Pitt's genius raised the country from the depths of humiliation to a position of world-wide power; and Walpole, like the rest of the nation, gratefully and almost incredulously applauded the measures of the great Minister.

He had a deep if somewhat reluctant admiration for Pitt. He could never, of course, entirely forget Pitt's furious attacks on his father in days gone by, though he extended to Pitt's open onslaughts a measure of forgiveness which he never accorded to the secret treachery of others. He also objected to Pitt's ruthlessness, both in political and personal matters; and at this juncture he particularly deplored his willingness to sacrifice British lives in desperate and unnecessary invasions of the coast of France. This was, in fact, one of the reasons he gave for his temporary retirement from politics: "being himself strongly tinctured with tenderness, he avoided any further intercourse with a minister, who was great with so little reluctance."[14] In one of these in-

[12] *Lewis,* ix. 207 (Walpole to Montagu, May 27, 1757).

[13] *Memoirs of George II,* ii. 138, 335.

[14] *Ibid.,* 335.

vasions, an unsuccessful attack on Rochefort, Conway had been in joint command; and while no doubts had been raised as to his personal bravery, his conduct of the expedition was strongly criticized, and Pitt had shown reluctance to employ him again. Walpole, of course, rushed to Conway's support, and published in the newspapers a poem ascribing the censures upon him to "Envy and her factious crew," and promising that time would bring full recognition of the services he had done to his country.

"Then, patient, let the thunder roll;
 Pity the blind you cannot hate;
Nor, blest with Aristides' soul,
 Repine at Aristides' fate."[15]

Pitt's failure to appreciate Conway naturally antagonized Walpole; but even his partisanship for his cousin could not blind him to the genius which the great statesman was displaying during these critical years. In an elaborate letter of compliment, written in 1759, he showed himself eager, almost to the point of obsequiousness, to express to Pitt his personal gratitude and admiration.[16]

For his own part, he welcomed the pleasures of retirement. By the end of 1758 he had withdrawn, "without disgrace, disappointment, or personal disgust," from public affairs. The *Anecdotes* were in contemplation, the press was in full activity, Strawberry Hill was about to be enlarged and adorned. With a thankful heart he returned to the pursuit of "arts, books, painting, architecture, antiquities, and those amiable employments of a tranquil life, to which in the warmest of his political hours he had been fondly addicted."[17] In the intervals of these pleasant activities, he watched with joy and amazement, like every Englishman of the time, as the fabulous tide of victory swept across the world. "Our bells are worn threadbare with ringing for victories," he wrote.[18] The humane and fastidious Whig became for a while an exultant imperialist, as British armies and fleets triumphed in

[15] *Toynbee,* iv. 113–4 (Walpole to Conway and Grosvenor Bedford, November 1757).
[16] *Ibid.,* 324–5 (Walpole to William Pitt, November 19, 1759).
[17] *Memoirs of George II,* ii. 334.
[18] *Lewis,* ix. 251 (Walpole to Montagu, October 21, 1759).

India and Africa, Canada and the Caribbean, as Quebec followed Plassey and Quiberon followed Quebec.

VI

In 1759 Walpole gained a new political connection, agreeable and potentially valuable, by the marriage of his niece Maria, his brother Edward's second daughter, to James Earl Waldegrave. Her elder sister, Laura, was already married to the Hon. and Rev. Frederick Keppel, Canon of Windsor and presently Bishop of Exeter. Apart from young Lord Orford, the bastard children of Edward Walpole were Sir Robert's only descendants in the third generation; and their marriages into the houses of Albemarle and Waldegrave gave their uncle Horace considerable satisfaction; for Lord Waldegrave was the great-grandson of James II and Arabella Churchill, as Mr. Keppel was of Charles II and Louise de Kéroualle. Maria was the beauty of the family, and his favourite among the three girls. He had long respected Lord Waldegrave as an able and uncorrupt politician, and liked him warmly as a man; and he welcomed the marriage, which indeed he claimed to have been instrumental in bringing about, with the greatest pleasure. At the time of the marriage Lord Waldegrave, who was some twenty years older than his bride, had retired for a period from political life. A few years earlier, being a devoted personal friend of George II, he had reluctantly acceded to the King's request that he should act as Governor to his grandson, the youthful Prince of Wales. He had found this position an extremely irksome one, and had not managed to endear himself either to the Prince or to his mother the Princess Dowager of Wales, who was completely under the political and personal domination of Lord Bute, and was eager that her friend should also become the Governor of her son.[19] Waldegrave had been thankful to resign after four years of this uncongenial duty; and after a period of political activity, during which, at the urgent request of the King, he had made a spirited but transient attempt to form a ministry, he had retired into private life, being rewarded for his services with the Garter. His political views and conduct, and his difficulties as Governor to the young Prince, were admirably set out in

[19] *Waldegrave,* 38–9, 63–78.

the *Memoirs* which he composed after his resignation.[20] Deriving a considerable income from his place as Teller of the Exchequer, he resisted all attempts to bring him back into active politics, and to the end of his life he preferred to live in comparative seclusion with his lovely wife and his young children. His political experience and wisdom, as well as his outstanding personal qualities, made him a most acceptable friend to Walpole; and when he died unexpectedly four years after his marriage, no man lamented him more sincerely.

VII

The year 1760, while less stirring than its predecessor, was an eventful one in many ways. The impetus of the war seemed momentarily to slacken; in February, Walpole was writing to Mann: "I think there is a glimmering of peace! God send the world some repose from its woes!"[21] But in the absence of momentous news from abroad, Englishmen were consoled by the excitement of two sensational trials at home. Lord George Sackville was court-martialled for his conduct at the battle of Minden; and Earl Ferrers was tried by his peers for the brutal murder of his steward. Walpole's descriptions of the latter trial, and of the conduct of Lord Ferrers after his condemnation and at his execution, are unsurpassed in their vividness and their profusion of detail. In one enormous letter to Mann[22] he gave the whole macabre narrative—Lord Ferrers' cool and unperturbed behaviour after the sentence, the reduction of his allowance of wine "agreeably to the late strict acts on murder," the attempts of his Methodist aunt Lady Huntingdon to convert him to her own views, his donning of his wedding clothes on the morning of execution, the incidents of the procession to Tyburn, the Sheriffs feasting on the scaffold after the hanging, the executioners fighting for the rope and the tears of the one who lost it. Walpole, of course, did not witness the execution; it may be that Selwyn, that *connoisseur* of horror,

[20] Walpole had access to the manuscript of these *Memoirs* (which remained unpublished till 1821) and made use of them in the composition of his own *Memoirs.*

[21] *Lewis,* xxi. 365–6 (Walpole to Mann, February 3, 1760).

[22] *Ibid.,* 394–403 (Walpole to Mann, May 7, 1760).

furnished him with the details which he handled in so masterly a fashion; in any case, the letter is one of his most memorable performances.

In the summer, Walpole went for his customary sightseeing tour. His northward progress was somewhat delayed owing to an attack of gout; but in the course of his tour he stayed at Ragley and Chatsworth, visited Lichfield Cathedral, passed with averted eyes through Sheffield, and explored Hardwicke and Newstead and Althorp. Soon after his return to Strawberry Hill, he was surprised to learn of the engagement of his youngest niece, Charlotte, to Lord Huntingtower; a prudent if rather prosaic niece who accepted her suitor, before she knew him by sight, because "I am likely to be large and to go off soon—it is dangerous to refuse so great a match."[23] Shortly after their marriage, a greater event took place. Early on the morning of October 26, King George II died suddenly of apoplexy.

Horace Walpole's reaction to this calamity was one of extreme relief—relief, however, quite unconnected with the personality or actions of the dead King. He had recently had an unexpected visit at Strawberry Hill from the Duke of York. For some while he had known the Duke, had joked with him about their rivalry in the affections of Lady Mary Coke, and had been one of a party which had attended him on a visit to the Magdalen House, where they and the assembled penitents listened to an impressive sermon from the ill-fated Doctor Dodd.[24] The visit to Strawberry Hill had been a very informal one, the Duke turning up casually one morning and Walpole receiving him "in the utmost confusion, undressed, in my slippers, and with my hair about my ears," and kneeling, in that dishevelled state, to kiss his hand.[25] But custom and politeness required that even this most informal visit should be returned, and that Walpole should make his appearance at Leicester House, where the Prince of Wales, his brothers, his mother and Lord Bute held their Court. He was appalled at the necessity. He had not been to Court for ten years, he had not been to Leicester House at all, every one was aware of his republican principles; and even if the motives of this sudden act of homage

[23] *Ibid.*, 439 (Walpole to Mann, October 5, 1760).
[24] *Ibid.*, ix. 273–4 (Walpole to Montagu, January 28, 1760).
[25] *Ibid.*, 303–5 (Walpole to Montagu, October 14, 1760).

were not misrepresented, they would be ridiculed, which was worse. There were letters to the Duke's equerry and to Lord Bute, consultations with "a jury of Court matrons," worries about clothes; an hour was fixed for his presentation. Then, on the day before the dreaded interview, the old King considerately died; and he was able to pay his homage to the new King with the rest of the world, without criticism or remark.

Apart from this fortuitous sense of relief, Walpole's emotions were not deeply stirred by the death of George II. But his curiosity led him to attend the royal obsequies in Westminster Abbey, taking advantage of his rank and walking in the funeral procession "as a rag of quality." He sent Montagu his impressions of the scene in the wonderful letter of November 13, 1760. This, like all Walpole's finest letters, has grown familiar by much quotation, with its descriptions of the torchlit Abbey, the superb setting in which the human actors so unworthily played their part, and of the Duke of Newcastle, whose conduct on this occasion plumbed the depths of the grotesque.[26]

He was favourably impressed by the new King. "This young man don't stand in one spot, with his eyes fixed royally on the ground, and dropping bits of German news; he walks about, and speaks to everybody." Everything at the outset of the new reign seemed auspicious—victory abroad, the nation united behind Pitt at home, political faction quite dormant, and a popular and likeable young King on the throne. All these advantages presently vanished. "A passionate, domineering woman, and a Favourite, without talents, soon drew a cloud over this shining prospect."[27] As a minor result of their machinations, Walpole before long would think himself obliged to emerge from his literary retirement and plunge into active politics once more. But at present no political issue disturbed his peace, except the necessity of placating his constituents at Lynn, in view of the coming election. Lord Orford had urged him to do this directly after the King's death; but he managed to postpone the disagreeable necessity until the following year. He paid a hurried visit to Lynn in February 1761, and went down to Norfolk again at the end of March, when the election took place.

[26] *Ibid.*, 320–3 (Walpole to Montagu, November 13, 1760).
[27] *Memoirs of George III*, i. 4.

He had left London in deep depression after parting with Conway, who was joining the army in Germany as second-in-command to Lord Granby; and his arrival at Houghton filled him with a still deeper melancholy. A sense of doom, the outcome of Lord Orford's mismanagement and extravagance, already brooded over the place. He wandered through the overgrown gardens, encountering gamekeepers and hares; he looked with pride at the splendid pictures, poor securities against the ever-mounting pile of his nephew's debts; memories of Sir Robert, of his geniality and wisdom and the state he kept, came flooding back to him. That night, in the solitude of the great house, he sat late in his father's little dressing-room, at the desk which his father had used, and wrote to Montagu his long and eloquent lament for Houghton's decline, his epitaph on all Sir Robert's magnificence and ambition. "...Here I am, probably for the last time of my life, though not for the last time—every clock that strikes tells me I am an hour nearer to yonder church—that church, into which I have not yet had courage to enter, where lies that mother on whom I doted, and who doted on me! There are the two rival mistresses of Houghton, neither of whom ever wished to enjoy it! There too lies he who founded its greatness, to contribute to whose fall Europe was embroiled—there he sleeps in quiet and dignity, while his friend and his foe, rather his false ally and real enemy, Newcastle and Bath, are exhausting the dregs of their pitiful lives in squabbles and pamphlets!...For what has he built Houghton? for his grandson to annihilate, or for his son to mourn over!"[28]

On the following morning he went over to Lynn, and passed the next few days in the midst of his enthusiastic constituents. It was not a contested election; he was returned unopposed, together with Sir John Turner; but he had to undergo a number of experiences which were unfamiliar and exhausting, though in retrospect not altogether disagreeable. "It is plain I never knew for how many trades I was formed, when at this time of day I can begin electioneering and succeed in my new vocation. Think of me, the subject of a mob, who was scarce ever before in a mob! addressing them in the town-hall, riding at the head of two

[28] *Lewis,* ix. 347–9 (Walpole to Montagu, March 25, 1761).

thousand people through such a town as Lynn, dining with above two hundred of them amid bumpers, huzzas, songs and tobacco, and finishing with country dancing at a ball and sixpenny whisk! I have borne it all cheerfully; nay, have sat hours in *conversation,* the thing upon earth that I hate, have been to hear misses play on the harpsichord, and to see an alderman's copies of Rubens and Carlo Marat. Yet to do the folks justice, they are sensible and reasonable, and civilized; their very language is polished since I lived among them. . . . Well! how comfortable it will be to-morrow, to see my perroquet, to play at loo, and not to be obliged to talk seriously."

In the course of his week of electioneering he had an amusing encounter with his father's sister, old Mrs. Hamond, who came over to Lynn especially to see him, "not from any affection, but curiosity." In eighteenth-century Norfolk elections, the chairs for the victorious candidates were provided with a kind of platform in front; and on these the representatives of the people were expected to stand, bowing gracefully as their conveyances lurched through the roaring crowd. Walpole remained indifferent to this honoured custom and subsided thankfully into his chair, thereby providing his aunt with a first-rate example of the inferiority of the younger generation. "The first thing she said to me, though we have not met these sixteen years, was, 'Child, you have done a thing to-day, that your father never did in all his life; you sat as they carried you; he always stood the whole time.' 'Madam,' said I, 'when I am placed in a chair, I conclude I am to sit in it—besides, as I cannot imitate my father in great things, I am not at all ambitious of mimicking him in little ones.'"[29]

VIII

For the first two years of George III's reign, Walpole remained more or less indifferent to politics. His chief political aversions were out of office; Conway was absent in Germany; and for a time he was willing to observe the ever-growing power of Bute with a lenient eye. "The truth was, I had been civilly treated on the King's accession, and had so much disliked Newcastle and

[29] *Ibid.,* 350–1 (Walpole to Montagu, March 31, 1761).

Hardwicke, that few men were better pleased than myself to see a new administration; and had not the standard of Prerogative been hoisted, and disgrace brought on this triumphant country, I should probably have remained a satisfied spectator."[30] His standards for the conduct of a constitutional monarch were perhaps a little distorted by the glamour and pageantry of an opening reign. The young King's marriage and coronation had provided him with material for endless gossip and correspondence. On the day of the coronation he had entertained some friends at the house of his deputy, Mr. Grosvenor Bedford, in Palace Yard, from which the company watched the splendid procession pass into Westminster Abbey and return to Westminster Hall.[31] And the impression of George III as an amiable and enlightened young monarch, moving amid the devoted homage of his subjects, took some time to fade. In fact, for a short while Walpole seems actively to have played the unaccustomed *rôle* of a courtier. Admittedly *The Garland,* the rather foolish poem which he wrote in praise of the King, was sent anonymously and in Grosvenor Bedford's handwriting to Lady Bute, and its authorship was never admitted:[32] but his letter to Lord Bute, in reply to a suggestion by that nobleman that he should undertake a sort of English equivalent of Montfaucon, is a surprising piece of obsequiousness to be addressed by even "a quiet republican" to the favourite of a dictatorial young King.[33]

The year 1761 brought yet another series of triumphs for the British arms all over the world; and yet again Walpole exulted in the spectacle of "St. James's Street crowded with nabobs and American chiefs, and Mr. Pitt attended in his Sabine farm by Eastern monarchs and Borealian electors, waiting, till the gout is gone out of his foot, for an audience."[34] The resignation of Pitt at the beginning of October, on the refusal of his colleagues to

[30] *Memoirs of George III,* i. 167.

[31] Walpole's guests were, according to a list given by Mr. Bedford: "Lady Hervey, Lady Hertford, Lady Anne Conway, Mr. Chute, Mrs. Clive, Mr. Raftor, Lady Townshend and Master, Miss Hotham and her maid." *(Toynbee,* v. 110 n.)

[32] *Toynbee,* v. 79–80 (Walpole to Grosvenor Bedford [July 19, 1761]).

[33] *Ibid.,* 174–6 (Walpole to the Earl of Bute, February 15, 1762).

[34] *Lewis,* xxi. 518 (Walpole to Mann, July 23, 1761).

consent to the declaration of war against Spain, distressed him considerably; but when, without the guiding genius of Pitt, the war dragged on through the following year, he became ever more eager for peace. Conway, in the meantime, had acquitted himself excellently in Germany; he had amply retrieved the reputation he had lost at Rochefort; and Walpole's only anxiety now was to see him home once more. He therefore welcomed, in November 1762, the Peace of Paris; its disadvantages and its mistakes were outweighed by two supreme considerations—"the miserable world will have some repose, and Mr. Conway is safe."[35]

Conway had to superintend the withdrawal of the army from Germany, and it was some while before he returned to England and was able to resume his Parliamentary activities. In the meantime Walpole's attention had been forcibly recalled to the vagaries of political life by a disagreeable *imbroglio* with Fox. His old ally had long ago ceased to compete with the genius of Pitt, and had found consolation for some years past in the unspectacular but extremely lucrative office of Paymaster. Now he was brought to the forefront of affairs again, in a desperate attempt to bolster up the increasingly unpopular administration of Bute. In October 1762 he entered the Cabinet and became leader of the House of Commons, and embarked at once on a policy of lavish propitiation of all those who might be possible supporters, and of vindictive proscription of opponents. Walpole was fated to experience both aspects of this policy. Fox addressed to him, on November 21, a suspiciously jocular letter, expressing willingness to offer to his impoverished nephew, Lord Orford, a valuable sinecure, the Rangership of St. James's and Hyde Parks, which had lately fallen vacant; and asking Walpole to act as intermediary in the matter. "If he does choose it," ran the letter, "I doubt not of his and his friend Boone's[36] hearty assistance, and believe I shall see you, too, much oftener in the House of Commons. This is offering you a bribe, but 'tis such a one as one honest good-natured man may without offence offer to another. . . . You'll believe me when I tell you that goodness of heart has as much share in this to the full as policy."[37]

[35] *Ibid.*, xxii. 96 (Walpole to Mann, November 9, 1762).

[36] Boone was Lord Orford's nominated member for Castle Rising.

[37] *Memoirs of George III,* i. 169 (Fox to Walpole, November 21, 1762).

This "artful and disingenuous letter," as Walpole called it, was delivered by hand, with a request for an immediate answer. It certainly put Walpole into a difficult position. He was ready to seize any opportunity of relieving his nephew's embarrassments, and perhaps of averting the catastrophe which was approaching Houghton; but at the same time he distrusted Fox profoundly, and was determined not to be indebted to him for any kind of favour. He therefore composed a reply in which he undertook merely to convey Fox's offer to Lord Orford, without giving his nephew any advice about its acceptance, or suggesting to him any means by which he could show his gratitude to his benefactor. This letter, "under the appearance of the same insincere cordiality which Fox affected to wear," contained several passages which were designed to show its recipient that Walpole was determined not to act with him in any way, or to give any support to the administration in Parliament or elsewhere.[38]

Fox's irritation at this reply was not diminished by the fact that Lord Orford, after accepting the Rangership of the Parks, never supported the ministry by a single vote, or showed the least sense of obligation to those who had bestowed this useful sinecure upon him. He therefore determined to punish Walpole, and did so by instructing the Secretary of the Treasury to delay the payments of his place as Usher of the Exchequer. This could put Walpole to considerable inconvenience, as it obliged him to advance large sums of money from his own pocket to provide the stationery and other requisites of the Exchequer. When five months had elapsed and his payments were still withheld, he appealed to Bute, who knew nothing of the private persecution which Fox was carrying on, and who ordered the immediate payment of the money.[39]

All through 1762 the popular resentment against Bute was rising. Wilkes gave brilliant and audacious expression to the general feeling in the *North Briton;* and in the second number of that periodical great play was made with Walpole's unlucky tribute to the Scottish nation in the *Catalogue of Royal and Noble Authors.*[40] Walpole reappeared in the *North Briton* eight months

[38] *Ibid.,* 170–1. *Lewis,* xxx. 168–70 (Walpole to Fox, November 21, 1762).
[39] *Toynbee,* v. 292 (Walpole to Bute, March 14 and 16, 1763).
[40] *The North Briton,* No. ii (June 12, 1762).

later, when the eulogistic character of Fox, which he had published in *The World,* was subjected to some admirable mockery.[41] But on this second occasion he deliberately drew Wilkes's ridicule upon himself. In his exasperation at his recent treatment by Fox, he had sent an anonymous letter to Wilkes, drawing his attention to the paper in *The World,* and "inciting the *North Briton* to take notice both of the author and the subject of the character."[42] Wilkes took the bait, and made Walpole's eulogy the theme of a vindictive attack on Fox, while treating Walpole himself with comparative leniency. This was precisely the sort of mystification that Walpole enjoyed; and his pleasure was enhanced by the report that Wilkes, on learning of the equanimity with which he had received the supposed attack, had said that "if he had thought I should have taken it so well, he would have been damned before he would have written it."[43] By this time, quite apart from his private satisfaction at any attack on Fox, he was becoming increasingly sympathetic to the point of view represented by Wilkes; and events were presently to make him a wholehearted supporter of the opposition. But he persisted for the time being in his resolve to keep out of active politics. He was feeling ill, and talked of visiting Italy again; and when there was a probability of his cousin Lord Hertford going as ambassador to Paris, he thought of accompanying him.

IX

Conway returned to England from Germany at the beginning of April 1763. For many months Walpole had eagerly looked forward to his arrival; but his joy was immediately darkened by the news that Lord Waldegrave was gravely ill with smallpox. To his great sorrow, Waldegrave died on April 8. On the same day the country heard with amazement that Bute had resigned.

Walpole retired with his widowed niece to Strawberry Hill, and watched with interest the political developments which followed Bute's unexpected action. Fox received a peerage, and will henceforth be known as Lord Holland; after an undignified squabble

[41] *Ibid.*, No. xxxvi (February 5, 1763).

[42] *Memoirs of George III,* ii. 20 (n).

[43] *Toynbee,* v. 289 (Walpole to Conway, February 28, 1763).

he was also allowed to retain his lucrative office of Paymaster. George Grenville succeeded Bute as First Lord of the Treasury and Chancellor of the Exchequer. Lord Hertford, Conway's elder brother, who had always adopted a neutral attitude in politics, was appointed Ambassador at Paris. This distinction to his cousin from the new ministers gave great pleasure to Walpole; but certain dispositions which Bute had made on his retirement caused him an equal degree of annoyance. He had obtained the reversion of Walpole's place of Usher of the Exchequer for Samuel Martin, the Secretary of the Treasury who at Fox's instigation had recently delayed the payment of Walpole's bills. This seems only to have mildly irritated Walpole, who in any case was destined to get the better of Martin by outliving him by several years; but he was deeply offended at the reversion of his brother Edward's place in the Custom House, in which he himself held the greater share under his father's will, being granted to Jenkinson, Bute's private secretary. Although he had refused to accept the grant of his reversion from Fox, and had made it clear to Bute that he would receive no favour from him, he had nevertheless always hoped that it would be continued to him in the event of his brother's death; and the grant to Jenkinson, which now excluded him from the possibility of obtaining it, was a bitter grievance to him.[44]

He was thus in every way disposed to welcome Bute's supersession by Grenville, for whose sincerity and integrity he had a great respect. He regarded Grenville as all that a Whig should be: he even referred to him as "scarce a less Whig saint" than Algernon Sidney.[45] But the Whig saint soon began to display very decided inclinations towards arbitrary government. His methods were hardly more scrupulous than those employed by Bute; and Algernon Sidney would have regarded with violent disapproval the political and private standards of many of the men who supported him. One of the earliest acts of his administration was the arrest and imprisonment of Wilkes under a general warrant, after the publication of number 45 of the *North Briton*. The legality of general warrants was exceedingly doubtful; and Walpole was among the many people who felt that vital principles of liberty

[44] *Memoirs of George III,* i. 210. [45] *Ibid.,* 269.

were involved in the question. He watched with anxiety the increasing strength of prerogative and arbitrary power; he strongly disliked the methods used against Wilkes, culminating in the persecution over the *Essay on Woman* towards the end of the year; and he distrusted and wished to prevent the alliance which Grenville formed with the hated Bedford faction. All these circumstances disposed him to return to active politics. During the summer he informed Grenville, through the medium of his neighbour the Gothic enthusiast Thomas Pitt, that he would probably differ from him over general warrants when that matter came to be debated in Parliament. And he determined to persuade Conway to take an active part in the House on the same question.[46]

Lord Hertford, the only other person whose influence over his brother was comparable to Walpole's, had always preferred to remain outside party politics, and hoped to persuade Conway to adopt the same attitude. Walpole therefore waited till October, when Hertford was safely installed as Ambassador in Paris. He then approached Conway on the subject of general warrants, and had no difficulty in persuading him to oppose them, and to take a firm line against all proposed extensions of arbitrary power. Conway voted against the Court on questions of privilege on November 15 and again on November 24. This conduct infuriated the King, who regarded an adverse vote in Parliament, from a Groom of the Bedchamber and an officer commanding one of his regiments of dragoons, as an act of unpardonable defiance. On each occasion he wrote to Grenville, to propose "dismissing General Conway both from his civil and military Commissions . . . and any others who have gone steadily against us, and giving it out that the rest would have the same fate if they do not amend their conduct."[47] Grenville calmed the King's wrath, and prudently suggested that Conway's dismissal should be postponed until the Christmas recess, "as a more usual time, and not so obnoxious"; and in the interval he decided to make a private attempt to conciliate Walpole and Conway. Thomas Pitt was first deputed to see Walpole, and hinted very clearly the lengths to which the Court was prepared to go if Conway persisted in his

[46] *Ibid.*, 270.

[47] *Grenville*, ii. 162, 166 (The King to Grenville, November 16 and 25, 1763).

defiance. Such phrases as "the King could not trust his army in such hands" only had the effect of stiffening Walpole's resistance, and he refused to make any attempt to influence Conway's attitude. Grenville then had an interview with Walpole, and held forth almost uninterruptedly from seven till ten at night without making the slightest impression on him. An interview with Conway had no greater effect.[48]

Conway was not, however, removed from his posts at the Christmas recess. This may have been in some measure due to consideration for the ambassadorial dignity of Lord Hertford, who did his best to excuse his brother's conduct to Grenville.[49] Hertford's position was certainly difficult: and Walpole, while sending him superb news-letters throughout his years in France, did not disguise his personal satisfaction at the line Conway was taking. Hertford, in Walpole's eyes, was a "perfect courtier"; and his replies to Walpole's news-letters are full of plaintive and very natural expressions of embarrassment at his brother's obstinate defiance of the King whom he himself was representing at Paris.[50] But nothing could check Conway now. Throughout the winter he consistently voted and spoke against the Government on general warrants, the prosecution of Wilkes, and all related questions of privilege and liberty. Still Grenville held his hand; and it was not until April 22, 1764, that Conway was officially informed that he had been dismissed from the command of his regiment and from his post as Groom of the Bedchamber.

This announcement, coming some two months after the last of the debates on general warrants, took every one by surprise. At first Walpole was incredulous: he then retired for three days to Strawberry Hill to "conquer the first ebullitions of my rage." He felt deeply responsible for having induced Conway to risk this blow to his career. He believed that Grenville's action was directed as much against himself as against Conway, not knowing that the King had been urging Conway's dismissal on Grenville ever since the previous November. He made substantial offers of money to Conway, which were refused; altered his will in his favour; and set himself to avenge his friend by every means in his

[48] *Memoirs of George III,* i. 271–4. *Grenville,* ii. 232–6, 320–7, 335–44, 346–60.
[49] *Grenville,* ii. 247–50 (Lord Hertford to Grenville, January 4, 1764).
[50] Add. MS. 23218, *passim.*

power. He gave up his project of visiting Lord Hertford in Paris, and turned with almost extravagant zeal to the work of building the random and disunited elements opposed to the Government into a force that could turn Grenville and the Bedfords out of office.[51]

All through the year he laboured to unite the Opposition. There were many potential allies; yet so divided were their ambitions, so conflicting their personal rivalries, that "I could not prevail on any three to assemble and enter into concert." In his eagerness to form a common front of the enemies of the Government, he actually made friends with the detested Duke of Newcastle. But his efforts met with every sort of discouragement and misfortune. Legge died; the Duke of Devonshire died; Pitt remained grandly aloof; and even the faction-loving Lord Temple would not join the Opposition. He also had frequent occasion to complain of the "supineness of my confederates."[52] There can be little doubt that his confederates grew somewhat resentful of the incessant activity, the frantic partisanship, that Walpole had suddenly begun to display. Rather cruelly he was made aware of this feeling by the very man on whose behalf he had undertaken the whole unprofitable crusade. He had been making some unauthorized endeavours to bring about a *rapprochement* between Conway and Pitt, forgetting the old-standing antagonism that existed between the two men; and Conway, finding himself likely to be drawn into a false position of deference towards Pitt, rebuked his cousin's ardour in a rather mortifying fashion. Walpole was deeply hurt at this behaviour; and although he concealed his feelings, he now began to meditate that final withdrawal from active politics which was precipitated a year later by another and a graver act of ingratitude on Conway's part.[53]

Walpole's private friends were somewhat disconcerted by the extraordinary vigour of his "political frenzy." They had not realized the lengths to which his partisanship for Conway could go. But any insult to Conway, any hostile pamphlet or insignificant newspaper abuse, pierced Walpole like an arrow; and no expedient was too trivial for him to adopt in defence or counter-attack. The extent of his anonymous activity in the press will

[51] *Memoirs of George III,* i. 320–6.
[52] *Ibid.,* 326–9. [53] *Ibid.,* ii. 21–3.

never be known; but he certainly advanced his championship of Conway through some rather ignoble channels, and did not think it beneath him to spread a newspaper *canard* that the Duke of Bedford had been the originator of the movement to abolish the custom of giving vails to servants.[54] His pamphlet in defence of Conway, written at white heat in a few days in June 1764, and published later in the summer, was a worthier piece of work.[55] From the mass of Government propaganda he singled out an *Address on the late Dismission of a General Officer,* in which an experienced pamphleteer named William Guthrie had defended the treatment of Conway with considerable skill and without any noticeable scurrility or rancour. He analysed this pamphlet carefully in his *Counter-Address,* meeting Guthrie's points fairly and effectively; but he encumbered his argument with a great deal of fulsome verbiage about Conway's bravery and virtue, and made a number of ill-tempered references to the "half-converted Jacobite" who had dared to assail him. Guthrie retaliated with a *Reply to the Counter-Address,* in which Walpole was severely handled, particularly on the score of his personal affection for Conway. Walpole sent Conway a copy of this pamphlet, with the comment that it was "the lowest of all Grub Street, and I hear is treated so. They have nothing better to say than that I am in love with you, have been so these twenty years, and am no giant. I am a very constant old swain: they might have made the years above thirty; it is so long I have had the same unalterable friendship for you, independent of being near relations and bred up together."[56]

He was also involved in a warfare of private letters with Thomas Pitt, and indirectly with Grenville, over certain disputed details of their negotiations and interviews with Conway and himself in the previous December.[57] A prolonged battle of recriminations and denials ended in a complete breach of his friendship with Thomas Pitt, and he was thereafter only on terms of distant courtesy with his agreeable neighbour. He was already in open

[54] *Ibid.,* 2–3. [55] Reprinted in *Works,* ii. 549–76.

[56] *Toynbee,* vi. 119 (Walpole to Conway, September 1, 1764).

[57] *Grenville,* ii. 320–7 (Grenville to Thomas Pitt, May 15; Pitt to Grenville, May 25, 1764), 335–44 (Walpole to Pitt, June 5; Pitt to Walpole, June 10, 1764), 353–60 (Grenville to Pitt, June 19, 1764).

Parliamentary opposition against Grenville, and was trying to discredit the Minister by every means in his power. Grenville retaliated by repeating Fox's trick of delaying the payments of Walpole's place at the Exchequer; and Walpole also suspected him of assisting Guthrie in writing the *Reply to the Counter-Address,* and of furnishing him with confidential information for that purpose.[58]

It was a strange year for Walpole, a year of tireless effort and protracted nervous tension, of incessant political intrigues mingling with the unique visionary mood that produced *The Castle of Otranto.* But all his whirlwind activity, his quarrels and whisperings and pamphleteering, distasteful reconciliations with old enemies and tedious political dinners with new friends, contributed little to the eventual collapse of the Government. He did indeed claim to have been instrumental in detaching Lord Bute from the Ministers and so to have appreciably weakened the Government;[59] but Grenville and Bedford were finally brought down by circumstances altogether outside his control. Early in 1765 the King was taken seriously ill; his health had indeed caused anxiety for some while, and it was now thought advisable, as soon as he recovered, to determine upon the members of the Royal Family who should act as Regents in the event of his further incapacitation. A Regency Bill was introduced by the Government; and to the universal astonishment the name of the Princess Dowager was deliberately excluded from the Bill. The King's consent to this "indelible stigma on his own mother"[60] was somehow obtained by his Ministers. He soon came to realize the grossness of the insult which he had thus inexplicably sanctioned, and made every effort to have the Bill altered so as to include the name of the Princess; but the Ministers were obdurate. He had already begun to weary of their domination; and he now asked his uncle the Duke of Cumberland to sound the Opposition with a view to forming another Government. In the complicated series of negotiations which followed, Walpole took some part. Ever since his dismissal, Conway had opposed the Ministers with vigour

[58] *Memoirs of George III,* ii. 4, 5, 9.

[59] *Ibid.,* 69–71, 97. For Walpole's somewhat exaggerated estimate of his own part in the fall of the Government, see also 85 and 98.

[60] *Ibid.,* 89.

and ability; he was now one of the foremost personalities of the Opposition, and he relied on Walpole's advice in every step he took. Walpole's views as to the proper conduct of the Opposition were often at variance with those of the younger members of the party, "two or three frantic boys" headed by Lord John Cavendish;[61] and when Cumberland proposed that the alternative Government should be formed by Lord Rockingham, a young nobleman of high reputation but small political experience, he was strongly opposed to the scheme. But a violent attack of gout kept him away from the critical meeting of the Opposition leaders at the Duke of Newcastle's house on June 30, 1765; and in view of Conway's eagerness to take part in the new administration, and of the high position now offered to his friend, it is probable that he would not have given very strong expression to his forebodings.[62] On July 8 the new Ministry, mainly consisting of members of the old Whig guard, came into office. Lord Rockingham was First Lord of the Treasury; and Conway became one of the Secretaries of State, and Leader of the House of Commons.

X

The main objects of Walpole's "political frenzy" now seemed to have been attained. The Whigs were in favour, Conway was vindicated and in high office, Grenville and Bedford were overthrown. He was indeed doubtful of the staying-power of a Whig Government which was led by Rockingham and from which Pitt remained obstinately aloof; but, for the moment, the triumph of his party was complete. To most of his friends he expressed unclouded happiness at the outcome of events,[63] and at the justification and reward of all his labours: in actual fact he was undergoing the greatest disillusionment of his life.

He had always hoped that, on the change of administration, some important place or office would be offered to him. He

[61] *Toynbee,* vi. 231 (Walpole to Hertford, May 11, 1765). *Memoirs of George III,* ii. 91–8.

[62] *Memoirs of George III,* ii. 135–6, 139–40, 148. *Holland Letters,* 230, "Horry has been much consulted in all this..." (Selwyn to Holland, July 12, 1765).

[63] *Lewis,* x. 160–1 (Walpole to Montagu, July 11, 1765); xxii. 309–12 (Walpole to Mann, July 12, 1765). *Holland Letters,* 240 (Walpole to Holland, July 19, 1765).

would have refused it; he had always said that he would never accept any place; but the compliment of the offer would have given him immense pleasure. Conway knew this perfectly well; yet he did not make the slightest effort to repay Walpole in this manner for all his exertions on his behalf. Failing the offer of a place, Walpole would have been content if some arrangement had been devised by which hostile Ministers could not in future delay the payments of his office at the Exchequer, as Fox and Grenville had done. He had hinted to Conway that such a step would make his independence perfectly secure for life, and would be a source of great satisfaction to him. Conway did nothing whatever about it. Yet he was working energetically and successfully to have his very lukewarm brother, Lord Hertford, appointed Lord-Lieutenant of Ireland; and was assiduous in obtaining posts for several other relatives whose support in the days of his adversity had been even less conspicuous. Walpole had expected no gratitude from his other political associates, with whom his alliance was mainly one of expediency; but Conway's neglect wounded him bitterly. From the days of their childhood he had exalted Conway into a hero; and now the image built up during all those years of constant and rather pathetic devotion was shattered by an act of stupid ingratitude.[64]

Insensitiveness can be more hurtful than deliberate cruelty. Writing after his first indignation had died away, Walpole was at laborious pains to acquit Conway of intentional ingratitude; but he could not explain away the humiliating fact of his sheer indifference, the manner in which he had taken his hero-worship and his partisanship for granted, without thinking for a moment that so ardent a devotee might appreciate some acknowledgment from his idol. "It is justice to him to say, that I think he was incapable of ingratitude: his soul was good, virtuous, sincere; but his temper was chill, his mind absent; and he was so accustomed to my suggesting to him whatever I thought it was right for him to do, that he had no notion of my concealing a thought from him; and as I had too much delicacy to mention even my own security, I am persuaded it never came into his conception. His temper hurt me, but I forgave his virtue, of which I am confident, and

[64] *Memoirs of George III,* ii. 148–51.

know it was superior to my own. We have continued to this day on an easy and confidential footing. . . ."[65] All this was only an ineffective attempt to prop up the fallen hero. He remained indeed on friendly terms with Conway, saw him regularly, continued to support him in his political career: but he took "strict care never to give him decisive advice, when it might lead him to a precipice." Conway's successes and reverses were no longer to be his own.

Walpole faced his disappointment with complete outward stoicism. He was determined that Conway should have no idea of his suffering. He decided to go to Paris as soon as his health allowed him. Throughout the political activities of the last two years, he had promised himself this diversion directly he had achieved his purpose and seen his party in office; and recent events had only given him additional motives to leave England and seek the consolation of new scenes and an unfamiliar society. His recent attack of gout, which had prevented him from attending the fateful meeting of his party at the Duke of Newcastle's, was the most severe he had yet undergone; he emerged from it broken and exhausted, and hobbled about the garden at Strawberry Hill until he was well enough to set out for France. Conway, as soon as he heard that Walpole proposed to remain abroad for the whole winter, gave a further display of egotism. Still feeling himself entitled to the constant benefit of Walpole's political advice, he broke out into indignant protests: Walpole was leaving his friends in the lurch, he was forgetting his obligations to his party, he was deserting Conway himself. Walpole remained indifferent to his reproaches. After the agitations of the last two years, and the illness and unhappiness of the summer, his only wish was to get away from it all—"to see French plays and buy French china, not to know their ministers, to look into their government, or think of the interests of nations"[66]—to enjoy a few delicious months of idleness and frivolity.

On September 9 he set out from London. He had determined to keep a journal of his visit to France, and the opening entries show that already his spirits were rising, that he was leaving his troubles

[65] *Ibid.*, 152.

[66] *Lewis*, x. 171 (Walpole to Montagu, August 31, 1765).

STRAWBERRY HILL : THE NORTH FRONT
From a drawing by THOMAS ROWLANDSON at Farmington, Connecticut
By kind permission of Mr. W. S. Lewis

HORACE WALPOLE, FOURTH EARL OF ORFORD (1793)
From a drawing by GEORGE DANCE
By kind permission of the Trustees of the National Portrait Gallery

behind and observing even the commonplaces of the English scene with a livelier and happier eye. "Sept. 9. Set out from Arlington Street at half an hour after eight: found no beggars at the door: those of London are too voluptuous to be up and have drunk their tea so early. . . . The innkeeper at Rochester (I suppose a politician) asked my servant who I was? When he heard, he said, 'Oh! he is going envoy to Constantinople to replace Mr. Grenville.' . . . A hop-ground with men and women gathering the hops, raising the poles into pyramids, the baskets, the sacks, and the perspectives through the lines, would make a lively picture, and what I never saw painted. . . ."[67] On the following day he embarked at Dover and landed at Boulogne, and on the 13th he arrived at Paris.

[67] *Ibid.*, vii. 258. The original manuscript is in the Harvard University Library.

XI

Madame du Deffand: and the Later Writings (1765-71)

I

SINCE the signing of the Peace of Paris, there had been a stream of French visitors to London; and the English, deprived for seven years of their customary pilgrimages to France for health or economy or amusement, began to cross the Channel in still greater numbers. The social bonds between the two capitals were re-established; and the reconciled *beaux mondes* observed with eager interest the novelties of manners and outlook, of speech and dress and architecture, which their neighbours had adopted during the tedious years of war. Among the minor novelties of the English scene, Strawberry Hill and its owner now held a recognized position. "Horry is now as much a curiosity to all foreigners as the tombs and lions," wrote Gilly Williams.[1] A succession of rather bewildered Frenchmen and Frenchwomen strove to grasp the Gothic whimsicalities of Strawberry Hill, and to veil in polite compliments their profound disapproval. Walpole welcomed them delightfully, with clarionets and French horns playing in the cloister, and complimentary verses to the ladies set up in type at the printing-house.[2] But the visitors remained rather at sea. Monsieur de Nivernais, as we have seen, removed his hat in deference to the ecclesiastical shadows of the Tribune; and Madame de Boufflers murmured to Lady Holland that the house was by no means "digne de la solidité anglaise."[3]

[1] *Jesse,* i. 322 (Williams to Selwyn, November 13, 1764).
[2] *Lewis,* x. 72–3 (Walpole to Montagu, May 17, 1763).
[3] *Ibid.,* xxii. 270 (Walpole to Mann, December 20, 1764).

Whatever their opinion of Strawberry Hill, Walpole received a most friendly welcome in Paris from the French whom he had entertained there. Monsieur de Nivernais, Madame de Boufflers, the Guerchys, the Dussons, Elie de Beaumont, were all profuse in their attentions. Some of his English friends, Lady Hervey and George Selwyn in particular, spent much time in Paris, and Walpole's arrival was awaited with interest by their acquaintances. The Hertfords were just about to leave Paris for Dublin, but Lady Hertford was still at Paris to welcome him; and the new ambassador was to be the Duke of Richmond, whom he knew well and whose wife was Conway's step-daughter. He had no fear of lack of friends in Paris, although he was quite unprepared for the heights of popularity which he was presently to attain in French society. From the moment of his arrival he was completely happy, restored in health by his journey, restored in spirits by the friendliness and civility displayed by every one he met.

Only a month later, reports of his success were reaching England, and Gilly Williams was writing to Selwyn "Has Horry wrote? You do not know how popular he is,"[4] and Walpole himself was at pains to deny to Lady Mary Coke and Lady Hervey some mocking rumours that the French were struck by the beauty of his person.[5] Paris, a year or two before, had taken a violent fancy for David Hume: now another gifted and unconventional Briton had become the rage. Walpole's originality and wit, his friendliness and gaiety, the flights and lapses of his headlong stumbling French, were irresistible. He was in brilliant spirits, exulting in his release from the burden of politics: and every one responded to his mood. The full extent of his social activities can be realized only from the perusal of his journal, of those brief entries, crammed with names, which record the dinners, operas, plays and supper-parties to which he rolled night after night in his chariot decorated with Cupids, "looking like the grandfather of Adonis."[6] Occasional passages in some of his letters express petulance and boredom: but in general he was

[4] *Jesse,* i. 412 (Williams to Selwyn, October 17, 1765).

[5] *Lewis,* xxxi. 70, 73–4 (Walpole to Lady Mary Coke, November 17; to Lady Hervey, November 21, 1765).

[6] *Ibid.,* x. 176 (Walpole to Montagu, September 22, 1765).

delighted with his flattering reception in Paris, and found, as he told Selwyn, that it was "charming to totter into vogue."[7]

Certain features of Parisian life were by no means to his taste. He was considerably distressed by the dirtiness of the streets and houses, and by the outspoken manner in which people discussed, in mixed company and in the presence of their servants, such delicate topics as religion and the latest symptoms of the Dauphin's illness. He was not a religious man, but he did not see "why there is not as much bigotry in attempting conversions from any religion as to it;" and he did not like a discussion on matters of belief, "even on the Old Testament," being carried on at table in the hearing of the footmen.[8] Indeed, the main trend of intellectual activity in France, the crusade of the *philosophes* and *Encyclopédistes* against religious belief, was tedious and distasteful to him. He could forgive the French their admiration for Richardson's novels and the game of whist; it was harder to forgive them their admiration for Hume, and for their fanatical and over-bearing addiction to doctrines to which, in spite of his mildly agnostic and liberal opinions, he could not bring himself to subscribe. In his earlier years he would have been in sympathy with the onslaughts on superstition and bigotry, privilege and reaction, which well-dressed *philosophes* delivered in the drawing-rooms of exquisite hostesses. Now he began to view these elevated sentiments in their uglier and more realistic colours, and to have some inkling of the misery they would ultimately bring to the France he knew and loved. And not only were their exponents dangerous; they were profoundly boring and humourless as well, and cast a gloom over the whole of social life. "Laughing is as much out of fashion as *pantins* or *bilboquets*. Good folks, they have no time to laugh. There is God and the King to be pulled down first; and men and women, one and all, are devoutly employed in the demolition. They think me quite profane, for having any belief left."[9] He defined the *philosophes* in very similar terms in a letter to Conway. "Do you know who *the philosophers* are, or what the term means here? In the first place, it comprehends almost everybody; and in the next, means

[7] *Ibid.*, xxx. 204 (Walpole to Selwyn, December 2, 1765).

[8] *Ibid.*, x. 176 (Walpole to Montagu, September 22, 1765).

[9] *Toynbee*, vi. 332 (Walpole to Thomas Brand, October 19, 1765).

men who, avowing war against popery, aim, many of them, at a subversion of all religion, and still many more, at the destruction of regal power."[10]

Holding such views, Walpole naturally looked about for a society which was frivolous and light-hearted, where the uplifting doctrines of the *Encyclopédistes* were not the favourite subject of conversation, and where Hume was not regarded with veneration. He found it in the *salon* of Madame du Deffand.

II

On September 17th, four days after Walpole's arrival in Paris, the following entry occurs in his journal: "After dinner to visit Mme de Bouzols; to the opera; to Mme du Deffand, a blind old lady of wit. Supped there, with the Duchesse de la Vallière, still very handsome, Madame de Forcalquier, very handsome and pleasing, who reads English, the Président Hénault, very old, deaf and almost gone, Lord Ossory, Sir James Macdonald, Elliot, Craufurd, and other French. They played at whisk after supper, two tables: left several there at past one.... At Mme du Deffand's they proposed to me to translate to her a scene in Rowe's *Ambitious Step-Mother,* of which Mme Forcalquier, who understands English, is fond; but I took care not to expose myself."[11] Walpole was introduced to this famous *salon* through a letter from George Selwyn, an old friend of Madame du Deffand. A week later he supped with her again, and played at "silver hazard" till past three in the morning.[12] In another week or two he was a regular member of her circle, and soon his liking for the "old blind *debauchée* of wit"[13] ripened into a singular and eventful friendship.

Marie de Vichy-Champrond, Marquise du Deffand, was sixty-nine years of age at this time. She had married Jean-Baptiste de la Lande, Marquis du Deffand, in 1718; had played her part in the dazzling social life of the Regency, and for one memorable fortnight had been the mistress of the Regent himself. Separated from her husband, who died in 1750, she spent many years at the court of the Duchesse du Maine at Sceaux; and later she

[10] *Ibid.,* 335 (Walpole to Conway, October 28, 1765).

[11] *Lewis,* vii. 261. [12] *Ibid.,* vii. 262.

[13] *Toynbee,* vi. 312 (Walpole to Conway, October 6, 1765).

settled in Paris, occupying the apartments in the secular portion of the Convent of Saint Joseph which had belonged to Madame de Montespan, the founder of the Convent. Here she established her *salon;* and here, disregarding the complete blindness which descended upon her in 1754, she continued to receive all that was most distinguished in the social and intellectual life of France.

The year before Walpole's visit to Paris, Madame du Deffand's *salon* had been rent by a terrible schism. She had quarrelled with her companion, Julie de Lespinasse, whom she had brought as a friendless and persecuted girl out of the country. Mademoiselle de Lespinasse was accused of holding a preliminary *salon* each day before Madame du Deffand appeared, and of attempting to secure for herself both the allegiance of the older woman's guests and the first brilliance of their conversation. She had promptly left the Convent of Saint Joseph and set up a *salon* of her own, taking with her most of the younger and more intellectual members of her benefactor's circle, including d'Alembert and Turgot. When Walpole came upon the scene, Madame du Deffand was still bitterly resentful of the treachery of Mademoiselle de Lespinasse and the desertion, in particular, of d'Alembert. The episode had led to the absolute exclusion of the *philosophes* and their doctrines from her *salon,* and this was one of the features that first attracted Walpole most strongly to it.

Madame du Deffand, in 1765, was profoundly unhappy and intensely bored. The new currents of thought in contemporary life meant nothing to her; and since her desertion by the *philosophes,* she was actively hostile to them. She had never had the slightest religious belief; in her schooldays Massillon had attempted to reason with her, and had retired from the youthful infidel in despair. Her chief intellectual pleasure, apart from a regular correspondence with Voltaire, lay in endless conversation within her chosen circle of friends. And, besides the recent defection of so many members of her *salon,* it appears from Walpole's letters that she had good reason to suspect disloyalty and unkindness from some of those who remained outwardly faithful.[14] And, anyhow, they bored her almost without exception.

[14] *Ibid.,* 405, 432–3 (Walpole to Gray, January 25; to Craufurd, March 6, 1766).

The old Président Hénault, with whom she had maintained a prolonged *liaison* in the far-off days at Sceaux, was almost in his dotage now. Pont-de-Veyle, who had written comedies and improper tales, was gloomy in conversation and only cheered up when his writings were praised. The women were growing elderly and grave; and almost the only sympathetic figure among them was the Duchesse de Choiseul, who shines out in Walpole's descriptions as a solitary star, young, lovely, and kind-hearted, amid the shadows of that garrulous and decrepit *salon*.[15]

In those circumstances, Madame du Deffand was glad to receive Walpole as a distinguished and agreeable addition to her depleted circle. Here was a man whose conversational powers were comparable to her own, who could meet her wit and irony on equal terms. But behind her practised cynicism, behind her blistering savagery of speech, had always lain a craving for friendship and affection; and presently she began to realize that in Walpole she could find these infrequent attributes. The strongest sympathy and liking began to grow up between them. They had both been lately betrayed by trusted friends; they were lonely, they were out of harmony with the age, in general attitude and outlook they were in singular agreement. She was delighted by Walpole's originality, his freedom of taste and opinion, above all by his essential kindliness. He was unique in her experience: she had never known anybody in the least like him. "Ce n'est point flatterie, c'est que l'esprit, les talents, et l'extrême bonté ne se sont jamais trouvés réunis qu'en vous."[16] On his side, he looked upon her with fascination as the embodiment and chronicle of one of the most remarkable passages in the history of France. In her epigrams he caught the accents of a more agreeable age; and his heart warmed to her as she talked, indomitable amidst her dull and ageing friends, of the Regent and his radiant court.[17] More than ever he was growing to love the past. "I almost think there is no wisdom comparable to that of exchanging what is called the realities of life for dreams. Old castles, old pictures, old histories, and the babble of old people, make one

[15] *Ibid.*, 393, 408 (Walpole to Lady Hervey, January 11; to Gray, January 25, 1766).

[16] *Lewis*, iii. 22 (Mme du Deffand to Walpole, April 30, 1766).

[17] *Ibid.*, xxx. 204 (Walpole to Selwyn, December 2, 1765).

live back into centuries, that cannot disappoint one. One holds fast and surely what is past. The dead have exhausted their power of deceiving—one can trust Catherine of Medicis now."[18]

Twice a week, and soon more frequently, Walpole joined the circle in her drawing-room, where the fire glowed on the gold silk with flame-coloured knots, and on the escutcheon with Madame de Montespan's arms that shone above the chimney-piece. Madame de Mirepoix, the Maréchale de Luxembourg, the Président Hénault, Pont-de-Veyle, and other *habitués* would be there, and probably a few English visitors: Madame du Deffand herself occupied a great chair which she called her *tonneau,* her tub, from which she delivered cynicisms not unworthy of Diogenes. More and more she came to single out Walpole from the rest of the company: he was infinitely more amusing and agreeable than her ancient friends, more so even than the English youths, Lord Ossory and *le petit Craufurd.* She began to develop an affection for him which may have been partly maternal—after all she was married in the year after his birth, and at least once wrote to him as *vous dont je serais la mère*[19]—but which soon became adoring and possessive. For his own part, he was grateful for her admiration and confidence, which brought welcome solace to a badly shaken man. But before long he realized that her attitude was of a kind to which he could not conceivably respond. As he wrote to Craufurd, "I am not at all of Madame du Deffand's opinion, that one might as well be dead as not love somebody. I think one had better be dead than love anybody."[20] To his alarm and embarrassment he perceived that her affection for him, her sympathy, her maternal solicitude had suddenly flowered into this abhorrent passion of love.

III

Walpole's adoption into Madame du Deffand's circle did not prevent him from finding plenty of amusement elsewhere. He greatly enjoyed the company of her hated rival Madame Geoffrin; and his letters and journals are full of the names of people, par-

[18] *Ibid.,* x. 192 (Walpole to Montagu, January 5, 1766).

[19] *Ibid.,* vii. 214 (Madame du Deffand to Walpole, March 22, 1780).

[20] *Toynbee,* vi. 434 (Walpole to Craufurd, March 6, 1766).

ticularly women, whom he found entertaining and agreeable. It was impossible for him to suppress a note of triumph in his letters to Conway, who was treading a somewhat thorny political path in London. "It would sound vain to tell you the honours and distinctions I receive, and how much I am in fashion; yet when they come from the handsomest women in France, and the most respectable in point of character, can one help being a little proud? If I was twenty years younger, I should wish they were not quite so respectable."[21] His popularity was much enhanced by the success of a mild *jeu d'esprit,* a letter which he wrote to Rousseau in the name of the King of Prussia, and which eventually led to the celebrated and resounding quarrel between Rousseau and Hume.

Hume had been taken to Paris by Lord Hertford a few years before as his private secretary. Walpole had shared in the general surprise that his pious and conventional cousin should select for this post the infidel philosopher, whom he had never even seen; but Hume had proved so capable that he was later made secretary to the Embassy, and after Lord Hertford's departure had acted as *chargé d'affaires* until the new ambassador arrived. He achieved a great personal success in Paris, and there appears to have been a little veiled antagonism between him and Walpole when the latter first appeared on the scene.[22] Hume had no great opinion of Walpole as a historian, and Walpole was always inclined to ridicule Hume's social triumphs and his Tory politics: but their general relations were friendly enough.

At the end of 1765 Hume was about to return to England, and was going to escort the much-persecuted Rousseau to a refuge on our tolerant shores. Rousseau had been obliged to leave Switzerland after his quarrel with the inhabitants of Motiers; his wrongs had been proclaimed far and wide, and were the subject of endless discussion. One evening at Madame Geoffrin's it was mentioned that the King of Prussia had offered Rousseau an asylum

[21] *Ibid.,* 395 (Walpole to Conway, January 12, 1766).

[22] Hume said "he concluded I had been sent to assist and moderate the Duke of Richmond, and owned he wondered I had not talked to him on that head. I desired to be excused from knowing anything of the matter, and assured him, as is true, that I was come to France to avoid politics, not to get farther into them. I supposed he had been jealous of my coming, and was glad to satisfy him." *Lewis,* vii. 262 (Walpole's *Journal*).

in his dominions, and that the offer had been refused. Walpole thereupon wrote a short letter purporting to be the King's invitation to the philosopher, an amusing trifle with some effective hits at Rousseau's clamorous self-pity and his constant sense of imaginary wrongs. The letter concluded: "Si vous persistez à vous creuser l'esprit pour trouver de nouveaux malheurs, choisissez-les tels que vous voudrez. Je suis roi, je puis vous en procurer au gré de vos souhaits: et ce qui surement ne vous arrivera pas vis-à vis de vos ennemis, je cesserai de vous persecuter quand vous cesserez de mettre votre gloire à l'être.

"Votre bon ami
"FREDERIC."

The woes of Jean-Jacques were not a kind to command much pity from Walpole. He could of course know nothing of the psychological bases of Rousseau's mania; he saw his life-story as one long series of supposed persecutions, unfounded grievances, and shameless ingratitude to a variety of benefactors. He showed the letter to a few people, to Helvétius and Diderot, and to the du Deffand circle: but out of respect to Hume he would not allow it to be more widely circulated until the two philosophers had left for England. Hume carried with him a letter from Walpole to Lady Hervey, which expressed a hope that he "may not repent having engaged with [Rousseau], who contradicts and quarrels with all mankind, in order to obtain their admiration."[23] Walpole could hardly foresee that his pretended letter from Frederick, which was nothing more than a piece of mild chaff, would be the means of bringing about the breach between Rousseau and Hume which he so clearly anticipated.

The letter was handed about and copied, and brought Walpole very much into the public eye. Some of Rousseau's partisans, amongst them the Prince de Conti and Madame de Boufflers, who had protected Rousseau in Paris before he set out for London, were highly indignant: but most people were highly amused. Before long the letter was copied into an English newspaper. Rousseau saw it, and the wildest suspicions blazed up in his mind. He leapt to the conclusion that Hume, Voltaire and d'Alembert had formed a conspiracy against him, and that the letter was the

[23] *Ibid.*, xxxi. 92 (Walpole to Lady Hervey, January 2, 1766).

composition of d'Alembert with the connivance of the other two. He wrote pages of frenzied denunciation to Hume, who had treated him with the greatest confidence and kindness; and who at the time was actually engaged in obtaining through Conway, with Walpole's assistance, a pension for him from the King of a hundred pounds a year. The affair ended in a complete breach between Rousseau and his benefactor. Hume took Rousseau's accusations very seriously; and at the instigation of d'Alembert and others in Paris, though strongly against Walpole's advice, he insisted on publishing an account of the whole affair. The English newspapers, which had already derived much welcome copy from Rousseau's eccentricities of appearance and conduct, were full of the controversy; and several pamphleteers joined in the fray. Walpole was himself attacked by literary busybodies on both sides of the Channel—amongst others, by Boswell in England and by Fréron in France; and finally he also thought it necessary to draw up a statement of his part in the controversy.[24] In short, his very harmless *jeu d'esprit* resulted in considerable annoyance to himself, and in a noisy and much-publicized *imbroglio* between the two most celebrated philosophers of the age.

IV

Walpole made no effort to associate with the many Englishmen who were in Paris during this winter. He saw a good deal of the new ambassador and his Duchess, and at Madame du Deffand's he became acquainted with Lord Ossory and John Craufurd, both of whom he afterwards knew well in England. But in general he avoided companies in which the English predominated; and an amusing description of one such party shows that he had some excuse for doing so. In a letter to George Selwyn he wrote. "The French amuse me, and the English you may swear divert me. Two nights ago I received an invitation to a ball at Lord Massareen's. As I have never visited him, for I keep as clear as possible of most of my countrymen whom I certainly did not come hither

[24] *A Narrative of what passed relative to the Quarrel of Mr. David Hume and Jean Jacques Rousseau, as far as Mr. Horace Walpole was concerned in it.* Printed, together with the letters between Walpole and Hume, in *Works*, iv. 249–69.

to know, I could not avoid going for an hour. I went at seven; found four or five English, no Lord Massareen; was told he was not up, at least was at his toilette. Gentlemen arrived, Ladies arrived, the Countesses of Berkeley and Fife &c. Still no Lord Massareen. I should tell you, that as we were in the height of the mourning for the Dauphin, the ball itself was very improper. However, some English swains came in coloured frocks, sattin wastecoats and breeches, and huge nosegays with bunches of ribbands. As to their flocks, they would have perished with cold, for the chimnies in that dirty *hôtel garni* smoaked so much, that to save our eyes, we were forced to put out the fires and open the windows. However, to display to the French valets our victorious constitutions, both ball and cards began, tho half the candles were blown out, and the fingers of the violins so frozen, that they missed every other note. In short, my athletic part of the British Constitution bore it for an hour, and then I came away, before Adonis himself made his appearance."[25]

During an attack of gout he was twice visited by Wilkes, with whom he was now on terms of politeness. Wilkes was very civil, he told Montagu, but far from entertaining: "his conversation shows how little he has lived in good company, and the chief turn of it is the grossest bawdy."[26] An even less acceptable visitor was James Boswell, now returning to England after his grand tour and his famous visit to Paoli in Corsica. He insisted on becoming acquainted with Walpole, in spite of a rather chilling response.[27] The visit which he eventually paid is recorded in his *Journal*.[28] Walpole, "a lean genteel man," asked about Paoli and gave his recollections of that other Corsican potentate, King Theodore; suggested that Boswell should write something about Paoli, and was told that he fully intended to do so; and referred to Rousseau

[25] *Lewis,* xxx. 211 (Walpole to Selwyn, January 12, 1766).

[26] *Ibid.,* x. 180 (Walpole to Montagu, October 16, 1765).

[27] A note of unenthusiastic courtesy is printed in *Boswell Papers,* vii. 61. Walpole tells Boswell that he "...shall be very glad of the honour of his acquaintance, and will endeavour to find him at home or hopes to meet him: Is very sorry it has not happened but as Mr. Walpole, from conforming to the French hours while he is here, and living much with the people, rises very late, and is seldom at home afterwards till very late too. He has been so unlucky as not to see Mr. Boswell...."

[28] *Boswell Papers,* vii. 60–1.

as "a Mountebank with great parts." Perhaps this nettled Boswell, who had paid an emotional visit to Rousseau in his Swiss retirement in the previous year, and was just preparing to escort Thérèse Levasseur to rejoin him in England. Anyhow, in the controversy which presently ensued he thought fit to forget Walpole's polite reception, and to attack him in the public press.

By far the most agreeable of the Englishmen whom Walpole saw in Paris was the Rev. William Cole. For ever hankering after a monastic life, Cole had seriously considered giving up his parish and spending the rest of his days in studious and frugal retirement, perhaps in association with a religious house, in "some agreeable Retreat, either in Flanders, Artois, or Normandy, where I thought I could with Comfort and Satisfaction finish my earthly Pilgrimage."[29] Walpole had tried to discourage this project by reminding him of the *droit d'aubaine,* by which the possessions of foreigners dying in France became the property of the French king: and when Cole thought of such a fate befalling the precious antiquarian collections which he had spent his life in compiling, his desire to live abroad began to fade. His visit to France was therefore mainly a holiday undertaken from curiosity and antiquarian zeal; and the "general Spirit of Infidelity and Scepticism so prevalent thro'out France," which he encountered almost from the moment of his arrival, finally dissuaded him from settling in that unhappy country.

Cole reached Paris at the end of October 1765, to find Walpole gradually recovering from a sharp attack of gout. The strangely assorted pair had intended to explore together the ancient monuments of Paris; but Walpole's health prevented him from sharing the prolonged inspections of damp churches and mouldering convents in which Cole indulged. They frequently dined and drove about together, and Cole's *Journal of my Journey to Paris* contains some most amusing glimpses of Walpole and his circle. He watched Walpole's extravagant purchases of china, was taken by him to Saint-Denis, and gazed with him at the house where Madame de Sévigné used to live. He describes his celebrated friend's lodgings at the Hotel du Parc Royal in the Rue du Colombier, and records that he paid fourteen guineas a month

[29] *Cole,* i.

for them. In one of his characteristic digressions he tells us how unjust it was that Walpole should have the gout in "one of the most puny, thin, delicate and meagre Constitutions and Frame of Body this Day in England," especially in view of his extreme temperance in food and drink. His unflagging pen delineates the remarkable men and women whom he met in Walpole's company. D'Holbach appears, and Madame Geoffrin, entertaining and agreeable, though negligently dressed and without any stays. Wilkes is announced, and Cole is all eagerness to see the infamous figure: but the servant has made a highly unflattering mistake, and the visitor turns out to be Lord Ossory.[30] But the most remarkable occasion, in Cole's opinion, was an evening when the conversation turned upon Rousseau, with the Chevalier de Lorenzi ardently upholding the libertine philosopher, and the Chevalier de Dromgold hardly able to mention his name with patience. In a long and warm dispute, Walpole entered the fray in support of Dromgold. "I was not a little pleased to hear my friend argue so warmly in Defense of Religion," Cole recorded: adding, a little wistfully, "and should have been completely so, had it proceeded, as in Mr. Drumgold's Case, who was a zealous Catholic and Christian, from a Conviction of the Truth of Revelation, than merely from Political Consideration."[31]

V

With the coming of spring, Walpole's sojourn in Paris drew to an end. It had been a period of extraordinary enjoyment and success: but "the civilities, the kindnesses, the honours I receive" could not detain him for ever, and the vernal beauty of Strawberry Hill was awaiting his return. He had made numbers of new friends, had passed through a variety of interesting experiences, and had satiated himself with sightseeing and conversation and the purchase of exquisite objects of *virtù*. His self-confidence was fully restored: Paris had put things into their right perspective, and had shown him that English party politics, and even the ingratitude of his dearest friend, were not preoccupations to be brooded upon to the exclusion of all enjoyment in life. Above all, he had come to realize that the world still holds pleasures and

[30] *Ibid.*, 53, 56, 82, 92.

[31] *Ibid.*, 62–70.

consolations for a man who was soon to enter on his fiftieth year, and who had lately been reminded of the fact by savage and persistent attacks of gout. In an unpublished letter to Selwyn, written a few days before his departure for England, he summed up the general effect of his months in Paris, and dwelt with particular gratitude on the congeniality of the French way of life to people of his increasing years in infirmities. "I leave Paris, I own, with regret: it is a paradise for age and wrinkles. One is never too old for a sort of society, nor neglected because one totters. Madame du Deffand has proposed to me to take an apartment in the convent where she lodges, and it tempts me for next winter, as she is much better company than Sir John Cust [the Speaker]. I played at cavagnol there two nights ago with the survivors of the last century; the youngest was Madame de Segur, a natural daughter of the Regent, who can be no chicken, and I did not once wish myself at a debate on the Stamp-act. An old woman that cheats at berlan is to me as respectable a personage as a patriot that cheats at eloquence; and if Livy had been a matron and writ the memories of the Roman dowagers that played at par and impar, as well as he has done the history of consuls and tribunes, I had as lief read them."[32]

Madame du Deffand, surrounded by her septuagenarian circle, would have justifiably ridiculed Walpole's lamenations about his age and wrinkles. In that society he figured as a youth; in her own estimation he was a brilliant and attractive boy; and as such she wished to address him, to his extreme discomfort, in the correspondence on which they proposed to embark as soon as they were parted. It is doubtful whether Walpole realized, until her letters began to arrive, the overwhelming violence of her devotion to him; but he was certainly aware that she loved him in a pathetic and embarrassing fashion; and before he left for England he insisted that she should confine her expressions of affection within limits which he regarded as suitable. Her first surviving letter to him, a touching note written before he set out from Paris, mentions "ce mot que vous m'avez interdit."[33] The forbidden word was *l'amour*. He wrote from Amiens to remind her of her promises of discretion. His letter has not been preserved;

[32] *Lewis,* xxx (Walpole to Selwyn, April 3, 1766).

[33] *Ibid.,* iii. 1 (Madame du Deffand to Walpole, April 16, 1766).

but it is evident from her exasperated reply that he adopted the mortifyingly superior tone which she came to know so well. "Si vous étiez français," she wrote, "je ne balancerais pas à vous croire un grand fat; vous êtes anglais, vous n'êtes donc qu'un grand fou. Où prenez-vous, je vous prie, que *je suis livrée à des indiscrétions et des emportements romanesques*? Des *indiscrétions,* encore passe: à toute force cela se peut dire; mais pour des *emportements romanesques,* cela me met en fureur, et je vous arracherais volontiers ces yeux qu'on dit être si beaux, mais qu'assurément vous ne pouvez pas soupçonner de m'avoir tourné la tête."[34] From these inauspicious beginnings developed a correspondence which lasted until her death fourteen years later, a weekly interchange of wit, adulation, embarrassment and upbraiding which finally extended to more than eight hundred letters on either side.

Walpole has been almost universally condemned for his conduct towards Madame du Deffand. He has been blamed for his caution and his fear of ridicule; he has been accused of consistent unkindness and heartlessness. In a protracted affair in which his heart was untouched, and which placed him in an almost unique position of embarrassment and absurdity, it would have been surprising if he did not occasionally display irritation and even resentment. He was anxious to show his old friend all possible kindness and sympathy: but, bewildered as he was by the violence of her passion, what more could he do? Her affection was of a type to which he could make no adequate response. He fulfilled a need in her life; he was a belated consolation for the loneliness, the boredom, the blindness, the frustration of so many years. But in his life she filled no corresponding need. It was this essential inequality that intensified her demands, drove Walpole into clumsiness and impatience, and turned their friendship into a prolonged and nerve-racking tragedy.

Walpole might indeed have been more kind in his responses. He might at least have flattered her with such easy gallantries as he bestowed on Lady Mary Coke and Miss Anne Pitt. But admiration for these ladies, however insincere at heart, was conventionally possible; while flowery devotion in response to the passionate overtures of a blind old woman, even though she was

[34] *Ibid.,* 7 (Madame du Deffand to Walpole, April 21, 1766).

the wittiest woman in France, was, in the eyes of the world, ridiculous. Walpole was perfectly frank to Madame du Deffand about his fear of ridicule; and it was quite well-founded. Their relationship was so abnormal as to be an obvious subject for mockery. Common prudence, and not an ignoble timidity, dictated the precautions which she found so irksome. He knew how her attachment could be handled by the virulent English press; and how his letters, in their unidiomatic French, might be passed round the drawing-rooms of Paris. The *cabinet noir* was known to open and copy correspondence passing between the two countries; and letters so copied might eventually pass into more general circulation. Madame du Deffand, always contemptuous of Walpole's fear of ridicule, was particularly scornful about his apprehensions of the *cabinet noir;* but his suspicions on this score were justified, and copies of fourteen of his letters, or of portions of them, taken by that efficient department of the secret service, survive to-day among the archives of France. Almost all the rest of his letters to Madame du Deffand are lost to us. At first he used to demand their return at intervals, just as he was accustomed to do with his letters to Mann; later he asked Madame du Deffand to destroy them; and after her death he was careful to secure the few that remained. Miss Berry printed some rather meagre extracts from them in the selection of Madame du Deffand's letters to Walpole which she published in 1810: later, acting presumably on Walpole's private instructions, she destroyed them all.

The rigidity of the sanctions imposed by Walpole on Madame du Deffand's phrasing of her letters has undoubtedly robbed them of much of their spontaneity and charm. They fall, in consequence, into a set formula, a pattern which Mr. W. S. Lewis has admirably compared to that of a "wall-paper composed of three or four figures which, looked at as a whole, gives the effect of variety, but examined in detail proves to be decorated with only the three or four figures." Mr. Lewis simplifies the pattern thus: "(1) affectionate statement, mingled with self-analysis, (2) bewildered and angry defence of herself, (3) impersonal recital of the "proper names" demanded by Walpole."[35] The "proper names" are the social chronicles that Walpole was always eager

[35] *Ibid.*, xxxi–ii.

to hear; and their recital was usually followed by a recurrence to the first theme, the tentative expressions of affection and the self-analysis that accompanied them. When these expressions seemed to Walpole to be excessive, he rebuked her, often impatiently, sometimes cruelly. She usually received his remonstrances meekly enough; he was *mon tuteur, mon gouverneur,* she was *votre pupille;* she must submit to his will. Now and then she was moved to a pathetic or an indignant protest, or to some despairing reflection on the tragedy of all human relations. "Ah, mon Dieu! que vous avez bien raison! l'abominable, la détestable chose que l'amitié! Par où vient-elle? à quoi mène-t-elle? sur quoi est-elle fondée? quel bien en peut-on attendre ou espérer? Ce que vous m'avez dit est vrai, mais pourquoi sommes-nous sur terre, et surtout pourquoi vieillit-on? Oh, mon tuteur, pardonnez-le-moi, je déteste la vie."[36]

It is odd that these letters, with all their varied burden of affection, of irritation and of remonstrance, had to pass through the medium of Wiart, Madame du Deffand's secretary, to whom she dictated her letters to Walpole and who read Walpole's letters to her. Wiart was the most faithful and devoted of servants: but the two friends could only enjoy unreserved freedom of intercourse when Walpole himself came to Paris. He visited Paris on four subsequent occasions, in 1767, 1769, 1771 and 1775, almost solely for the purpose of seeing her; a proposed visit in 1777 was prevented by the war; and after her death in 1780 he never crossed the Channel again. However impatient his letters might occasionally sound, he never failed in these visits; and in the long evenings of boredom and melancholy she could at least look forward to the time when the well-loved voice would next be pouring out those voluble and ill-accented syllables, 'Ah! po-int du tout, c'est tout au con-traire," beside her great arm-chair by the fireside in the Convent of Saint Joseph.[37]

VI

Walpole arrived back in London on April 22, 1766, and found himself plunged into politics immediately on his return. He had

[36] *Ibid.,* 156 (Madame du Deffand to Walpole, October 20, 1766).
[37] *Ibid.,* 375 (Madame du Deffand to Walpole, November 11, 1767).

forsworn politics; but his indignation against Conway, the main cause of that renunciation, had cooled during the last few months. Conway, as Secretary of State, had become Mann's official superior; and at Walpole's request he had arranged the promotion of Mann, who had hitherto been Resident at Florence, to the rank of Envoy. Walpole, wintering in Paris against Conway's will, had been doubtful whether he retained sufficient influence with his cousin to ensure Mann's promotion; and his letters to Mann are full of anxiety on this head.[38] But all was well in the end, and Conway announced to Mann his increase of rank in a private letter, "in which he makes the most affectionate mention of you. . . pray help me to make Mr. Conway sensible of my gratitude to him for so signal a proof of his friendship both to you and me."[39] Walpole was much cheered by this demonstration that his influence with Conway had not entirely collapsed; and when, on returning to England, he found his advice anxiously sought by a much-perplexed Secretary of State, the temptation to interpose in politics once more proved irresistible. Although he never again felt the old affection for Conway, and although he kept, so far as one can see, his resolution "never to give him decisive advice, when it might lead him to a precipice," he gladly resumed the *rôle* of political mentor to his cousin.

He found the Rockingham Ministry on the verge of collapse. The Duke of Grafton, Conway's fellow Secretary of State, was determined to resign unless Rockingham was replaced by Pitt: and Pitt now appeared willing to leave his retirement and return to the head of affairs. Conway himself was weary of his office, the duties of which he fulfilled with extreme conscientiousness; and he was uncertain how to act in the negotiations that lay ahead. Accustomed as he was to rely on Walpole's advice, he welcomed his return as though no coolness had ever arisen between them; indeed, it is quite possible that he was never aware of Walpole's resentment in the previous year. Now once more he had that quick intelligence, that experience and foresight, to direct his course and steady his vacillations.

[38] *Ibid.*, xxii. 347–8, 358–60 (Walpole to Mann, October 16 and November 2, 1765).

[39] *Ibid.*, 375–6 (Mann to Walpole, December 14, 1765).

Without any pronounced political aims, save the continued exclusion from office of Grenville and the Bedford faction, Walpole set himself to guide Conway in public life. When Rockingham fell and Pitt came into power, he persuaded Conway to accept Pitt's offer that he should remain in his former office. When friction arose between Conway and Pitt, and later when Pitt retired into mysterious seclusion and left his followers bewildered and leaderless, he still prevented Conway from resigning. He also became the political adviser of the Duke of Richmond, who had returned to England and had succeeded the Duke of Grafton as Secretary of State during the dying struggles of the Rockingham Ministry. Although he had not spoken in the House for many years, he now became something of a power behind the scenes, a figure of accepted importance in the ever-fluctuating political world.[40] Conway and Richmond were known to be directed by him. Pitt consulted him about the state of politics in France, and astounded him by asking him to move the Address.[41] The King, when anxious to prevent Conway from resigning, sent messages through Lord Hertford to urge Mr. Walpole to persevere to this end.[42] But Walpole, in what he described as "this favourable shining hour," followed a policy of complete personal disinterestedness. He might have obtained from the King at this juncture the assurance of the regular payment of his Exchequer salary: but he tells us that he would not ask it.[43] And when Mann aspired to the red ribbon of a Knight of the Bath—he had received a baronetcy some years previously—Walpole refused, kindly but firmly, to exert his influence any further on his behalf.[44]

[40] The Duke of Grafton emphasized this in a passage of his autobiography. "There was no one from whom I received so just accounts of the schemes of the various factions...than from Mr. Horace Walpole, who since became Earl of Orford. His friendship, and attachment to Mr. Conway had been constant, and he was well known; and his zealous desire that we two should be more closely united, urged him to sift out the designs of those who were counter-acting his active endeavours: and no person had so good means of getting the knowledge of what was passing, as himself." (*Grafton*, 140–1.)

[41] *Toynbee*, vii. 52 (Walpole to Conway, October 18, 1766).

[42] *Memoirs of George III*, ii. 287; iii. 54, 63.

[43] *Ibid.*, iii. 58.

[44] *Lewis*, xxii. 478–80 (Walpole to Mann, January 21, 1767). Mann received the coveted honour in 1768.

Perhaps the greatest triumph of Walpole's brief spell of political influence was attained when Lord Holland begged him "in the most flattering terms" to use his influence with the Duke of Grafton to obtain him an earldom. Walpole had for some years been on the old terms of friendship with Holland; but he could not quite forget Holland's treatment of him in 1763, and it was with a gratifying sense of his own magnanimity that he made the desired application to Grafton.[45] Towards the end of 1767, however, his efforts to bolster up Conway finally collapsed, and his political influence waned once more. Grafton, who for practical purposes had by now supplanted Chatham in the conduct of affairs, wished to strengthen his government by the inclusion of the Bedford faction; and the Bedfords practically made it a condition that Conway should resign the seals of Secretary of State. Conway, to Walpole's bitter disappointment, gave way; he was weary of office, and wanted to serve the country in some military capacity once again. He resigned in January 1768, and in the revised Cabinet accepted the office of Lieutenant-General of the Ordnance.[46]

Walpole deeply regretted Conway's resignation, and particularly resented that it should have been brought about by the detested Bedford group. To see his friend elbowed out of office by Sandwich and Rigby was almost more than he could bear. But it gave him an opportunity for his own final withdrawal from active politics, a step which he had contemplated for several years and had only postponed for Conway's sake. Already, in March 1767, he had told the Mayor of King's Lynn, in a dignified and courteous letter, that he did not propose to stand again for the borough at the next election, owing to the state of his health and his desire to withdraw from all public business.[47] A year later, when the country was in the turmoil of a general election, he was able to remain quietly in Arlington Street, writing to Montagu that "the comfort I feel in sitting peaceably here, instead of being at Lynn in the high fever of a contested

[45] *Memoirs of George III,* iii. 68–9. The King refused to grant Holland the earldom he desired.

[46] *Ibid.,* 89–91, 106. *Grafton,* 172.

[47] *Toynbee,* vii. 92–4 (Walpole to William Langley, Mayor of King's Lynn, March 13, 1767).

election, which at best would end in my being carried about that large town like the figure of a pope at a bonfire, is very great."[48]

He never regretted his retirement from Parliament. But he retained his interest in current politics, and still liked to be consulted and to do a little unobtrusive wire-pulling when he had an opportunity. Conway withdrew from the Cabinet when the Duke of Grafton was succeeded in office by Lord North; but he remained in Parliament, and continued to rely on Walpole's advice on most occasions. Walpole did not set foot in the House of Commons, after he had resigned his seat, until 1772, when curiosity led him to go and listen to a speech by that youthful prodigy, Charles Fox;[49] but he carried on his political memoirs, with gradually diminishing enthusiasm, until 1783. The later memoirs, and especially the *Last Journals,* are naturally less vivid and amusing, since he was no longer present at the speeches and debates which he was recording; such passages as his wonderful description of Charles Townshend's "champagne speech" were no longer possible.[50] But when, occasionally, political events affected his intimate friends, or he himself became momentarily an actor in them, the old fire returned. A very large part of the *Last Journals* is occupied with a narrative of the marriage of his niece, Lady Waldegrave, with the Duke of Gloucester, the King's brother, and an elaborate recital of his own conduct in this delicate situation. When there was trouble about a seat for Conway in Parliament, and Walpole thought that Lord Hertford was not doing his best for his brother, intense feeling is displayed—"on the stairs I trembled so with passion that I had like to have fallen from the top to the bottom."[51] And the same spirit and indignation flash out in the narrative of Burke's surprising attempt to obtain from Sir Edward Walpole, for his own benefit, the lucrative sinecure of the Clerkship of the Pells. "Can one but smile at a reformer of abuses reserving the second greatest abuse for himself."[52]

[48] *Lewis,* x. 254 (Walpole to Montagu, March 12, 1768).
[49] *Last Journals,* i. 80.
[50] *Memoirs of George III,* iii. 17–9.
[51] *Last Journals,* i. 388–96.
[52] *Ibid.,* ii. 453–6.

VII

On Christmas Day 1766 Walpole began a five-act tragedy, *The Mysterious Mother.* This work was presently laid aside, and was not finished until March 15, 1768. Its composition was interrupted because Walpole had embarked on another book, *Historic Doubts on the Life and Reign of King Richard the Third,* on which he worked at intervals throughout 1767 and which he published on February 1, 1768.[53]

It had occurred to Walpole, some years before, that Richard III had been unjustly treated by historians. "Many of the crimes imputed to Richard seemed improbable; and, what was stronger, contrary to his interest...and as it was easy to perceive, under all the glare of encomiums which historians have heaped on the wisdom of Henry VII, that he was a mean and unfeeling tyrant, I suspected that they had blackened his rival, till Henry, by the contrast, should appear in a kind of amiable light."[54] His scepticism about the murder of the little princes, Richard's nephews, was strengthened by certain entries in the Coronation Roll of the King, "an original and important instrument" hitherto unknown to historians, whose existence was pointed out to him by his old schoolfellow Charles Lyttelton, now Bishop of Carlisle and President of the Society of Antiquaries.[55] With his preconceptions fortified by this document, Walpole undertook the complete rehabilitation of Richard III. In *Historic Doubts* he proved, to his own satisfaction, that Richard was innocent of the murders of Henry VI and his son Prince Edward, of the Duke of Clarence, of the two young Princes, and of his own Queen: that the younger of the two Princes was almost certainly the youth who was later executed as an impostor under the name of Perkin Warbeck: that Richard's personal deformity had been grossly exaggerated: and in general that the grisly tyrant and usurper, enthroned in popular tradition and immortalized by Shakespeare, was a creation of Tudor propaganda, of 'mob-stories or Lancastrian forgeries."

[53] *Lewis,* xiii. 43 *(Short Notes of my Life).*
[54] *Works,* ii. 109 (Preface to *Historic Doubts*).
[55] *Ibid.,* 141, 146 n.

A modern historian would at least give Richard the benefit of the doubt on several of the charges against which Walpole defended him. Whether he would do so on the strength of Walpole's arguments is more doubtful. *Historic Doubts* was an original and spirited piece of special pleading, but its theories were based on inadequate material, and were often supported by decidedly flimsy reasoning. Walpole had undoubtedly devoted much deep thought and industrious research to the book; it was nevertheless marked with the same disdainful amateurishness that had drawn upon his earlier works the criticism of his more pedantic contemporaries. "If I do not flatter myself, I have unravelled a considerable part of that dark period," he wrote in the preface. "Whether satisfactorily or not, my readers must decide. Nor is it of any importance whether I have or not. The attempt was mere matter of curiosity and speculation. If any man, as idle as myself, should take the trouble to review and canvass my arguments, I am ready to yield so indifferent a point to better reasons. . . ."[56]

The book, which he did not print at Strawberry Hill, was an immediate success: it was an invitation to the pleasures of argument and controversy, and a second edition was called for at once. Selwyn, to his own surprise, was convinced by its arguments; Gray, a more expert judge, warmly commended it, but was unconvinced on several points and distressed by various crudities of style.[57] The most general reaction was probably that expressed by Lord Carlisle: "The Emperor Nero's character wants a little white-washing, and so does Mrs. Brownrigg's, who was hanged for murdering her apprentices the other day. I hope he will undertake them next, as they seem, next to his hero, to want it the most."[58] Rejoinders soon appeared in the magazines. William Guthrie, Walpole's opponent in the Conway controversy, attacked the book at some length in the *Critical Review*. Another adversary took the field in the *London Chronicle*. A lawyer named Guydickens published an *Answer to Mr. Horace Walpole's late Work. . . or an Attempt to Confute him from his own Arguments*, a production written in a highly obsequious

[56] *Works*, ii. 110 (Preface to *Historic Doubts*).
[57] *Gray*, iii. 1006–7 (Gray to Walpole, February 14, 1768).
[58] *Jesse*, ii. 286 (Lord Carlisle to Selwyn, March 5, 1768).

strain and enlivened by indifferent jokes, which nevertheless reveals how effectively a trained legal mind could combat some of Walpole's gossamer arguments.[59] Walpole for the present ignored these critics. In the following year he received from Gibbon's Swiss friend, Deyverdun, a copy of his critical journal *Mémoires Littéraires de la Grande Bretagne,* containing an unsigned review of *Historic Doubts.* The review was written by Gibbon himself,[60] who courteously hinted that Walpole's arguments were over-ingenious, and dazzled the reader without convincing him. At the end were printed some observations specially communicated by Hume, in which Walpole's conclusions about the fate of the little princes were disputed. Of all the crimes imputed to Richard, there is least doubt of his direct responsibility for the death of these children: but their murder was also the very crime of which Walpole thought he had most convincingly acquitted him. Walpole had already discussed with Hume the points raised in these notes, and did not expect to have them publicly urged against him in this fashion. He therefore wrote a lengthy defence of his book, analysing Hume's notes point by point, and taking the opportunity of replying to the other writers who had attacked him. He showed Hume the manuscript of this spirited and able defence of his views: but he felt that, though he had treated his opponent with "the severity he deserved," it would be better not to print his rejoinder, and it was not published until after his own death.[61]

The historians had taken particular exception to the flimsiness of Walpole's arguments and the weakness of his deductions; the antiquarians were just as pained by his carelessness over minor details and matters of fact. In 1770 the Society of Antiquaries began to publish an annual volume of papers contributed by its

[59] Walpole thought at first that this work, signed "F.W.G. of the Middle Temple," was also the work of Guthrie. It is a substantial quarto pamphlet, designed by its publishers to be bound up with Walpole's book: and the two are often found so bound.

[60] It is printed in Gibbon's *Miscellaneous Works* (1815), iii. 156–67. It does not appear that Walpole ever knew that Gibbon, and not Deyverdun, was the author.

[61] *Lewis,* xiii. 44–5 *(Short Notes of my Life).* It was printed in *Works,* ii. 185–220.

members: and both the first and the second of these imposing quarto volumes contained confutations of *Historic Doubts.* These attacks were peculiarly irritating to Walpole. They appeared in the official records of a Society of which he was an honoured member, accustomed to be treated with considerable deference; and they were written, not in the tone of courtesy adopted by men of the polite world such as Hume and Gibbon, but with the habitual peevishness of the provincial antiquary. It was an additional source of grievance that the first of these papers was the work of the President of the Society, Dr. Jeremiah Milles, Dean of Exeter, who had succeeded to the presidential chair after the death of Bishop Lyttelton in 1768. The second paper was written by the Rev. Robert Masters, a Cambridgeshire parson and an associate, though by no means a friend, of William Cole.[62] Dr. Milles confined his observations to the document which Walpole had described as Richard's Coronation Roll, and on which he had optimistically based much of his belief in the King's innocence of the death of the young princes. The Dean restored this so-called Roll to its proper significance as a volume of Wardrobe Accounts not exclusively associated with Richard's coronation, and demolished effectively the conclusions that Walpole had derived from it. Mr. Masters attacked *Historic Doubts* on a wider front, and was extremely offensive about Walpole's "boasted discoveries" and the small conviction they would bring to any one "who does not wilfully shut his eyes, and prefer ridiculous tradition to true history."[63]

Walpole composed rejoinders to both these papers, but did not publish them.[64] Although he had not attended the meetings of the Society for some years, and was now determined to resign, he did not wish to appear to have been driven out by the triumphant pen of Dr. Milles. His opportunity came when the Society decided to investigate the history of Dick Whittington and his cat, and Foote introduced their discussions on this important theme into one of his farces. He then informed the secretary

[62] Dr. Milles's paper was printed in *Archæologia,* i. 361–83, and Masters' in ii. 198–215.

[63] *Archæologia,* ii. 215.

[64] They are printed in *Works,* ii. 221–51. Walpole also printed six copies of the *Letter to Dr. Milles* at Strawberry Hill.

that he felt obliged to withdraw from a learned body which had allowed itself to become the subject of public ridicule.[65]

VIII

Walpole's other original work of these years was his tragedy, *The Mysterious Mother*. As we have already seen, this play was written at intervals over some fifteen months, during which time he was occupied with politics, amusement, *virtù*, a visit to Paris, and the preparation and writing of *Historic Doubts*. Yet it bears no sign of its dilatory composition. A nightmare of violent emotion and protracted suspense, it might have been thrown off at fever-heat as was *The Castle of Otranto*. Tense, powerful and authentic, this extraordinary drama of incestuous passion is unlike anything else that Walpole wrote, and unlike anything else written in his century.

The theme of *The Mysterious Mother* was suggested to Walpole by a story he had heard in his youth, of a gentlewoman who came to Archbishop Tillotson "under uncommon agonies of mind" and made a confession of matchless horror. She had secretly taken the place of a maid-servant with whom her son had arranged an assignation, and had borne him a daughter: and her son had subsequently fallen in love with this girl and married her, unaware that she was both his daughter and his sister. "The prelate charged her never to let her son and daughter know what had passed, as they were innocent of any criminal intention. For herself, he bade her almost despair."[66]

It is difficult to explain why, apart from its obvious dramatic qualities, this repulsive story should have held so much interest for Walpole. A psycho-analyst might perhaps connect his attraction to the theme of incest with his youthful devotion to his own mother, which exerted so profound an influence on his life. A subconscious urge of this sort would certainly explain both his choice of a theme and the intense feeling with which the theme was handled. Be that as it may, Walpole determined to dramatize the situation, in spite of its obvious unsuitability for

[65] *Lewis*, xiii. 47 *(Short Notes of my Life)*. *Works*, ii. 251 and n. The farce in which Foote ridiculed the Society of Antiquaries was *The Nabob*.

[66] *Works*, i. 125–6 (postscript to *The Mysterious Mother*).

exhibition on the polite stage of the eighteenth century. He transferred Archbishop Tillotson's despairing penitent and her unhappy children to a period shortly before the Reformation, and laid the scene at Narbonne. The guilty mother, the Countess of Narbonne, has exiled her son Edmund to the wars, while bringing up Adeliza, her daughter by him, "fruit of that monstrous night," as her ward. Edmund returns home, unheralded and disguised, and falls in love with Adeliza. Meanwhile Benedict, the Countess's sinister and malignant confessor, professes to have detected heretical leanings in his penitent: and these tendencies, combined with her obstinate refusal to reveal the source of her life-long anguish, determine him to destroy her. She recognizes Edmund as her son, and her horror at his presence causes the friar to suspect the nature of her secret. With devilish malice he urges Edmund and Adeliza to marry immediately, and joins their hands himself. The Countess, distracted by the news of the marriage of her children, reveals the whole hideous secret, and finally stabs herself. Adeliza retires to a nunnery: Edmund returns to the wars—

> "to th' embattled foe I will present
> This hated form—and welcome be the sabre
> That leaves no atom of it undefac'd!"

This playbill summary can give no idea of the skill with which Walpole constructed his play. The dramatic unities are most carefully observed: the final revelation and catastrophe are postponed, through gradually mounting suspicion and tension, until the last scene of all, and in the meantime he has "bestowed every ornament of sense, unbigoted piety, and interesting contrition, on the character that was at last to raise universal indignation."[67] The figure of the Countess, vainly trying to expiate her guilt in a life of charity and mortification, is movingly drawn; and her submissive penitence is in powerful contrast to the odious activities of Benedict, into whose character Walpole poured his wholehearted loathing of the bigotry and fraudulence which he so persistently attributed to the church of Rome. The sole digressions in this swiftly moving drama are the debates on superstition and belief which Edmund and his friend Florian conduct with

[67] *Ibid.*, 127 (postcript to *The Mysterious Mother*).

Benedict and Martin, the cunning and unscrupulous friars. The Countess and her confessor dominate the play; but the other characters, Edmund and Adeliza and Martin, are clear-cut and definite; and if the echoes of Shakespeare are occasionally a little too obvious, if Florian is a pale shade of Mercutio and the Porter gossips in the accents of Juliet's Nurse, the fault was a rare one in the eighteenth century. The extent of Walpole's knowledge and understanding of Shakespeare has never been fully realized. He read him incessantly: he had defended him publicly against the mockery of Voltaire, and privately against the incomprehension of Madame du Deffand. His blank verse, like his characterization, is filled with Shakespearian reminiscences: persistent echoes, often absurd, but sometimes striking the ear with an unexpected beauty.

Walpole had *The Mysterious Mother* printed at Strawberry Hill in 1768 in a severely limited edition of fifty copies. Some of his friends, including those fastidious critics Chute and Gray, approved of it; others, George Montagu among them, could not bear the subject;[68] and in general there was a feeling of surprise that Walpole should have chosen a theme odious in itself and quite impossible for presentation on the stage. Uncritical people allowed their emotions of horror and disgust to extend to the author. Fanny Burney, for example, was allowed to borrow the Queen's copy, and bore it away in high expectation; but a reading in mixed company proved unexpectedly embarrassing. "I felt a sort of indignant aversion rise fast and warm in my mind, against the wilful author of a story so horrible: all the entertainment and pleasure I had received from Mr. Walpole seemed extinguished by this lecture, which almost made me regard him as the patron of the vices he had been pleased to record."[69] To this verdict may well be opposed the striking tribute of Byron: "It is the fashion to under-rate Horace Walpole; firstly, because he was a nobleman, and secondly, because he was a gentleman; but, to say nothing of the composition of his incomparable letters, and of *The Castle of Otranto,* he is the "Ultimus Romanorum," the author of *The Mysterious Mother,* a tragedy of the highest order,

[68] *Lewis,* x. 259 (Walpole to Montagu, April 15, 1768).

[69] *D'Arblay,* iii. 234–6.

and not a puling love-play. He is the father of the first romance and of the last tragedy in our language, and surely worthy of a higher place than any living writer, be he who he may."[70]

IX

In 1767 and on three occasions afterwards, Walpole went to France, and spent a few weeks of the summer and autumn with Madame du Deffand and his other friends in Paris. Apart from this innovation, his life continued to pass much as it had done for many years before. The hours of inconspicuous but diligent attendance in Parliament were over: masquerades and dancing had given place to loo, and he had his recognized seat among the dowagers and elderly gentlemen round Princess Emily's card-table. But he still passed the same endless hours, both in London and at Twickenham, in visiting and conversation; still continued to load the walls of Strawberry Hill with pictures, the cabinets with *bibelots,* the shelves with prints and books; still went on his antiquarian tours all over England, and brought his wit and gaiety to the country-houses of his friends. The worry and unhappiness of 1765 had vanished. Lady Townshend's remark, "Mr. Walpole is spirits of hartshorn," was as true in 1770 as it had been twenty years before. Lady Mary Coke gives an amusing illustration of Walpole's irrepressible high spirits during a party at Conway's house, Park Place near Henley, where the presence of Princess Emily was shedding an air of constraint on the company. "Before we sat down to cards a set of Morris dancers, with a fool at their Head, appear'd upon the green before the windows, and danced exceedingly well. Mr. Walpole was so delighted that he began dancing about the room to the great surprise of the Princess, but She desired me to dance with him: not being able to obey her commands, She pulled me into the middle of the room and would have danced with me, if I had not begged H.R.H. to honour me with any other commands."[71]

In 1767 he lost his old friend Lady Suffolk: and Lady Hervey died in the following year. No longer could he pass evening after tranquil evening with one or other of these celebrated dowagers, listening to their stories of the forgotten courts where they had

[70] Preface to *Marino Faliero.* [71] Coke, iii. 249 (June 25, 1770).

shone in their brilliant youth. He paid what tribute he could to their memory, in an elegy for Lady Hervey's monument at Ickworth, and later, in his *Reminiscences,* to the goodness and charm of Lady Suffolk. Two more breaches in the circle of his friends soon followed—in 1770 his mysterious estrangement from George Montagu, and in 1771 the death of Gray.

The termination of Walpole's friendship with Montagu has never been explained. For thirty years he had showered upon him a constant stream of his liveliest, longest and most carefully polished letters. In his whimsical country retirement at Greatworth or Adderbury, amid the squires and the parsons and the port, Montagu had been the first reader of descriptions which are now pre-eminent in the social history of his time: the funeral of George II and the coronation of his grandson, Princess Emily at the card-table and at the unforgettable house-party at Stowe, Walpole himself brooding amid the vanished glories of Houghton, the gaiety and movement of a hundred fêtes and masquerades, the antiquities and curiosities of scores of cathedrals and mansions and ruined castles. Nor was Montagu unconscious of his good fortune. "Your letters are always agreeable and charming to me, and I should be all encrusted with rusticity did you not now and then polish me with an epistle."[72] "I have lost few of my old friends; many I have of thirty years standing, but there are none who I can more surely trust, and none of half the value, comfort, and delight to me in comparison of you."[73] If ever a friendship was well-established, rooted in congeniality and ancient habit, it was the friendship between Walpole and Montagu. Yet in the autumn of 1770 their interchange of letters ceased abruptly, inexplicably and completely. Montagu had somewhat emerged from his shell on the accession of his relative, Lord North, to power in this year: he had received a sinecure post from him, and was thinking of living in London. Walpole had shown political and personal courtesies to North, and on October 6 Montagu wrote to express his pleasure on this subject. "You cannot tell how thankful Lord North and Lord Guilford are for your kindness and noble dispositions towards them. I cannot remember half the obliging things Lord North has always said to me on the occasion

[72] *Lewis,* x. 81 (Montagu to Walpole, June 4, 1763).
[73] *Ibid.,* 164–5 (Montagu to Walpole, August 1, 1765).

whenever I have seen him, and it is the greatest pleasure imaginable to me that my oldest and best friend is so well with my new one."[74] Walpole, who was enduring an attack of gout, sent a brief but perfectly amiable reply a few days later.[75] Yet from this moment they appear to have had no further contact of any sort, although Montagu did finally settle in London, as his friend had been urging him to do for so many years past.

Ten years afterwards Montagu died, and Walpole mentioned his death in a letter to Cole. "I should have been exceedingly concerned for him a few years ago—but he had dropped me, partly from politics and partly from caprice, for we never had any quarrel—but he was grown an excessive humourist, and had shed almost all his friends as well as me. He had parts and infinite vivacity and originality till of late years—and it grieved me much that he had changed towards me after a friendship of between thirty and forty years."[76] Undoubtedly there are signs in Walpole's later letters of impatience with Montagu's "humours," his vagueness and irresolution, his habit of putting Walpole to endless trouble in choosing him a Thames-side house and then settling ever deeper into "Squireland." Undoubtedly his letters in return were often slapdash and perfunctory, though occasionally they break into coruscations of wit and gay absurdity. But there is nothing in the letters of either to suggest that an estrangement was at hand; and one can only regret that the friendship which produced so brilliant and delightful a correspondence should have finally petered out in this depressing way.

The glittering succession of Walpole's social chronicles was not seriously checked by this breach with their long-established recipient. He had corresponded for several years past with the Duchess of Grafton, who was now the Countess of Upper Ossory. His letters to her now became more elaborate and more frequent, until she had entirely replaced Montagu in the circle of his most favoured correspondents.

Anne Liddell, daughter of the first Lord Ravensworth, had married the Duke of Grafton in 1756. Walpole had always admired her, and was never weary of praising her beauty and

[74] *Ibid.*, 321 (Montagu to Walpole, October 6, 1770).

[75] *Ibid.*, 322 (Walpole to Montagu, October 16, 1770).

[76] *Ibid.*, ii. 211 (Walpole to Cole, May 11, 1780).

dignity. She and Lady Mary Coke were for some years his "two sovereigns," his "Polly and Lucy;"[77] he showered compliments, verses, and high-flown but innocuous gallantries upon them in equal profusion. The Duke and Duchess of Grafton had constant disagreements, and they finally separated in 1765. Four years later the Duchess was divorced by her husband on account of a love affair with John Fitzpatrick, second Earl of Upper Ossory, whom she then married. This marriage was a completely happy one: and it gave great satisfaction to Walpole, who had known and liked Lord Ossory since they first met in Madame du Deffand's *salon*. Moreover Lady Ossory now fulfilled, perhaps even more appropriately than George Montagu, the conditions he required from the chief recipient of his records of social life; she spent much of her time in the country, was grateful for London news, and was personally acquainted with most of the people and places he described. For the rest of his days she was one of his most frequent correspondents, and one of the best-loved; and it was to her that he addressed, six weeks before he died, the letter of farewell which concludes with so perfect a cadence the varied records of his life.

Less than a year after his estrangement from Montagu, Walpole lost another of his oldest friends. In the summer of 1771 he was in Paris, and one day opened the newspapers from England to find an announcement of the death of Gray. "I started up from my chair when I read the paragraph—a cannon-ball would not have surprised me more!"[78] He had left Gray looking rather unwell, but suspected as little as Gray himself that actual danger was threatening; and he was deeply shocked and grieved at the loss of his friend. The death of a close contemporary always provides food for reflection, and Walpole's reflections were given a still more sombre colour by his belief that Gray's fate would also be his own.[79] So many of his earliest friends had already

[77] *Toynbee,* v. 242–3 (Walpole to Conway, September 9, 1762).

[78] *Lewis,* i. 228–9 (Walpole to Cole, August 12, 1771).

[79] *Toynbee,* viii. 71 (Walpole to Conway, August 11, 1771). Gray's illness was called "gout in the stomach," though it is now thought he suffered from chronic kidney disease which terminated uræmia (*Gray,* iii. 1272 n). Eighteenth-century physicians were liable to attribute any violent abdominal attack to gout settling in the stomach: and persons of gouty constitution often anticipated such a development of their malady.

passed out of his life: West and Lyttelton were dead, Montagu was his friend no longer, Ashton was an ageing and disagreeable clergyman whom he had not seen for twenty years. Now Gray had also vanished, and the last effective link with so many scenes of the past—Eton, Cambridge, the first happy months in Italy—was broken by his death. The wounds of their quarrel had long since healed, and had healed completely. For years past Gray had been the most agreeable of correspondents, the most welcome of guests, the candid and somewhat astringent critic of the literary and architectural novelties of Strawberry Hill. And the obscure Eton friend, the moody and sensitive companion of the Grand Tour, had become, beyond fear of rivalry or comparison, the foremost poet of his age: so that Walpole could proudly boast, when the claims of other writers were mentioned, "Recollect that I have seen Pope, and lived with Gray."[80]

[80] *Lewis,* i. 310 (Walpole to Cole, April 27, 1773).

XII

Chatterton: and the Later Decades (1769-88)

IN 1769 an incident took place, apparently unimportant at the time, which was nevertheless fated to cause Walpole endless embarrassment and unhappiness. Throughout the affair he was in no way to blame: yet it clouded many years of his life, and gravely lowered his reputation in the eyes of his contemporaries and of posterity.[1]

On March 28 he received the following letter.

"Sir

Being versed a little in antiquitys, I have met with several Curious Manuscripts among which the following may be of Service to you, in any future Edition of your truly entertaining Anecdotes of Painting—In correcting the Mistakes (if any) in the Notes you will greatly oblige.

Your most humble Servant
Thomas Chatterton
Bristol, March 25th
Corn Street."[2]

The rest of the paper was filled with a prose discourse headed "The Ryse of Peyncteynge yn Englāde, wroten bie T. Rowleie, 1469 for Mastre Canynge." This essay purported to give a history of painting in England, from the self-adornment of the ancient

[1] I would like to acknowledge here my debt to the late E. H. W. Meyerstein's admirable *Life of Thomas Chatterton* (1930), in which Chatterton's relations with Walpole are treated with a wealth of detail and documentation.

[2] Add. MS. 5766B, f. 44.

Britons with "the hearbe Woade" down to Henrie a Thornton, Henrie a Londre, John de Bohuna and other mediæval celebrities. There was a spirited piece of Ossianic twaddle about a painter called Afflem who had been kidnapped by the Danes; and from the pen of "Johne seconde Abbate of Seyncte Austyns Mynsterre the fyrste Englyshe Paynctere yn Oyles," who was also a poet, there was a short but vigorous poem about Richard I.

> Harte of Lyone! shake thie Sworde,
> Bare thie mortheynge steinede honde:
> Quace whol Armies to the Queede,
> Worke thie Wylle yn burlie bronde.
> Barons here on bankers-browded,
> Fyghte yn Furres gaynste the Cale;
> Whilest thou ynne thonderynge Armes,
> Warriketh whole Cyttyes bale....

It is a little surprising that Walpole, the Fellow of the Society of Antiquaries, the author of *Historic Doubts,* should have been deceived by such gibberish as this. Admittedly he was hasty and uncritical, and could in any case have had no views as to the sort of poetry that was written in the time of Richard I; but he should at least have recognized that the style and spelling of Rowley bore singularly little resemblance to the almost contemporary documents which he had lately utilized in his work on Richard III. However, he seized the bait with the greatest eagerness, and at once dispatched a most courteous letter[3] to his unknown correspondent at Bristol. Chatterton, in a note on Rowley, whom he described as a secular priest of St. John's in Bristol, had mentioned that many remarkable poems by him were still in existence; and Walpole's enthusiasm may have been partly due to his hopes of obtaining these as material for his press. In his letter he asked for further details of them—"I should not be sorry to print them, or at least a specimen of them, if they have never been printed." He thanked Chatterton for his notes on Rowley's text, which had been very helpful, as "I have not the happiness of understanding the Saxon language." He was much struck by Abbot John's verses, "wonderful for their harmony and spirit,"

[3] Add. MS. 40015, f. 11. *Lewis,* xvi. 105–6 (Walpole to Chatterton, March 28, 1769).

and also by the fact that the Abbot's introduction of oil-painting into England confirmed his own theory that the art was known long before the days of "John ab Eyck." He concluded with a shower of compliments about Chatterton's "humanity and politenes."

Thomas Chatterton, the recipient of this flattering letter, was a boy of sixteen, the son of a Bristol schoolmaster. His father's early death had left the family in poverty; and Chatterton, after an education at Colston's Hospital in Bristol, had been apprenticed to an attorney of that city. During his childhood he had amused himself by playing with a collection of legal parchments in the muniment-room of the Church of St. Mary Redcliffe, and in particular with those relating to William Canynges, the fifteenth-century Mayor of Bristol and benefactor to the Church. Chatterton was a child of surprising precocity, and from an early age had written verses of remarkable merit. Eager for public attention, and for the recognition of his powers which would certainly have been withheld from an obscure apprentice, he had begun to cast some of his poems into a strange mediæval diction, and to display them to the *literati* of Bristol as the work of Thomas Rowley, an imaginary monk supposed to have been patronized by Canynges. He claimed to have discovered quantities of Rowley's writings, both in prose and verse, among the Canynges parchments, although these were in actual fact all legal documents of the most ordinary description. He soon built up a strange and elaborate fantasy around "Canynge," Rowley, and the glories of mediæval Bristol, of which St. Mary's Church was so noble an example; and his astounding poetic gift became inextricably involved with this shadow-world of his own creation. Before long he was hopelessly caught in the net of his ill-considered deception. His Bristol patrons were naturally demanding to see the Rowley originals, which he could not produce, although he satisfied them at intervals with a few forged stanzas. He longed to reap the reward, in celebrity and in some improvement in his circumstances, of the poetic genius which he unquestionably possessed: yet he had to attribute his productions to Rowley, or accept the certain consequences of exposure and ridicule.

He was naturally overjoyed by Walpole's letter. Here at last was recognition, and the possibility of fame. The best-known amateur antiquary of the day had addressed him as an equal, was struck with his verses, had accepted as genuine every word of his fantastic prose. Even if the glittering prospect of a Strawberry Hill imprint should not materialize, Walpole's patronage and notice might at least help him to a literary career in London, whither his ambitions were now tending. Directly he received Walpole's letter he wrote again to him, enclosing a further instalment of Rowley's history of painting, and several more specimens of his poetry. Only a portion of this letter survives: but it seems that the missing part contained an account of his circumstances and his ambitions, and a request to Walpole to use his influence to find him a more congenial post. There was no plea of poverty. As Walpole wrote later in his own defence, "Chatterton was neither indigent nor distressed at the time of his correspondence with me. He was maintained by his mother, and lived with a lawyer. His pleas to my assistance were, disgust to his profession, inclination to poetry, and communication of some suspicious MSS."[4] Chatterton's second letter thoroughly aroused his suspicions, as indeed a further consideration of the earlier batch of manuscripts may have done. He asked a relative living at Bath, Lady Malpas, to verify Chatterton's account of himself, which she was able to do.[5] He also showed the poems to Gray and Mason, who at once recognized them as the most obvious of forgeries. He was still uncertain whether Chatterton was merely attempting to obtain money or advancement from him by this imposture, or whether the whole business was an elaborate hoax designed to bring him into public ridicule; in neither case could he have supposed that a boy of sixteen was the sole contriver of the scheme, and he probably regarded Chatterton as the decoy put forward by a gang of swindlers or of practical jokers. However, he wrote to Chatterton "with as much kindness and tenderness as if I had been his guardian," but probably in a tone of maddening superiority, advising him for his mother's sake to continue in the profession she had chosen for him, and adding

[4] *Works,* iv. 217 *(Letter to the Editor of the Miscellanies of Chatterton).*

[5] *Ibid.,* 219. The identity of the "noble lady of virtue and character" is given in a manuscript note by Walpole in his own copy of the *Letter to the Editor of the Miscellanies,* in the possession of Mr. W. S. Lewis.

that "when he should have made a fortune he might unbend himself with the studies consonant to his inclinations."[6] He also said that better judges than himself had rejected the authenticity of the manuscripts.

This letter exasperated Chatterton as much as Walpole's earlier letter had delighted him. Stung by its lofty tone, he decided that Walpole, on learning of his unknown correspondent's real origin and circumstances, had changed his attitude from motives of sheer snobbery. And as for deception, had not Walpole himself pretended that *The Castle of Otranto* was a translation from an Italian original, and had he not veiled his authorship of the story in every sort of plausible mystification? Conscious that his own creative powers were of an order that Walpole could not approach, he bitterly resented the failure of his scheme; and he swore vengeance on the wealthy *dilettante* who had raised his hopes so high and had then, full of self-righteousness and good advice, dashed them once more to the ground. For Chatterton was not the gentle, ill-used boy-poet envisaged by Coleridge and by Keats. Tormented always by the sense of his unappreciated genius, this "acrimonious prodigy"—to use Meyerstein's admirable phrase—behaved throughout his short life, to almost every one with whom he came in contact, with spitefulness and dishonesty.[7]

On receiving Walpole's second letter, Chatterton sent a brief reply, maintaining the genuineness of Rowley's productions, and concluding thus: "Though I am but sixteen years of age, I have lived long enough to know that poverty attends literature. I am obliged to you, sir, for your advice, and will go a little beyond it, by destroying all my useless lumber of literature, and never using my pen again but in the law."[8] Six days later, he wrote again to ask for the return of his manuscripts; and as Walpole did not return them, he wrote once more in July, upbraiding him for his insolence in not replying. "I think myself injured, sir: and, did not you know my circumstances, you would not dare to treat me

[6] *Ibid.*, 223 (*Letter to the Editor of the Miscellanies of Chatterton*). The actual text of this letter of Walpole to Chatterton has not survived.

[7] *Meyerstein*, xii.

[8] *Works*, iv. 236 (Chatterton to Walpole, April 8, 1769).

thus."[9] Walpole drafted a reply to this last letter, pointing out that Chatterton had access to the alleged originals of the manuscripts he had sent. "If you want them, sir, I will have them copied, and will send you the copy. But having a little suspicion that your letters may have been designed to laugh at me, if I had fallen into the snare, you will allow me to preserve your original letters, as an ingenious contrivance, however unsuccessful."[10] He did not send this letter, however, but packed up all Chatterton's letters and manuscripts and despatched them to the troublesome youth without even taking copies—a lack of precaution which he afterwards greatly regretted.[11]

After this, he expected to hear no more of Chatterton. But the young poet continued to brood over his wrongs, and voiced his resentment against Walpole in some savage lines which he would have sent to Strawberry Hill, but for the dissuasion of his sister.

> "Walpole! I thought not I should ever see
> So mean a heart as thine has proved to be;
> Thou who in Luxury nurs'd behold'st with Scorn
> The Boy, who Friendless, Penniless, Forlorn,
> Asks thy high Favour—thou mayst call me Cheat—
> Say, didst thou ne'er indulge in such Deceit?
> Who wrote Otranto? But I will not chide,
> Scorn I will repay with Scorn, and Pride with Pride.
> Still, Walpole, still thy Prosy Chapters write,
> And twaddling Letters to some Fair indite,
> Laud all above thee—Fawn and Cringe to those
> Who for thy Fame, were better Friends than Foes
> Still spurn the incautious Fool, who dares ——
>
> ——————
>
> Had I the Gifts of Wealth and Lux'ry shar'd
> Not poor and mean—Walpole! thou hadst not dared
> Thus to insult. But I shall live and stand
> By Rowley's side—When *Thou* are dead and damned."[12]

[9] *Ibid.*, 237 (Chatterton to Walpole, July 24, 1769).

[10] *Ibid.*, 238.

[11] *Ibid.*, 224 *(Letter to the Editor of the Miscellanies of Chatterton).*

[12] MS. now at the Bristol Museum. I have copied the text from *Meyerstein*, 271. It is surprising to learn, from the line about the "twaddling Letters," that Walpole's epistolary fame, which one would have supposed to be more or less private knowledge during his life-time, had reached anyone so remote from his own circle as Chatterton.

In April of the following year Chatterton came to London, intending to support himself by miscellaneous journalism. He had already contributed a good deal of prose and verse to various newspapers and magazines—satires, lampoons, songs, political essays, mostly of a highly contemporary type. After he had arrived in London, he continued to turn out the same kind of copy, with a particular bias in the direction of satire and libel; and he did not forget his sworn vendetta against Horace Walpole. Much of his work was done for the *Town and Country Magazine,* a recently established periodical which had met with great successs, chiefly owing to its *Tête-à-Têtes,* a regular monthly feature in which well-known *liaisons* of the day were dissected and held up to ridicule, with every circumstance of impertinence and scurrility. The victims of the *Tête-à-Tête* for December 1769 had been Horace Walpole and Mrs. Clive, under the names of Baron Otranto and Mrs. Heidelburgh, the latter name being taken from Kitty's celebrated part in Colman's *Clandestine Marriage.*[13] It is unlikely that Chatterton had anything to do with this performance, though the raillery of Walpole's "Gothic taste for Mrs. Heidelburgh" was hostile and insolent enough to satisfy even his thirst for vengeance: he was still at Bristol at the time, and the *Tête-à-Têtes* were too important a feature of the magazine to be entrusted to a country contributor. But after he came to London, he made use of the name of Baron Otranto and the pages of the *Town and Country Magazine* for several attacks on Walpole. Among these is an amusing piece of mockery on his antiquarian activities, where Baron Otranto, "who has spent his whole life in conjectures," discovers a mutilated gravestone originally inscribed "James Hicks lieth here, with Hester his wife," and with great labour interprets this legend as "Hic jacet corpus Kenelmae Sancto Legero. Requiescat, etc., etc.;" after which effort of scholarship he has an elegant engraving made of the stone, for presentation to the Society of Antiquaries.[14] It is unlikely that

[13] *Town and Country Magazine* (1769), 617–20.

[14] *Ibid.,* (1770), 431–2. Another of Chatterton's attacks was a poem which touched on the relations of Walpole and Kitty Clive. In his copy of Chatterton's *Miscellanies* (in the possession of Mr. W. S. Lewis) Walpole has written the following note: "A little before this celebrated Actress left the Stage in her old age, Mr. Walpole gave her a House near Strawberry Hill. On this

at this time Walpole suspected Chatterton of being the author of these attacks, or even gave that ambitious but shady young man another thought. And when Chatterton killed himself, on August 24, 1770, after four feverish months in London, he heard nothing of it.

A crop of legends has risen around the circumstances of Chatterton's suicide. His first weeks in London had been successful, and by no means unprofitable. Later he had met with disappointments; he was hard pressed for money, and there seems little doubt that he was suffering from venereal disease. Pain, weariness, melancholy, pride, the agonizing consciousness of his unappreciated genius, there were plenty of motives for the sudden impulse by which he put an end to his life. In Meyerstein's view, his mental condition was so unstable that he might have killed himself at any time after his arrival in London, and there is no evidence that starvation or penury brought about his fatal act. The whole story is most tragic. Chatterton's poetic genius might have blossomed into something unique in the English language, whether he freed himself from the Rowley formula or whether he perfected it; but an agonizing death by poison and an unknown grave awaited him before he reached his eighteenth year.

In the following April, Walpole was at the banquet of the Royal Academy, and heard Goldsmith commending some ancient poems which had been lately discovered at Bristol. He told Goldsmith of his correspondence with Chatterton, and heard from him, for the first time, that Chatterton had come to London and had killed himself. Walpole was surprised and concerned, as any humane man would have been. "I heartily wished then that I had been the dupe of all the poor young man had written to me; for who would not have his understanding imposed on to save a fellow being from the utmost wretchedness, despair and suicide!"[15] But he felt no sense of responsibility for the catastrophe. After all, he had never seen Chatterton; he could scarcely have estimated, from the few pieces submitted to him, the full beauty and originality of the Rowley poems; he could only regard their

---

foundation she was represented as his Mistress, tho they were both between fifty & sixty, in a monthly magazine, whence Chatterton took the story."

[15] *Works,* iv. 224 *(Letter to the Editor of the Miscellanies of Chatterton).*

author as a tiresome boy who had tried to palm off some forgeries upon him. And, happily for his peace of mind, he did not foresee that in a few years' time he would be assailed as the murderer of a youthful genius on whom he had never set eyes, and who had only come to his notice as the unsuccessful perpetrator of a gross piece of fraud.

Almost from the day of Chatterton's death, interest in the Rowley poems began to grow. Copies were handed about; scholars pondered over them; the first shots were fired in the controversy that was presently to agitate the learned world, as to whether the obscure young apprentice could possibly have been the author of those wonderful poems, or whether they really were the genuine productions of Rowley, the forgotten monk of Bristol. Early in 1777 Thomas Tyrwhitt published his edition of *Poems, supposed to have been written at Bristol by Thomas Rowley, and others, in the Fifteenth Century*. Tyrwhitt did not pretend to decide on the real authorship of the poems: he preferred to leave the matter to the judgment of the learned, although his private belief was that they were the work of Chatterton. The literary world, realizing for the first time the full extent and beauty of those poems, was divided on the issue, and remained divided. Walpole, as astonished as every one else by the quality of the poems, nevertheless believed that they were written by Chatterton. He was more immediately concerned, however, by a notice of the book in the *Monthly Review* for April 1777, which brought his name into the controversy by mentioning that Chatterton had submitted the poems to him and that he had disbelieved in their authenticity.[16] This reference, though perhaps rather officious, was fair enough: but a continuation of the notice, in the next issue of the *Monthly Review,* included an account of Chatterton's discovery of the poems, the work of George Catcott, a foolish Bristol antiquary who had patronized Chatterton and professed to believe implicitly in Rowley; and in this account Walpole was treated in a very different style. "In 1770," wrote Catcott, "Chatterton went to London, and carried all this treasure with him, in hopes, as we may very reasonably suppose, of disposing of it to his advantage; he

[16] *Monthly Review* (1777), 259.

accordingly applied, as I have been informed, to that learned antiquary, Mr. Horace Walpole, but met with little or no encouragement from him; soon after *which,* in a fit of despair, as it is supposed, he put an end to his unhappy life, having first cut to pieces and destroyed all the MSS. he had in his possession."[17] Such statements were, of course, as unjust as they were inaccurate. Yet these two downright lies—that Chatterton in person submitted his poems to Walpole during his few months in London, and that Walpole by spurning him was directly responsible for his suicide—were taken up by others, and soon came to be believed by a large section of the public.

Walpole was naturally much upset by these accusations. He took no immediate action, but in May 1778 he drew up an account of his part in the affair in a letter to William Bewley, a surgeon living at Massingham, near Houghton, with whom he had some acquaintance, and who contributed to the *Monthly Review.*[18] While anxious to justify himself in the eyes of people interested in the matter, he was reluctant to publish any sort of defence, for fear of embroiling himself in further controversy. In the next year, however, a certain John Broughton of Bristol published a volume of *Miscellanies in Prose and Verse by Thomas Chatterton,* with a preface strongly condemning the "gentleman well known in the republic of letters" who had rejected the overtures of the youthful genius. The reader of the *Miscellanies* was invited to "feel some indignation against the person to whom his first application was made, and by whom he was treated with neglect and contempt." The preface continued: "It were to be wished that the public was fully informed of all the circumstances attending that unhappy application; the event of which deprived the world of works which might have contributed to the honour of the nation, as well as to the comfort and happiness of their unfortunate author."[19]

This was really more than Walpole's patience would stand. He composed a stinging reply, in the form of a letter to the editor of the *Miscellanies,* and subjoined to it the letter which he had written to William Bewley, explaining and justifying his conduct

[17] *Monthly Review* (1777), 323.
[18] *Works,* iv. 220–7. *Lewis,* xvi. 121–34.
[19] Chatterton's *Miscellanies,* xviii, xx–i.

in the whole affair. Even so, he was reluctant to submit his defence to the world. He hesitated, consulted friends, rewrote and enlarged his narrative. In January 1779 he printed at Strawberry Hill a private edition of two hundred copies of *A Letter to the Editor of the Miscellanies of Thomas Chatterton;* but it was not until 1782 that he was goaded by constant attacks into justifying his conduct before the general public. In that year his *Letter to the Editor of the Miscellanies of Chatterton* was reprinted in four instalments in *The Gentleman's Magazine,*[20] and became available to every one. It was a spirited and well-argued defence, and to any unprejudiced person should have been perfectly convincing. Walpole had been greatly hurt at the accusations of arrogance and inhumanity towards Chatterton, and was particularly careful and patient in his reply; but occasionally he would give way to indignation at becoming "perhaps the first instance of a person consigned to judgement for not having been made a fool of!" In one of these bursts of anger he made the suggestion that Chatterton, had he lived, might have proceeded to other and more criminal branches of forgery; but this remark is almost pardonable if his exasperation and strong sense of injustice are taken into account, and it is the only remark which is not scrupulously just to Chatterton. Throughout the miserable wrangling in which he had become involved, Walpole never failed to acknowledge, publicly and privately, his admiration for Chatterton's genius, his regret that he had not been given a fairer chance of assisting him, and his conviction that he was the sole author of the poems attributed to Rowley.

For year after year the Rowleian controversy rumbled on. Did Chatterton write the poems attributed to Rowley? Did Rowley write them? Did Rowley write them and Chatterton rewrite them? Walpole's old antagonist Dr. Milles, and his old schoolfellow Jacob Bryant, were the leaders of those who upheld the claims of Rowley. Warton, Malone, Steevens, Percy, Tyrwhitt, Lort and many others maintained that Chatterton was alone responsible; and most of them rushed into print in support of their views. Pamphlets multiplied, columns of the newspapers and magazines were filled with the arguments of the contending

[20] *Gentleman's Magazine* (1782), 189–95, 247–50, 300, 347–8.

parties. Walpole took no part in the fray. He collected the pamphlets and annotated them,[21] from the anti-Rowleian standpoint, but otherwise he preferred to be disassociated from an affair which can only have caused him pain. He never had the slightest remorse for his part in it, and had no possible reason to blame his own conduct. But he was pursued to his grave and beyond by the accusation that he had turned away a youthful genius from his doors, to despair and to die.[22] According to Miss Hawkins, he "began to go down in public favour from the time when he resisted the imposition of Chatterton;"[23] and to the end of his days he might open a new book and discover some indefensible sentence about "the Starvation Act, dated at Strawberry Hill."[24]

II

At the time of the publication of *Historic Doubts,* Selwyn told Walpole that, if he pleased, he might write Historic Doubts on the present Duke of Gloucester too.[25] This was a reference to the mysterious relations of Walpole's niece, Lady Waldegrave, with the King's younger brother. The Duke had fallen in love with Lady Waldegrave when she reappeared in the world a year after her husband's death; and she did not receive his attentions with disfavour. Walpole did not wish to see his niece installed as a royal mistress, and he thought it highly unlikely that the King would allow his brother to marry her. Moreover, she was the mother of three daughters by Lord Waldegrave, while the Duke

[21] Four volumes of *Chattertoniana,* with Walpole's notes, are now in Mr. W. S. Lewis's library at Farmington. See *Lewis,* xvi. 331–63.

[22] He did not publicly answer any further attacks: but the material about Chatterton left for posthumous publication (*Works,* iv. 234–45), and the letters to Dr. Lort in *Toynbee, Supplement,* ii. 26–9, 33–7, are examples of his continued anxiety to justify his conduct. Meyerstein discussed in his *Life of Chatterton* (pp. 278–82) Walpole's inexplicable denial, in his letter to Lort of July 27, 1789, that he ever received Chatterton's letters of March 25 and 30, 1769. Since Walpole had publicly admitted in 1782, in his *Letter to the Editor of the Miscellanies of Chatterton,* that he had received these letters, his denial seems absolutely pointless; and I am inclined to think that it was due to some lapse of memory on the part of an ageing man.

[23] *Hawkins,* i. 104–5.

[24] Mathias, *Pursuits of Literature* (1794), Dialogue I, 151 and n.

[25] *Lewis,* xiv. 171 (Walpole to Gray, February 18, 1768).

was seven years her junior and had not yet come of age. Walpole, reviewing all these circumstances, decided to do his best to end their association. In 1764 he persuaded her to send a letter, written by himself, decisively rejecting the Duke's advances and announcing her "final and unalterable resolution" never to see him again. This impressive effort at separation lasted less than a fortnight; and Walpole, having failed thus ignominiously, did not make a second attempt. In September 1766 the Duke and Lady Waldegrave were secretly married; but although they henceforward lived together openly, the marriage was not made public owing to the Duke's reluctance to face his brother's displeasure. It was, however, generally assumed that their marriage had taken place. Walpole himself had little doubt of it; but he refused to meet the Duke, saw as little as possible of Lady Waldegrave, and made a point of showing the world that his niece's position was gratifying neither to his personal ambition nor to his family pride. "Indeed my own father's obligations to the royal family forbade me to endeavour to place a natural daughter of our house so near the Throne."[26]

So matters rested, until in 1771 the King's youngest brother, the Duke of Cumberland, announced his marriage to a widow named Mrs. Horton. The Duke of Cumberland was a byword for foolish and disreputable behaviour; his bride was the daughter of Simon Luttrell, Lord Irnham, concisely described by Lady Louisa Stuart as "the greatest reprobate in England," while the same authority pronounced his daughters to be "noisy, vulgar, indelicate, and intrepid."[27] They were a very different couple from the Duke and Duchess of Gloucester, but the King's displeasure against his erring brothers drew no distinction between them. They had both married, or were believed to have married, against his will; and that was unpardonable. In a desperate attempt to prevent the Duke of Gloucester's marriage, or to intimidate him into disavowing it, he directed that a Royal Marriage Bill should be introduced into Parliament, providing that the descendants of George II should not marry without the approbation of the Sovereign. The Duke of Gloucester then gave permission to his wife to notify their marriage to her relations; and this she did in

[26] *Memoirs of George III,* iii. 267–71. [27] *Coke,* i. xcv.

a letter to her father, of which Horace Walpole said that "I, a writer in some esteem, and all my life a letter-writer, never penned anything like this letter of my niece. It is great, it is pathetic, it is severe, and it is more than all these—it is the language of Virtue in the mouth of Love."[28]

Now that the marriage was established, Walpole rallied decisively to his niece's side. Later in the year, she found herself with child; and the Duke therefore decided to notify the marriage formally to the King, and to endure his brother's indignation and the exclusion from Court which had already been pronounced on the Duke of Cumberland. This sentence of exclusion was thought likely to be extended to all who paid their court to the Duke and Duchess of Gloucester; but Walpole was ready to incur the royal displeasure, and immediately wrote asking if he might come and kiss their hands. He had no particular liking for the Duke; indeed he was at this time extremely displeased with him, as he had lately been at Florence and had been ungrateful and uncivil to Sir Horace Mann. But he felt obliged to support his niece, now completely involved in the atmosphere of hatred and feud which ever prevailed in the family circles of the Hanoverian monarchy; and he paid them an infinitely ceremonious first visit, kissing hands, replying to the Duke in monosyllables, filled with poignant anxiety that "he might not think I assumed the familiarity of a near relation."[29] When this position had once been established, things became easier. He grew proud of his royal niece and of the two royal children who were born to her. She constantly sought his advice in later years, in all the embarrassments and humiliations that the King's hostility entailed, in her constant anxieties about her situation if the Duke, frequently in ill-health and almost always in debt, should die before her. The last of all his surviving letters, a brief note about his health dictated a month before he died, was addressed to her.[30]

The avowal of Lady Waldegrave's marriage was a subject of extreme displeasure to Lady Mary Coke, and her anger was vented on Walpole. She had come to regard herself, with singularly little reason, as the chosen bride of the Duke of York: and since his

[28] *Last Journals,* i. 92–107. [29] *Ibid.,* 129–38.

[30] Walpole to the Duchess of Gloucester, February 6, 1797: MS. at Chewton Priory.

death had regarded herself almost as his widow. Her grief at failing to become a Royal Duchess was cruelly embittered when the Duke of Cumberland married Mrs. Horton, and the Duke of Gloucester acknowledged his marriage to Lady Waldegrave. It was dreadful to her that women with the shady family connections of Mrs. Horton, and the ignominious birth of Lady Waldegrave, should occupy the dazzling position which she had longed in vain to reach. Walpole had offended her by something he wrote in a letter to her when she was in Vienna in the autumn of 1771; but she would have forgiven him if she could have forgotten his niece's splendid marriage. No longer, in her diary, is he "more agreeable than it is possible to tell you." He is disagreeable, out of humour, backward in settling his card debts, and does not thank her for inquiring after his health. Only once does she speak of him with any sympathy, when she recounts, after the birth of the Duchess of Gloucester's daughter, how some one officiously asked him if his royal great-niece was a pretty baby; to which he coldly replied "It looked very red when I saw it," and then talked about the weather.[31]

At this time Lady Mary's persecution-mania was steadily gaining ground, and she was quarrelling with every one. She went to Vienna again in 1773; but on this occasion she considered that the Empress Maria Theresa, who had formerly been most gracious to her, received her coldly. She instantly formed the conviction that the Empress had ordered her assassination. As long as she remained in the Austrian domains, she was haunted by this fear; and when in Tuscany the postboys drove her into a river, it was obvious that the Empress had ordered them to drown her.[32] She went on to Florence, where Sir Horace Mann, at Walpole's request, was waiting to show her every possible courtesy; but nothing that he did could please her. He "join'd with my enemies in that particular of setting every body to pillage me as much as possible;" he was "very false to me, and certainly in the secrets of my enemies;"[33] he recommended servants who were extortionate and probably murderous, and treated Mrs. Fulford "with much more politeness and distinction on purpose to vex me."

[31] *Coke*, iv. 178 (June 20, 1773).
[32] *Ibid.*, 254–6 (November 3, 1773).
[33] *Ibid.*, 296, 302 (January 23 and February 1, 1774).

Behind his conduct she could perceive, once again, the hand of Maria Theresa.

In France, whose Queen was the daughter of this vindictive Empress, she was equally uneasy; and she could not feel secure from assassination till she was in England once more. Nevertheless, she went to Paris again in 1775; and it was during this visit that her long-standing friendship with Walpole came to a violent end. Walpole related his version of their quarrel to Lady Louisa Stuart, who repeated it with great vivacity in her memoir of Lady Mary.[34] Walpole, it appears, was aroused at five o'clock one morning by his Swiss valet. "Miladi Coke—il lui est arrivé quelque malheur; elle est toute éplorée." Walpole dressed and hurried downstairs, and was informed by the agitated Lady Mary that, just as she was setting out for England, Lady Barrymore had enticed her confidential courier into her own service. Walpole, who had been sleepily expecting some fearful tale of robbery or worse, was so ungallant as to say "Is that all?" It was not all. He was informed, amidst violent denunciations of his indifference and cold-heartedness, that Lady Barrymore had been bribed by Marie Antoinette to entice away the faithful courier; and that, deprived of the courier's protection, Lady Mary would be murdered by order of the Empress on the road to Calais. Still unable to make him really conscious of the gravity of her plight, Lady Mary left the house in a towering rage; and although she reached England unharmed by any Imperial assassins, she never forgave him. They continued to meet on rather frigid terms at the card-tables of other people; she even went again once or twice to Strawberry Hill; but there was no genuine reconciliation between them. She outlived Walpole by fourteen years, dying in 1811, eccentric to the last, sitting up in bed with a high-crowned beaver hat on her head.

III

After the completion of the important new additions which had

[34] *Ibid.*, i. cv–ix. Lady Mary's printed journals do not extend beyond 1774, so we do not possess her version of the quarrel. Lady Louisa adds: "I will not answer for the strict accuracy of the narrative; but one part of it—that respecting the Imperial plots conjured up by Lady Mary's imagination—Lord Orford neither invented nor exaggerated."

been begun in 1760, Strawberry Hill was as large as Walpole required. With the Gallery, the Cloister, the Round Tower and the Tribune, it had reached the limits he had planned. Finished and complete in every detail, the beloved house greeted him as he drove down from London, its pinnacles and battlements rising above the wall which separated it from the highway, its straggling length bordered on the further side by lawns and flower-beds and trees.

But his passion for building could not be satisfied. Before the interior decoration of the Round Tower was completed, he had started on the Great North Bedchamber or State Bedchamber. This addition looked out into the charming little garden, the Prior's Garden with its elegant Gothic screen, which lay between the house and the wall which bounded the road. Its ground floor was divided into a Servant's Hall and Wine Cellar; above these rooms the State Bedchamber revealed its sombre glories. It was a room of great magnificence. Two large bow-windows held ten coats of arms, executed in painted glass by Peckitt, displaying the principal matches of the Walpole family. The walls were hung with crimson Norwich damask; the bed was of Aubusson tapestry, with plumes of ostrich feathers at the corners. Walpole had designed the chimney-piece from the tomb of Dudley, Bishop of Durham, in Westminster Abbey; it was carved in Portland stone, which was afterwards gilded; and over it was his celebrated picture of Henry VIII and his children. Portraits by Mytens and Van Dyck hung on the walls. A cabinet held an extraordinary and characteristic medley of objects, including the gloves of James I, the wedding gloves of John Hampden's wife, an armorial seal which had belonged to Gray, an apostle spoon presented by Cole, the "speculum of kennel-coal" which Doctor Dee had used to call up spirits, the spurs worn by William III at the battle of the Boyne, and the tortoiseshell case in which Van Tromp used to carry his pipes to sea.[35]

In 1776 Walpole built "one of those tall thin Flemish towers, that are crowned with a roof like an extinguisher,"[36] in the northern angle between the Round Tower and the main body of the house. This tower, designed by James Essex, the talented

[35] *Works,* ii. 494–503 *(Description of Strawberry Hill).*

[36] *Toynbee,* ix. 421 (Walpole to Lady Ossory, October 9, 1776).

Cambridge architect, rose several feet above the Round Tower, forming a conspicuous feature of the house and effectively breaking its rather monotonous horizontal lines. It contained a small hexagonal closet specially designed to receive seven drawings in soot-water by Lady Diana Beauclerk, illustrating *The Mysterious Mother;* and was accordingly called the Beauclerk Tower. The closet was hung with Indian blue damask; and Lady Diana's drawings, which Walpole described as incomparable, inimitable, and sublime, and all of which had been conceived and executed in a fortnight, were naturally its most conspicuous feature. But, as in all the rooms at Strawberry Hill, the walls soon became covered with a miscellany of other pictures; and even in this tiny closet a generous assortment of objects of *virtù* filled all the available space.[37] Walpole liked to make a certain amount of mystification over the Beauclerk Closet, and only the most favoured visitors to the house were allowed to see it.

His collections increased steadily, with an almost relentless pressure. Again and again he protested that he had not a farthing or an inch of space left; but irresistible objects turned up at sales, were offered to him by dealers, were showered upon him by his friends. Death or circumstances broke up the collections of other men, and pictures and relics which he had long coveted were added to the treasures of Strawberry Hill. Sometimes he would grace his walls with a masterpiece such as Sir Joshua's superb painting of his great-nieces the three Ladies Waldegrave; sometimes he would stuff another cabinet with dubious curios, the shoes and gloves and snuff-boxes of the great. He built a Chapel in the garden to house some of his more cumbrous acquisitions. It was of brick with a front of Portland stone, copied from a chapel-tomb in Salisbury Cathedral. Chute designed the roof, Mann sent a relief of Saint John the Baptist by Donatello, and Selwyn presented a holy-water stoup in earthenware. Here, among other treasures, he placed a remarkable thirteenth-century mosaic shrine from the church of Santa Maria Maggiore in Rome, and the stained-glass window representing Henry III and Eleanor of Provence, which Lord Ashburnham had taken out of Bexhill church and given to him.[38]

[37] *Works,* ii. 503–5 *(Description of Strawberry Hill).*
[38] *Ibid.,* 507–8.

He drew up a detailed catalogue of his collection, and printed a small edition of it at his press in 1774. This *Description of Strawberry Hill* was reprinted ten years later, with additions and a number of plates; and there was also an abbreviated version for the use of the servants who showed the house to the public. It is a fascinating compilation, in which every picture and drawing on the walls, and almost every cup and saucer in the China Closet, is mentioned with affectionate particularity. From "a large old white china tea-pot, that was the Duke of Monmouth's; a present from Simon second Earl of Harcourt," to the "extraordinary large brainstone; a present from Mr. Grosvenor Bedford" which he placed in the garden,[39] every object, great or small, beautiful or ridiculous, is carefully listed by its admiring owner.

When Strawberry Hill first began to be talked about, and strangers asked permission to see the house, Walpole was rather flattered; but soon he was deluged with applications, and found himself hunted from room to room by constant parties of sight-seers. He therefore printed at his press a set of rules which were to be strictly observed by intending visitors. People had to apply for a ticket a day or two in advance; each party was limited to four persons; only one party was admitted each day, and between certain hours, and in certain months of the year; and children were not to be brought. In the library of Harvard University are some notes by Walpole giving lists of his visitors, and occasional comments on their behaviour, from 1784 onwards. His rules seem to have worked smoothly, although occasionally there was trouble with such people as Mr. Perkins, who "very rude, abused James, gave Margaret nothing, because his servant had been made to wait while I was at dinner." To show the frequency and the variety of these visitors, it is perhaps of interest to print Walpole's entries for a typical month; and July 1788 has been selected for this purpose.

2. Mrs. Plumer and 3.
3. Mr. Hatsell and 3.
5. Sir H. Englefield, his mother and sister. *Myself.*
6. Comte and Comtesse Czernin.
8. Prince and Princess Rospigliosi. *Myself.*

[39] *Ibid.*, 415, 510.

10. Colonel Ironside and 3.
11. Mrs. Yates and 2.
13. Mr. Ford, printer and 3 more.
14. Mr. and 2 Misses Berry. *Myself.*
15. Mr. Railton and 3. a Distiller at Hampton: tho had printed ticket, brought 6.
16. Mr. Willock of Putney and 3.
17. Sir Watkin Lewes and 3.
18. Mr. and Mrs. Scott and 2, from Mr. Hare.
19. Ld. Clifden and Son, *myself.* Mr. Astle and Son, *myself.*
20. Count D'hane and two.
21. Monsieur Boissier.
24. Colonel Blair and 3, from Mr. Lysons.
25. Monsieur de Pavie and 2 more French.
28. Four from Lady Charleville.
30. Mrs. Olier and 3.
31. Lady Astley and 3.[40]

IV

Since the printing of Lord Herbert of Cherbury's *Autobiography* in 1764, the history of the Strawberry Hill press had been rather uneventful. A second edition of the *Anecdotes of Painting,* begun in 1763, was finished in 1765 by his latest printer Thomas Kirgate. A slender pamphlet of *Poems by Anna Chamber, Countess Temple,* with some introductory lines by Walpole, was issued in 1764; and a few songs and poems were printed as single leaflets. In 1765, before he went to France, Walpole discharged Kirgate, but re-engaged him in 1768; and he remained henceforward at Strawberry Hill, as Walpole's printer and later as his secretary, until his master's death.

After Kirgate's return, the press resumed its activities. In 1768 Walpole printed two hundred copies of *Cornélie, Vestale,* a tragedy by the Président Hénault, most of which were sent to Paris; and in the same year the fifty copies of *The Mysterious Mother* were struck off. Walpole also began to print a quarto edition of his own works, a project which he abandoned after he

[40] *Lewis,* xii. 231. The word "myself" after certain names indicates that he showed those privileged visitors round the house himself.

had completed a very few copies of the first two volumes, and which was the foundation of the splendid five-volume edition of his *Works* which appeared in the year after his death. In 1769 he printed three hundred copies of the *Poems* of Francis Hoyland, an impoverished clergyman, to be sold for his benefit. And in 1772 he published a new edition of the *Mémoires du Comte de Grammont.*

He had been contemplating this edition of Count Anthony Hamilton's delightful work for more than twenty years.[41] He had been gradually identifying the people mentioned by Hamilton, in whose text the English names were often wildly misspelt; and he had hoped to illustrate his book with the portraits of "the principal beauties and heroes." In the latter attempt he was not very successful, and the volume appeared with engravings of Grammont, Hamilton, and Miss Hamilton alone; but his identifications were made with great skill, and have been of considerable service to later editors of the *Mémoires.* He corrected the names of people and places, and added notes and some prefatory matter, but did not touch the text in any way.

Hamilton's exquisite style, and the gaiety and gallantry of his subject-matter, appealed strongly to Walpole; and his new connections with Paris led him to appreciate, more warmly than ever, the blending in Hamilton's pages of the cultural and social life of England and France. As a symbol of the relations between the two countries, and as a tribute to their personal friendship, he dedicated the volume to Madame du Deffand. "L'Editeur vous consacre cette Edition, comme un monument de son Amitié, de son Admiration, et de son Respect; à Vous, dont les Graces, l'Esprit, et le Goût retracent au siècle présent le siècle de Louis Quatorze et les agremens de l'Auteur de ces Mémoires."

In 1772, also, he printed at Strawberry Hill seven most interesting letters written by Edward VI to Barnaby Fitzpatrick, a youth with whom he had been brought up and to whom he was much attached. Fitzpatrick was of the same family as Lord Ossory, who lent Walpole the letters; and Cole had undertaken the work of transcribing them. In the same year Walpole formed the scheme of printing at occasional intervals copies of original manu-

[41] *Ibid.,* ix. 118 (Walpole to Montagu, July 22, 1751).

scripts or of scarce tracts of an antiquarian nature, in imitation of Peck's *Desiderata Curiosa.* This series was called *Miscellaneous Antiquities,* and the greater part of the edition was for sale. Two instalments were issued, both in 1772: the first consisted of extracts from William Segar's *Honour Military and Civill,* printed in 1602, relating to jousts and tournaments; the second was a copy, made many years before by Gray from the original in the British Museum, of the defence of Sir Thomas Wyatt the elder when accused of high treason, together with his life written by Walpole. But the sale of these two parts was disappointingly slow, and Walpole decided not to carry the project any further.

The next two years were occupied with the printing of the *Description of Strawberry Hill.* There were constant interruptions to its progress; Kirgate injured his hand, Walpole was frequently prostrated with gout. After the appearance of the *Description* in 1774, the press slumbered completely until 1778, except for the printing of *Dorinda, a Town Eclogue,* by Lord Ossory's brother Richard Fitzpatrick, and a few leaflets, including Charles Fox's well-known verses to Mrs. Crewe. In 1778 Walpole printed *The Sleep-Walker,* a translation by Lady Craven of a comedy by Madame du Deffand's friend Pont-de-Veyle; and in the next year he printed his *Letter to the Editor of the Miscellanies of Thomas Chatterton.*

It was long since Walpole had given to the public any of the original research and criticism in which he had first made his name as an author; but in 1780 he issued a fourth volume of the *Anecdotes of Painting.* This volume had been completed and printed in 1771, but its publication was delayed so long "from motives of tenderness" towards the surviving relatives of artists whom he could not whole-heartedly praise. It covered the reigns of the first two Georges, and did not include any artists who were still alive at the date of its publication. Among the painters, therefore, Hogarth was supreme, towering above the competent if somewhat uninspiring Hudsons and Highmores: and Walpole devoted to his works a chapter of criticism which undervalued the splendid quality of his painting, but made full amends when considering him as "a writer of comedy with a pencil," as a humorist, a satirist and a reformer. If these two reigns could only furnish a single great name in painting, Walpole found ample compensation in the architectural revival which then took place under those magnificent patrons the Earls of Pembroke and Burlington. In earlier chapters he had treated Vanbrugh with gross injustice, and had not been much fairer to Hawksmoor and Gibbs; but the Palladian enthusiasts had the entire sympathy of the celebrated amateur of Gothic. He proclaimed further that Lord Burlington, "the Apollo of arts, found a proper priest in the person of Mr. Kent;" and his chapter on Kent was a fine and deserved tribute to that great man. He referred to his paintings with contempt; but as an architect, and still more as a landscape gardener, he gave him the fullest measure of praise. The development of landscape gardening was, in Walpole's eyes, as important as the revival of pure classical architecture. Kent was the father of modern gardening—"an original, and the inventor of an art that realizes painting and improves nature. Mahomet imagined an Elysium, but Kent created many."[42] For Kent's experiments in Gothic he had no sympathy; in fact, throughout the *Anecdotes* there is no word of praise for modern Gothic work, whether by Hawksmoor, Kent or any other architect.

Walpole prefixed to the fourth volume of the *Anecdotes of Painting* an "Advertisement" which, if taken too seriously, would bring about his final damnation as a critic. In reviewing the flourishing condition of contemporary art, he gave due applause to the architects of the day, but passed over Adam and Chambers, and only mentioned by name the comparatively youthful Wyatt. A single paragraph about the painters of the age bestowed some commendation on Reynolds, Gainsborough and Zoffany. But it took Walpole several pages to do justice to the achievements of certain talented amateurs who happened to be members of his own set. Lady Lucan had recently learned to copy Cooper and the Olivers "with a genius that almost depreciates those masters, when we consider that they spent their lives in attaining perfection:" she had, moreover, transferred the vigour of Raphael to her copies in water-colours. Henry Bunbury, that delightful slapdash caricaturist, was "the second Hogarth, and first imitator who ever fully equalled his original." Lady Diana Beauclerk was, of course, fit to rank only with Shakespeare: "yet is there a

[42] *Works*, iii. 488.

pencil in a living hand as capable of pronouncing the passions as our unequalled poet; a pencil not only inspired by his insight into nature, but by the graces and taste of Grecian artists." The busts executed by that female genius, Mrs. Damer, were not inferior to the antique: her terra-cotta shock dog rivalled Bernini's marble one, and indeed all the animal sculpture that the ancients have left us—even the Barberini goat, the eagle at Strawberry Hill, and the dog that was formerly owned by Mr. Jennings, but was now in the collection of Mr. Duncombe.[43]

This preface reveals Walpole in one of his most irritating moods. Few men were more capable of appraising the splendid powers of Gainsborough and Reynolds; but he preferred to publish fulsome nonsense about Lady Lucan's water-colours and Mrs. Damer's terra-cotta dog. How much of what he wrote in these moods was mere amiable compliment, how much arose from his instinctive sympathy for the aristocratic amateur, and how much was serious appreciation of the works he was considering, it is impossible to judge. But these outbursts of facile enthusiasm have done great damage to his reputation as a critic, alike in the eyes of his contemporaries and of posterity.

Walpole brought the fourth volume of the *Anecdotes of Painting* to a close with an *Essay on Modern Gardening*, one of the most charming of his minor writings. In his lightest and gayest style, he traces the history of gardening from its biblical and mythological beginnings down to his own day. Rapidly surveying the garden of Eden and the garden of Alcinous, the hanging gardens of Babylon and the laborious pleasure-grounds laid out by Pliny, he arrives at Sir William Temple's classic description of Moor Park, and pronounces it to display every fault of taste that could be devised. In violent reaction against the architectural and formal tradition of English gardening, he will allow no merit to any practitioner of the art until he comes to William Kent. Le Nôtre is dismissed with scorn; indeed the masterpieces of French and Dutch taste were as contemptible in Walpole's eyes as the aspirations of some of his contemporaries towards a style of gardening which they believed to be practised by the Chinese. But with Kent, and the startling novelty of the Ha! Ha! which he

[43] *Ibid.*, 398–401.

popularized, a complete revolution took place. "He leaped the fence, and saw that all nature was a garden. He felt the delicious contrast of hill and valley changing imperceptibly into each other, tasted the beauty of the gentle swell, or concave scoop, and remarked how loose groves crowned an easy eminence with happy ornament, and while they called in the distant view between their graceful stems, removed and extended the perspective by delusive comparison."[44] He praises Kent's skill in the handling of light and shade, in veiling unattractive objects, in introducing buildings, and above all in the management of water; but he does not fail to touch upon his faults, the inconsiderable size of his woods and groves, the timidity of some of his conceptions, and such occasional aberrations as the planting of dead trees to add reality to a landscape. From the revolution initiated by Kent, landscape gardening in England, in Walpole's view, had gone from one triumph to another. He discusses the new trees which had been introduced during the last few years, the foreign pines and firs with their novel variations of colour and form, the exotic shrubs with their bold or delicate foliage. He comments on the passion for planting which was transforming the face of the country. "If no relapse to barbarism, formality, and seclusion is made, what landscapes will dignify every quarter of our island, when the daily plantations that are making have attained venerable maturity!" He hails the achievements of Kent's successor, Capability Brown; and looks forward to the establishment amid the ever-increasing beauties of England of "such a school of landscape as cannot be found on the face of the globe."[45]

The *Essay on Modern Gardening* was translated into French by the Duc de Nivernais. The excellence of this version, and the skill with which the quotations from Milton and Pope were rendered, induced Walpole to print it as a compliment to his friends in France. In 1785 he issued four hundred copies, with the French and English texts printed on opposite pages, two hundred of which were sent to France. In the same year he printed his smallest edition, six copies of his own *Hieroglyphic Tales.* These *Tales* were six short fairy stories which he had written between 1766 and 1772, partly to amuse Lady Ailesbury's little niece

[44] *Ibid.,* ii. 536. [45] *Ibid.,* 543.

Caroline Campbell, and partly to amuse himself. They are all in his maddest and most inconsequent vein. In a postscript he remarks how strange it was that "there should have been so little fancy, so little variety, and so little novelty, in writings in which the imagination is fettered by no rules, and by no obligation of speaking truth."[46] In his delirious little stories he attempts to supply these deficiencies. "There was formerly a King," one of them begins, "who had three daughters—that is, he would have had three, if he had had one more—but somehow or other the eldest was never born. She was extremely handsome, had a great deal of wit, and spoke French in perfection, as all the authors of that age affirm, and yet none of them pretend that she ever existed. It is very certain that the two other princesses were far from beauties; the second has a strong Yorkshire dialect, and the youngest had bad teeth and but one leg, which occasioned her dancing very ill."[47]

The same vein of moonstruck nonsense was exploited in his little play, *Nature will Prevail*,[48] which he wrote in the year after the *Hieroglyphic Tales*. Here the scene is laid on a desert island, where two men, Current and Padlock, a fairy called Almadine, a country girl called Finette, and an Echo play out a fantastic little comedy of confusion and misunderstanding. Walpole called this production "A Moral Entertainment, in One Act," and did succeed in bringing out the moral that two people on a desert island will contrive to injure one another by malice and gossip just as they would do in a larger society—in fact, that Nature will Prevail. But the whole conception of the little piece is in the same vein of utter fantasy as the *Hieroglyphic Tales;* and it is faintly surprising that it should have been acted with applause on the London stage. Walpole sent it to George Colman, at first anonymously; Colman was much pleased with it, and urged Walpole to extend it to the normal length of a farce; and although Walpole refused to alter it, he produced it at the Little Theatre in the Haymarket, in June 1778, with considerable success.[49]

[46] *Ibid.*, iv. 352. [47] *Ibid.*, 330.
[48] *Ibid.*, ii. 291–304.
[49] *Lewis,* xiii. 48, 50 *(Short Notes of my Life).*

V

As the years went by, many of Walpole's oldest friends vanished from the scene. In the decade between 1776 and 1786, he had to mourn the deaths of Chute and Madame du Deffand, Cole and Lady Hertford, his brother Edward, Mrs. Clive and Sir Horace Mann. He filled the gaps in his circle as best he could; but younger men and women could never replace these lifelong friends.

Chute died, rather suddenly, in 1776. His friendship with Walpole had never undergone the slightest change since they first met at Florence thirty-five years before. He was the most entirely congenial of all Walpole's friends; their tastes, interests and opinions were in the completest harmony. In an almost heart-broken letter to Mann, Walpole described the magnitude of his loss. "He was my counsel in my affairs, was my oracle in taste, the standard to whom I submitted my trifles, and the genius that presided over poor Strawberry! His sense decided me in everything; his wit and quickness illuminated everything. I saw him oftener than any man; to him in every difficulty I had recourse, and him I loved to have here, as our friendship was so entire, and we knew one another so entirely, that he alone never was the least constraint to me. . . . My first thought will always be, 'I will go talk to Mr. Chute on this;' the second, 'alas! I cannot;' and therefore judge how my life is poisoned! I shall only seem to be staying behind one that is set out a little before me."[50]

Madame du Deffand died in September 1780. Walpole had not visited her for five years; but their correspondence, with its interminable repetitions of affectioin and reproof, of her love constantly rebuffed by his unrelenting caution, had proceeded without any serious check. She had been ailing during the whole summer, but had carried on her usual way of life almost until the end. Walpole was kept informed of the progress of her illness, both by her secretary Wiart and his cousin Thomas Walpole, who happened to be in Paris. He could have reached Paris in time to see her once more; but he felt that his presence would have been useless. The state of his own health made the long journey an ordeal which he felt unable to face. After all, their two countries

[50] *Toynbee*, ix. 365 (Walpole to Mann, May 27, 1776).

were at war, and even the courteous warfare of the eighteenth century added to the difficulties of civilian travel. She did not ask him to come to her; it is doubtful even whether she would have wished to see him. A full month before she died, and a fortnight before her illness had taken a critical turn, she had sent him a letter of farewell, a letter suggesting that she had at last achieved a mood of detachment which she would not have wished to surrender again. "Divertissez-vous, mon ami, le plus que vous pourrez; ne vous affligez point de mon état; nous étions presque perdus l'un pour l'autre; nous ne nous devions jamais revoir; vous me regretterez, parce qu'on est bien aise de se savoir aimé."[51] Wiart added to her letter a reassuring postscript to the effect that "Madame est fort faible, mais pas aussi malade qu'elle se le croit;" but Walpole had no doubt, on reading her letter, what the end would be.[52] She had wished to make him her heir, but he had firmly refused to accept any pecuniary legacy from her. She bequeathed to him all her papers, a large and precious consignment; and also her ferocious little dog, Tonton, who had long been the terror of her guests at the Convent of Saint Joseph. Tonton was transported to Strawberry Hill, where a life of luxury failed to sweeten his temper, and where he died nine years later at the advanced age of sixteen.

In 1782 Cole died at Milton near Cambridge. His correspondence with Walpole had continued with unabated vigour until a few weeks before his death. Although the principal subject of all their letters was antiquarian research, they did not neglect the personalities of their friends and enemies, for Cole in his quiet way was as fondly addicted to gossip as Walpole. As a rule they agreed to keep off the topics of Church and State, on which their views were profoundly opposed; but on all other subjects, and especially on their common affliction of the gout, they wrote with volubility and without reserve. Walpole, following his scheme of maintaining a dynasty of correspondents on each of the subjects on which he desired to enlighten posterity, selected Michael Lort as Cole's successor in the antiquarian field. Lort was an agreeable man and an able antiquary; but Walpole could never expect that

[51] *Lewis,* vii. 243 (Madame du Deffand to Walpole, August 22, 1780).
[52] *Toynbee,* xi. 270–2 (Walpole to Thomas Walpole, September 6, 1780).

he, or any one else, would fill the place in his affections so long occupied by the stalwart and combative figure of Cole.

Almost at the same time Lady Hertford died suddenly in London. However strongly he sometimes felt about Lord Hertford's courtier-like propensities, he never extended his condemnations to his wife. Although she does not come a great deal into the records of his life, he had always valued her friendliness and good humour, had admired the competence with which she managed her enormous family and household, and had appreciated the welcome he always received at her house—"one of the few houses on which I reckoned for my remaining time."[53] Her death made the first breach in what he had long regarded as his own family circle, the little set formed by his cousins Hertford and Conway and their wives and children. Early in 1784, another reminder of the lapse of time occurred with the death of his brother Sir Edward Walpole, which left him, with the exception of his half-sister Lady Mary Churchill, the sole survivor of his generation of the family. Sir Edward had lived so long in eccentric seclusion that Horace, although in latter years on the friendliest terms with him, could not be greatly moved at his death. The loss of his brother made a considerable difference to his financial position, for the place of Collector of the Customs, which Sir Edward held for life, and out of which Horace received £1,400 a year for the period of his brother's life, now lapsed entirely to a stranger.[54] But Walpole, who had made it a point of honour to refrain, except on two occasions, from asking ministers for the prolongation of this sinecure to cover his own life, accepted the reduction of income very philosophically; and he could after all console himself with the reflection that his brother had reached the age of seventy-seven, and that his own place of Usher of the Exchequer had increased to a far greater annual value than had been anticipated when it was first conferred upon him.

[53] *Ibid.*, xii. 370 (Walpole to Mann, November 12, 1782). There is an excellent character of Lady Hertford in *Last Journals*, i. 384; and many of her unpublished letters to him are in Add. MSS. 23218–9.

[54] *Toynbee*, xv. 103 (Walpole to Lady Ossory, January 18, 1792). *Works*, ii. 364–6 *(Account of my Conduct)*. See *ante*, 109.

Mrs. Clive died at the close of 1785. No more would she work carpets and embroider chairs for Strawberry Hill; no more would Walpole welcome her expansive presence in his garden, or stroll across to Cliveden for a chat at her tea-table. And less than a year later an even stronger link with the past was broken by the death at Florence of Sir Horace Mann.

From 1783 onwards the handwriting of Mann's letters begins to grow ever more shaky, and his spelling becomes a little erratic. At last his vitality was flagging, though he whose fragile physique Walpole had long ago likened to "wet brown paper" had displayed, like Walpole himself, astonishing powers of resistance as his life advanced. The ceremonial of the Tuscan court was growing ever more fatiguing to him, and the Grand Duke thought nothing of making him stand at an audience, when he was approaching eighty years of age, for an hour and three quarters. Bouts of illness wore down his strength; and by 1786 he began to have premonitions of the end. In February of that year he wrote to Walpole: "though I am not vehemently attached to this world I must do it the justice to own that I have no right to complain of my lot in it, during a very decent course of time and with more comforts than I had any pretensions to, at the beginning of it, upon the whole therefore I am perfectly well satisfied and look forward with a total indifference as to myself, though to the last hour of my existence I shall be anxious to hear of your welfare." He struggled on through the spring and summer, his letters ever growing more feeble and incoherent; till on September 5th he suddenly broke off a pathetic scrawl with "Adieu my Dear Sir, I am quite exhausted, Yrs. HM;"[55] and his last letter to Walpole had been written. His nephew and heir hurried out to Florence, and was with him till he died on November 16. He described in a touching letter how his uncle read and wept over Walpole's last letters, the final letters of their wonderful correspondence of forty-five years.[56]

[55] Mann to Walpole, August 2, 1783; February 6 and September 5, 1786. (MSS. at Farmington.)

[56] Horace Mann the younger to Walpole, September 25, 1786. (MS. at Farmington.)

VI

The new friends whom Walpole made in those years did not go very far towards repairing the havoc that death had created in his circle. Among men, perhaps the most important was William Mason, whom he had known for a number of years, but who did not become an intimate friend or a very regular correspondent until after the death of Gray. They then became closely associated over Mason's biography of his friend; and afterwards Mason gradually took Gray's place as Walpole's chief correspondent on all matters of contemporary literature.[57] Walpole greatly admired Mason's poems, and in particular the *Heroic Epistle to Sir William Chambers* and the other political and anti-Court satires which he published anonymously. He wrote a commentary on these pieces, and was privy to the complicated process of mystification by which Mason concealed his authorship of them.[58] The *Heroic Epistle* was attributed by many people to Walpole himself; and he derived a great deal of amusement from pretending to every one that he knew nothing at all about it. With Mason's patron, the second Earl Harcourt, he was also on very friendly terms. Lord Harcourt was an enthusiastic follower of literature and the arts. As a young man he had broken in upon Gray's retirement at Cambridge, "in a Solitaire, great Sleeves, jessamine-powder, and a large Bouquet of Jonquils," in order to express to the poet his profound admiration for his works.[59] He became a *connoisseur* and an accomplished artist, and his etchings were warmly praised by Walpole. Nuneham, under his rule, became the headquarters of a literary and artistic *côterie,* and it was one of the houses which Walpole visited with most pleasure. In 1784, however, Walpole and Mason quarrelled, owing to a divergence in their political views. Lord Harcourt was suddenly reconciled to the Court, after having been for a long while in vehement opposition to it; and Walpole was not only

[57] *The Correspondence of Walpole and Mason* was first published by the Rev. John Mitford in 1851, and now forms volumes xxviii and xxix of the Yale Edition.

[58] *Satirical Poems published anonymously by William Mason with notes by Horace Walpole, now first printed from his Manuscript,* edited by Paget Toynbee, 1926.

[59] *Gray,* ii. 499 (Gray to Mason, April 23, 1757).

indignant at the coolness with which Mason announced this step, but strongly suspected him of having encouraged Lord Harcourt to take it.[60] They were not reconciled until 1796, and both died in the following year. The friendship between Walpole and Harcourt remained in abeyance for almost as long a period.

Other friends of Walpole during his last years were George Hardinge and Edward Jerningham. Hardinge was a lawyer, and subsequently a politician, of considerable ability. He published several pamphlets on literary subjects, and corresponded with Walpole for some years.[61] After his marriage in 1777 he settled at Twickenham, in a house called Ragman's Castle, and Walpole found him a pleasant and serviceable, if somewhat intrusive neighbour. Edward Jerningham was the author of a great deal of sentimental poetry, and of several plays. His conversation was less mawkish than his verses, and he was known in Walpole's circle as "the charming man." Yet another new friend was Robert Jephson, an Irishman of literary tastes. He was the author of a play, *Braganza,* for which Walpole wrote an epilogue, and which also inspired the short discourse entitled *Thoughts on Tragedy* which Walpole cast into the form of three letters addressed to him.[62] In 1781, Jephson repaid these attentions by founding on *The Castle of Otranto* a tragedy, which he called *The Count of Narbonne.* Walpole took great interest in the production of this play. A letter has survived in which he implores the actress Mrs. Pope to take part in it. "Mr. Jephson, who has long been my friend, and who has proved himself so by making a rational and interesting tragedy out of my wild *Castle of Otranto,* cannot bring it on the stage to advantage unless you, Madam, will be pleased to appear in the character of Hortensia, the wife of the Count of Narbonne....Unless I were as great a master of the stage as you are a mistress, Madam, I could not describe half that you will call out from the part."[63] The play was produced at Covent Garden in the winter of 1781, and to Walpole's delight was extremely successful.

[60] *Lewis,* xxix. 327–33 (Walpole to Mason, February 2, 1784). *Walpoliana,* i. 88–93. *Berry,* ii. 39–40.

[61] Much of their correspondence is printed in *Nichols,* iii. 177–219.

[62] *Works,* ii. 304–14. The *Epilogue* is printed in *Works,* iv. 400–1.

[63] *Toynbee,* Supplement, i. 282–3 (Walpole to Elizabeth Younge [Mrs. Pope], October 22, 1781).

A less pleasant person than Jephson was John Pinkerton, the Scottish historian and antiquary, who managed to toady Walpole with some success. He frequently visited Strawberry Hill, elicited long letters on literary and antiquarian subjects from his host, and repaid his courtesy by compiling after his death the two little volumes of his table-talk published under the title of *Walpoliana*. The preface of this book contains a particularly vivid description of Walpole's appearance and way of life; and the malice of some of Pinkerton's comments, possibly actuated by disappointment at not being mentioned in Walpole's will, does not in any way detract from the value of this picture.

He was fortunate in some of his new women friends of whom two in particular, Lady Craven and Lady Diana Beauclerk, added greatly to the happiness of his life. Lady Craven, beautiful, foolish, with a varied succession of lovers and a passion for writing and acting plays, brought gaiety wherever she went. She dedicated to him, in terms of warm admiration, a nonsensical little book of her own composition;[64] and he printed her translation of *Le Somnambule* at Strawberry Hill. In 1783 she finally separated from her husband, wandered about Europe, lived with the Margrave of Anspach, and became his Margravine after the deaths of their respective spouses. Still more agreeable to Walpole was Lady Diana Beauclerk, for whose drawings he built the Beauclerk Closet. She had been the wife of Lord Bolingbroke, who had divorced her on account of her *liaison* with Topham Beauclerk, the friend of Johnson. Walpole could not endure Beauclerk, but was devoted to Lady Diana, and gave to her charming and spirited paintings and drawings a degree of praise that would have been excessive if applied to Gainsborough. After Beauclerk's death she came to live at Richmond, and remained always among the most valued of his friends.

Dearer than these was Mrs. Damer, the only child of Conway and Lady Ailesbury. He had adored her as a child, and she used to live at Strawberry Hill for long periods when her parents were abroad. She had been married at the age of eighteen to John Damer, the son and heir of Lord Milton. The marriage had not

[64] *Modern Anecdote of the Ancient Family of the Kinkvervankotsdarsprakengotchderns: a Tale for Christmas* 1779. *Dedicated to the Honourable Horace Walpole.*

been very happy, and had ended tragically; for Damer, the heir to a vast fortune, managed to pile up enormous debts, and in a sudden frenzy shot himself in 1776. Mrs. Damer afterwards spent a good deal of time abroad, and developed her talent for sculpture, of which Walpole used to speak in terms of the highest eulogy. The keystones of the arches of the bridge at Henley, representing Thames and Isis, are fine speciments of her work, Walpole saw more and more of her as his life drew to an end; and he bequeathed Strawberry Hill and all its contents to her for life.

VII

During these years he was often put to great inconvenience and perplexity by the vagaries of Lord Orford. For a long while his nephew's eccentricities had been verging upon madness. His affairs had drifted into utter confusion; Houghton, that once princely mansion, had sunk so low that a disreputable Newmarket character had kindly volunteered to live in it if he could have the use of all the game.[65] Lord Orford, attended by his mistress Mrs. Turk and a rabble of dubious hangers-on, camped in the parsonage at Eriswell near Newmarket. In 1773 he became completely insane, and Walpole felt obliged to assume entire charge of his affairs. He had to leave the summer tranquillity of Strawberry Hill for the melancholy confusion of Houghton. He found the pictures and furniture well preserved; but "all the rest is destruction and desolation! The two great staircases exposed to all weathers, every room in the wings rotting with wet, the ceiling of the gallery in danger, the chancel of the church unroofed, the water-house built by Lord Pembroke tumbling down, the garden a common, the park half-covered with nettles and weeds, the walls and pales in ruin, perpetuities of livings at the very gates sold, the interest of Lynn gone, mortgages swallowing the estate, and a debt of above £40,000 heaped on those of my father and brother. A crew of banditti were harboured in the house, stables, town, and every adjacent tenement . . . ." Into this chaos Walpole valiantly plunged, spending fifteen hours a day with lawyers and stewards, arguing with farmers

[65] *Lewis,* xxviii. 93 (Walpole to Mason, June 28, 1773).

over their leases, giving away pointers and greyhounds, selling bullocks and sheep, arranging for a sale of racehorses and carefully drawing up their pedigrees. "With all my heraldry," he told Lady Ossory, "I never thought to be the Anstis of Newmarket."[66]

After a few exhausting weeks, Walpole's diligence and good sense had effected great reforms in the management of Houghton, and in all Lord Orford's tangled affairs. Early next year his nephew recovered; he approved everything that Walpole had done, admitted that his reforms were what he had himself wished to carry out but could never bring himself to undertake, and promised to follow the scheme of economy and retrenchment that had been laid down for him.[67] Neither his gratitude nor his intended reformation lasted for more than a month or two. He soon resumed his old extravagant way of life; and when Walpole remonstrated with him, he "fairly washed his hands of me."[68] Most of the summer of 1774 he spent in sailing about the Cambridgeshire fens, demolishing the bridges when they were too low to admit the passage of his little fleet of boats.

Three years later Lord Orford again went raving mad. Walpole was summoned; and with the admirable family loyalty which he always displayed, he put aside the ingratitude with which his former efforts had been received, and instantly went to his nephew's aid. He found him in the tumbledown parsonage-house at Eriswell, where he spent most of his time. He installed himself in the inn at Barton Mills, sent for a doctor from Norwich and another from London, and succeeded, in spite of the protests of Mrs. Turk and the "jockey-parson" who owned the house, in having his nephew removed to a place nearer London. Lord Orford had put "a most worthless and conceited fellow" in charge of his affairs, and Walpole declined to collaborate in any way with this man; but he still did what he could to help his nephew. When, on his recovery from his second attack, Lord Orford made a genuine attempt to settle the whole of the family affairs and to pay off the still outstanding debts of his father and grandfather, both Horace and Sir Edward gave him all the assistance in their power. Their consent was necessary for the steps he wished to

[66] *Toynbee*, viii. 32 (Walpole to Lady Ossory, September 1, 1773).

[67] *Ibid.*, 414 (Walpole to Lady Ossory, January 29, 1774).

[68] *Ibid.*, 454 (Walpole to Mann, May 15, 1774).

take, and the transaction might have proved to be to their financial disadvantage; but both of them readily agreed, from family pride, from affection for the memory of Sir Robert, for the sake of Houghton which was his monument. "We are both old men now, and without sons to inspire us with future visions. We wish to leave your Lordship in as happy and respectable a situation as you were born to, and we have both given you all the proof in our power, by acquiescing in your proposal immediately."[69]

A few months later, Lord Orford requited the generosity of his uncles by despoiling Houghton of its supreme glory, Sir Robert's collection of pictures. He sold them, for a sum variously stated to be £40,000 or £45,000, to the Empress Catherine of Russia. Walpole had once resigned himself to the sacrifice of the pictures in order that the debts of his father and eldest brother should be paid; but when he learnt that Lord Orford had compounded with Sir Robert's creditors for £15,000, and had declined to settle his father's debts at all, not being legally obliged to do so, he naturally regarded the sale as totally unnecessary.[70] He was bitterly grieved and angry. "It is the most signal mortification to my idolatry for my father's memory, that it could receive. It is stripping the temple of his glory and of his affection. A madman excited by rascals has burnt his Ephesus. I must never cast a thought towards Norfolk more; nor will hear my nephew's name if I can avoid it."[71]

VIII

Certainly Walpole's advancing years brought sorrows in their train—the Chatterton affair, his nephew's folly and ingratitude, declining health, the loss of friends. But his life remained, on the whole, a peculiarly happy one—"a much happier life than I deserve, and than millions that deserve better."[72] Withdrawn from active participation in affairs, he still preserved the liveliest interest in events and men and books. His fingers almost disabled by the gout, with great chalk-stones working through the joints,

[69] *Ibid.*, x. 326 (Walpole to Lord Orford, October 5, 1778).
[70] *Ibid.*, 377 (Walpole to Mann, February 11, 1779).
[71] *Ibid.*, 369 (Walpole to Lady Ossory, February 1, 1779).
[72] *Ibid.*, 361 (Walpole to Conway, January 9, 1779).

he still scribbled his brilliant and unflagging letters; or, feverish with pain, dictated them from his bed to his printer Kirgate. He watched with undiminished fascination the political scene—the revolt of the American colonies, the Gordon Riots, the trial of Warren Hastings, the impassioned speeches of Burke, the duels of Pitt and Fox in the chamber where he had listened to the duels of their fathers. He carried on his journals of political events until six years before his death;[73] they grow briefer and more perfunctory, the handwriting becomes a painful scrawl, but he could not give them up. And he continued to indulge in his passion for annotating books. A large proportion of the books from his library contain marginal notes, often of great length and fullness of detail; some of his books are packed with them. He collected all the most remarkable plays, pamphlets and poems that appeared, had them bound into volumes, inserted a list of contents, filled them with marginalia, and stuffed them with newspaper-cuttings; then Kirgate would print special title-pages with one of the Strawberry Hill vignettes, and the volumes, with all the otherwise obscure and inaccessible details which they contained, would form a part of his legacy to posterity.[74]

He did not become in any way a recluse. He went out less and saw fewer people; but at many houses he was still a faithful and a welcome guest, and regularly appeared at the card-tables of certain congenial dowagers at Twickenham, and in the *salons* of the blue-stocking ladies in London. In 1778, the lease of his house in Arlington Street being about to fall in, he moved to another house on the east side of Berkeley Square, which remained his London residence till the end of his life, and in which he died. (This house, like all its neighbours, was pulled down some years ago; and a portentous block of office buildings now rises cliff-like upon the site.) It was a plain and homely house, he said, "but I am charmed with it, as men pretend to be when they

[73] The *Last Journals,* in their published form, end in 1783. The final portion from 1783 until 1791 is still unpublished, and is in the collection of Mr. W. S. Lewis at Farmington.

[74] At Farmington there are more than 150 volumes of pamphlets collected and annotated in this way; at Harvard 22 volumes of poems. Mr. Lewis also owns about 300 plays, extracted some twenty-five years ago from the volumes into which they were bound by Walpole.

marry a dowdy for convenience—and I shall return to my mistress Strawberry with double pleasure, when the honeymoon is over."[75] To Strawberry he always joyfully returned, to the verdant landscape without and the conventual gloom within, to his pictures and his painted glass, to the birds and squirrels in the garden, to his pleasant neighbours and to kind and sensible Margaret his housekeeper. Whatever troubles might be assailing him, he could forget them in that enchanted neighbourhood. At the height of his distress over the Chatterton affair, he described to Lady Ossory how a music-party at Hampton Court had carried him away from the wearisome attacks of his enemies into an older and more seemly world. A gentleman was singing Purcell. "His taste is equal to his voice, and his deep notes, the part I prefer, are calculated for the solemnity of Purcell's music, and for what I love particularly, his mad songs and the songs of sailors. It was moonlight and late, and very hot, and the lofty façade of the palace, and the trimmed yews and canal, made me fancy myself of a party in Grammont's time—so you don't wonder that by the help of imagination I never passed an evening more deliciously. When by the aid of some historic vision and local circumstance I can romance myself into pleasure, I know nothing transports me so much. . . . I sometimes dream, that one day or other somebody will stroll about poor Strawberry and talk of Lady Ossory—but alas! I am no poet, and my Castle is of paper, and my Castle and my attachments and I shall soon vanish and be forgotten together!"[76]

[75] Walpole to Lady Ossory, October 28, 1778 (unpublished).
[76] Walpole to Lady Ossory, August 11, 1778 (unpublished).

XIII

The Final Years (1788-97)

I

ON April 25, 1788 Boswell called on Horace Walpole, and found him at home, "just the same as ever: genteel, fastidious, priggish." They talked about Doctor Johnson and about the gout. Walpole had always detested Johnson, politically as a Tory pamphleteer and pensioner, socially as the embodiment of direct personal rudeness, violent and unreasonable prejudice, loud talk and coffee-house argument. He could never forgive him for his treatment of Gray in the *Lives of the Poets;* he refused ever to be introduced to him, and such terms as "odious and mean character," "saucy Caliban," and "old decrepit hireling" abound when he is mentioned in the *Memoirs* and letters. Nevertheless he told Boswell on this occasion that the recent publication of Johnson's letters to Mrs. Piozzi had given him a much better opinion of his character, "for they shewed him to have a great deal of affection." Gratified by this, Boswell took his leave; and recorded in his journal that *"Hory's* constitutional tranquillity, or affectation of it, and the *tout ensemble* of his connections and history, etc., etc., pleased me."[1]

Walpole had become an object of curiosity to many others besides Boswell. He was a celebrity many times over—as the son of the great Minister, as the creator of Strawberry Hill and the author of *The Castle of Otranto,* as a writer and printer and collector and antiquary. A number of people have recorded their impressions of him at this time; and Pinkerton's account of his appearance, his manners, and his way of life at Strawberry Hill is especially vivid.

[1] *Boswell Papers,* xvii. 102.

"The person of Horace Walpole was short and slender, but compact and neatly formed. When viewed from behind, he had somewhat of a boyish appearance, owing to the form of his person, and the simplicity of his dress. His features may be seen in many portraits; but none can express the placid goodness of his eyes, which would often sparkle with sudden rays of wit, or dart forth shafts of the most keen and intuitive intelligence. His laugh was forced and uncouth, and even his smile not the most pleasing.

"His walk was enfeebled by the gout... this painful complaint not only affected his feet, but attacked his hands to such a degree that his fingers were always swelled and deformed, and discharged large chalk-stones once or twice a year; upon which occasions he would observe with a smile, that he must set up an inn, for he could chalk up a score with more ease and rapidity than any man in England....

"Though he sat up very late, either writing or conversing, he generally rose about nine o'clock, and appeared in the breakfast-room, his constant and chosen apartment, with fine vistas towards the Thames. His approach was proclaimed, and attended, by a favourite little dog, the legacy of the Marquise du Deffand; and which ease and attention had rendered so fat that it could hardly move. This was placed beside him on a small sofa; the tea-kettle, stand and heater, were brought in, and he drank two or three cups of that liquor out of most rare and precious ancient porcelain of Japan, of a fine white embossed with large leaves.... The loaf and butter were not spared, for never tasting even what is called no-supper, he was appetised for breakfast; and the dog and the squirrels had a liberal share of his repast.

"Dinner was served up in the small parlour, or large dining-room, as it happened: in winter generally the former. His valet supported him downstairs; and he ate most moderately of chicken, pheasant, or any light food. Pastry he disliked, as difficult of digestion, though he would taste a morsel of venison-pye. Never, but once that he drank two glasses of white-wine, did the editor see him taste any liquor, except ice-water. A pail of ice was placed under the table, in which stood a decanter of water, from which he supplied himself with his favourite beverage....

"If his guest liked even a moderate quantity of wine, he must have called for it during dinner, for almost instantly after he rang the bell to order coffee upstairs. Thither he would pass about five o'clock and generally resuming his place on the sofa, would sit till two o'clock in the morning, in miscellaneous chit-chat, full of singular anecdotes, strokes of wit, and acute observations, occasionally sending for books, or curiosities, or passing to the library, as any reference happened to arise in conversation. After his coffee he tasted nothing; but the snuff box of *tabac d' etrennes,* from Fribourg's, was not forgotten, and was replenished from a canister lodged in an ancient marble urn of great thickness, which stood in the window seat, and served to secure its moisture and rich flavour.

"Such was a private rainy day of Horace Walpole. The forenoon quickly passed in roaming through the numerous apartments of the house, in which, after twenty visits, still something new would occur; and he was indeed constantly adding fresh acquisitions. Sometimes a walk in the grounds would intervene, on which occasions he would go out in his slippers through a thick dew; and he never wore a hat. He said that, on his first visit to Paris, he was ashamed of his effeminacy, when he saw every little meagre Frenchman, whom even he could have thrown down with a breath, walking without a hat, which he could not do, without a certainty of that disease, which the Germans say is endemial in England, and is termed by the natives *le catch-cold.* The first trial cost him a slight fever, but he got over it, and never caught cold afterwards: draughts of air, damp rooms, windows open at his back, all situations were alike to him in this respect. . . .

"His engaging manners, and gentle, endearing affability to his friends, exceed all praise. Not the smallest hauteur, or consciousness of rank or talents, appeared in his familiar conferences; and he was ever eager to dissipate any constraint that might occur, as imposing a constraint upon himself, and knowing that any such chain enfeebles and almost annihilates the mental powers. Endued with exquisite sensibility, his wit never gave the smallest wound even to the grossest ignorance of the world, or the most morbid hypochondriac bashfulness: *experto crede.*"[2]

To this detailed account of Walpole may be added a further

[2] *Walpoliana,* xl–iv, lxvi.

description of his appearance, although strictly speaking it belongs to an earlier date. It is from the *Memoirs* of Miss Lætitia-Matilda Hawkins, the daughter of Sir John Hawkins, Johnson's executor and biographer, who was a neighbour at Twickenham. "His figure was as has been told, and every one knows, not merely tall, but more properly *long* and slender to excess; his complexion and particularly his hands, of a most unhealthy paleness.... His eyes were remarkably bright and penetrating, very dark and lively:—his voice was not strong, but his tones were extremely pleasant, and if I may say so, highly gentlemanly. I do not remember his common gait; he always entered a room in that style of affected delicacy, which fashion had then made almost natural; *chapeau bras* between his hands as if he wished to compress it, or under his arm—knees bent, and feet on tip-toe, as if afraid of a wet floor.

"His dress in visiting was most usually, in summer when I most saw him a lavender suit, the waistcoat embroidered with a little silver or of white silk worked in the tambour, partridge silk stockings, and gold buckles, ruffles and frill generally lace. I remember when a child, thinking him very much underdressed, if at any time except in mourning, he wore hemmed cambric. In summer no powder, but his wig combed straight, and showing his very smooth pale forehead, and queued behind:—in winter powder."[3]

In his later years, Walpole was always happiest among women; or, as Pinkerton put it, "he was an elegant and devout admirer of the fair sex, in whose presence he would exceed his usual powers of conversation; his spirits were animated as if by a cordial, and he would scatter his wit and *petits mots* with dazzling profusion."[4] In the drawing-rooms of the ladies of the blue-stocking circle, Mrs. Montagu, Mrs. Vesey and the rest, his conversation was a source of unfailing delight, though Fanny Burney found him a rather alarming personage when they first met at Mrs. Vesey's.

[3] *Hawkins,* i. 105–6. It will be noticed that Pinkerton and Miss Hawkins contradict one another on the point of Walpole's height. It seems clear, from various references, that Walpole was rather over middle height, but that his extreme leanness made him look considerably taller. In his later years he stooped a good deal.

[4] *Walpoliana,* xlvi.

When she knew him a little better, she wrote in her diary: "In the evening came Mr. Walpole, gay, though caustic; polite, though sneering; and entertainingly epigrammatical. I like and admire, but I could not love, nor trust him."[5] He was on better terms with another literary woman of almost equal celebrity at that time, Hannah More, who used to frequent the blue-stocking assemblies, and whom he also used to meet when she stayed with Mrs. Garrick at Hampton. A warm friendship sprang up between the ageing wit and the serious young woman of letters. Although she displayed at this time little of the evangelical fervour which characterized her in later years, she nevertheless made constant attempts to persuade Walpole to think more deeply on matters of religion. Walpole would gently tease his "holy Hannah" about her puritanical views; but she admitted that in all their conversations she had never heard a sentence from him which savoured of infidelity.[6] The influence of Middleton's teachings remained with him to the end; a deist he remained, and the passionate convictions of Hannah More were as incomprehensible to him as the Popish ceremonies which he had observed in Italy and the Methodist "enthusiasm" which had repelled him in his own country. Two years before his death he presented her with a splendidly-bound Bible, inscribed by his old and gout-tormented hand with a touching tribute to her virtues.[7]

To his excellent Friend
Miss Hannah More
this Book,
which he knows to be the dearest Object of her Study,
and by which
to the great comfort and relief
of numberless afflicted and distressed Individuals
She has profited beyond any Person with whom he is acquainted,
is offered,
as a mark of his esteem and gratitude,
by her sincere

[5] *D'Arblay,* ii. 270, 272.

[6] *More,* ii. 11 (H. More to her sister, February 17, 1786).

[7] This Bible is now in the library of Mr. W. S. Lewis at Farmington. The inscription is only partly in Walpole's hand; at several points he has broken off, and words or lines are in another hand, probably Kirgate's. See also *More,* ii. 437.

and obliged humble Servant
Horace Earl of Orford
1795

After this, the reflections in which "Saint Hannah" indulged on hearing of his death appear a trifle forbidding. "His playful wit, his various knowledge, his polished manners, alas! what avail they now! The most serious thoughts are awakened. . . ."[8] It is pleasanter to return to the earlier stages of their friendship, when she dedicated *Florio* to him, and honoured him with a flattering couplet in *The Bas Bleu.* He returned these compliments by printing another of her poems, *Bishop Bonner's Ghost,* at Strawberry Hill. The Bishop of London, Dr. Porteus, had lately made a new walk in the gardens of Fulham Palace, cutting through a sombre thicket to a recess where stood a chair said to have belonged to Bishop Bonner. Hannah More's poem purported to be addressed by Bonner's ghost to his successor, reproving him for admitting light into the hallowed darkness where he had lurked so long. It was a perfect opportunity for introducing a great deal of Protestant symbolism, and Hannah More made the most of it.

"Just so your innovating hand
Let in the moral light;
So, chas'd from this bewilder'd land,
Fled intellectual night. . . ."

Bishop Bonner's Ghost was a very skilful piece of work, and Walpole was delighted with it. It was privately issued in 1789, and was the last work, except for one or two leaflets, to be printed at the Strawberry Hill press during his lifetime.

II

At the end of 1787 or the beginning of 1788 he first saw two young women, Mary and Agnes Berry, at an evening assembly. He would not be introduced to them, having heard so much in their praise that he expected to find them spoilt and pretentious. When he next met them at a more intimate party, he sat beside Mary Berry, "and found her an angel, both inside and out," a view which he continued to hold to the end of his life.

[8] *More,* iii. 13 (Hannah More to Martha More, March 1797).

Mr. Berry, the father of these two girls, had been disinherited by a wealthy great-uncle for marrying a woman with no money, and for refusing to marry again after her death. On a very small income he had educated his two daughters, and had travelled with them in France and Italy. Mary was twenty-five, and Agnes a year younger, when Walpole first met them. Beautiful and accomplished, with the romantic story of their father's sacrifice in the background, they had become popular directly they arrived in London. Mr. Berry took a house at Twickenham in 1788, and their acquaintance with Walpole ripened into a close friendship.

Before long, Walpole came to realize that Mary and Agnes Berry were perhaps the most agreeable companions he had ever known. They combined good looks with polite accomplishments, personal charm with intellectual ability; their manners were natural and unaffected; they were fashionable without moving in the hectic vanguard of fashion. They were able to appreciate Strawberry Hill, and at the same time they adorned it. They enjoyed, as few perhaps of the younger generation were disposed to do, the endless reminiscences and anecdotes of their host; and they looked so beautiful as they sat among his treasures in the Gallery or the Tribune, listening enraptured to his talk of Miss Bellenden and Miss Lepell, of the triumphs and storms of Sir Robert's administration, of George II and Queen Caroline. Their interest in his early recollections led him to set down some of them in a more permanent form; and the *Reminiscences, written in* 1788, *for the amusement of Miss Mary and Miss Agnes Berry,* was the last of his literary works, and one of the most agreeable.[9] Gay and colloquial in tone, as was fitting in a work designed to perpetuate his after-dinner conversation, it consists of nine chapters of random anecdotes about George I and his German mistresses, the courts of George II and Frederick Prince of Wales, and in particular about the career of his old friend Lady Suffolk. In a sense the little book is the memorial of his friendship with Lady Suffolk, and of their long talks about old times at Marble

[9] First published in *Works,* iv. 273–318. Reprinted by Dr. Paget Toynbee from the original MS. in the possession of Mr. J. Pierpont Morgan, with the restoration of some passages previously unpublished, and some notes by Walpole of his Conversations with Lady Suffolk. (Oxford University Press, 1924.)

Hill. But it is even more a tribute to his new friends, and Posterity was forgotten as he contemplated this smaller but more charming audience. "O Guicciardin!" he exclaimed, "is posthumous renown so valuable as the satisfaction of reading these court-tales to the lovely Berrys?"[10]

He made a point of professing an equal devotion for Mary and Agnes. They were his "twin wives," "my wife Rachel and my wife Leah," "mes très chères Fraises." Agnes was gentle, modest, retiring; he loved and admired her, and hung her unassuming water-colours in places of honour at Strawberry Hill. But it was towards Mary, more lively, more intellectual, more vivid and striking in her beauty, that his affections were really directed. All through the winter of 1788, and the following spring, the happy relationship continued. When they toured in England in the summer, he pursued them with devoted gossiping letters. The next autumn they took a house at Teddington, and the placid evenings of talk and anecdote were resumed at Strawberry Hill. But in 1790 the Berry family decided to travel abroad again. Walpole was in despair. He had come to realize that he could not be happy without Mary's frequent presence; and the prospect of losing her for months on end was almost more than he could endure. The French Revolution was proceeding on an ever more ominous course; even from Italy, where the Berrys proposed to travel, came rumours of disturbances which horrified him. He was able for a time to conquer his anxiety. In a touching letter of farewell he protested that his feeling was rational, pure, unpassionate: "I do pique myself on not being ridiculous at this very late period of my life." It was his "sweet consolation," in his last years, to have fallen into their society; and now all their graces "are lost to me, alas! when I have no time to lose!"[11] It was only later, when his nerves were strained by their long absence and the imagined dangers surrounding them, that his letters began to reveal the true situation. Gradually but surely it became evident, however warmly he denied the fact even to himself, that at last, after seventy years of emotional detachment, he had become the helpless victim of a love which he could neither deflect nor overcome.

[10] *Works,* iv. 299.
[11] *Lewis,* xi. 110–3 (Walpole to Mary Berry, October 10, 1790).

III

The French Revolution cast a gloom over Walpole's final years. He had known France well enough to realize the eventual necessity of far-reaching social changes; but even in 1765 he had foreseen that the changes would probably be violent and destructive. His forebodings were now justified. He saw authority pass into the hands of a set of murderous doctrinaires; he saw harmless people slaughtered in tens of thousands; and, like most English liberals of the day, he sickened at the senseless cruelty and destruction perpetrated in the name of Liberty. Men and women whom he had known familiarly, with whom he had talked and supped in Paris, were dragged through yelling crowds to the guillotine; or appeared in England as pitiful and helpless refugees. A nephew of Madame du Deffand, an innocent and worthy man, was taken from a bed of sickness and hanged by the mob at Avignon.[12] The old Whig, who had watched with sympathy the progress of the American Revolution, who had admired Washington and Franklin with all his heart, turned in despair from the spectacle presented by France.[13] The long persecution of the King and Queen was an agony to him. In letter after letter he denounced their tormentors—those tigers, hyenas, savages, Iroquois, that bloody and atrocious nation.... And the execution of the King inspired a letter to Lady Ossory, hitherto unpublished, in which his feelings of horror and indignation boil over in one tremendous flood of words. "Indeed, Madam, I write unwillingly; there is not a word left in my Dictionary that can express what I feel. *Savages, barbarians,* &c., were terms for poor ignorant Indians and Blacks and Hyænas, or, with some superlative epithets, for Spaniards in Peru and Mexico, for Inquisitors, or for Enthusiasts of every breed in religious wars. It remained for the enlightened eighteenth century to baffle language and invent horrors that can be found in no vocabulary. What tongue could be prepared to paint a Nation that should avow Atheism, profess Assassination, and practice Massacres on Massacres for four years together: and who, as if they had destroyed God as well as their King, and established Incredulity by law, give no symptom

[12] *Ibid.,* 76 (Walpole to Mary Berry, July 2, 1790).
[13] *Toynbee,* xiv. 256 (Walpole to Conway, July 1792).

of repentance! These Monsters talk of settling a Constitution—it may be a brief one, and couched in one Law, 'Thou shalt reverse every Precept of Morality and Justice, and do all the Wrong thou canst to all Mankind.'

"Yes, Madam, yes, the Eighteenth Century could not close without carrying its improvements into execution, and exhibiting the discoveries of Philosophy. It had extracted an Encyclopédie of all the guilt of former ages, and to avoid the charge of plagiarism, have piqued themselves on refining on the cruelty of every crime. Extracting the quintessence of all the tortures exercised on the early Christians, *the most August Senate of the World* (as the French Assemblies have called themselves) the Parisians for *four years* together have heaped every species of indignity, insult, terror, deliberate barbarity on five wretched persons, all the time in their power, and studiously augmented every dread of a Father and Mother for themselves and their two Children, and gone on in that meditated inhumanity by retrenching every poor comfort, inflicting cold and want of necessaries, and every now and then *enlivening* their sufferings that might have grown torpid by use, by exhibiting to their eyes the bleeding head of a butchered friend, or assailing their sensibility by massacres of hecatombs of their innocent friends—no matter whether women or men!

"Hardened as Rocks, these unepithetable Murderers have mounted to the height of their guilt—but, as if Providence had designed to turn their worst deed to their deeper confusion, what a Character they have brought to light, and cannot sully! The assembled Type of all the Virtues, heroic or Christian, that they have been persecuting and labouring to extirpate! Religion, spotless Virtue, Goodnature never impeached, abhorrence of spilling blood even to rescue himself and family, Courage unshaken, Dignity with not a shade of affection, Patience unexampled, and Charity unwearied by indignities, and all this Mass of Virtues evidently both the emanations of his heart and the result of a propriety of good sense, for in all his trials did he either utter one silly sentence, or not give the proper answers that Truth and Reason dictated?—Let the bloody Pedants, his butchers, name the Roman or Greek, the Antonine or the Socrates, who lived as innocently, or died so beautifully as Louis Seize!"[14]

IV

The Berrys remained abroad for thirteen months. In a darkening world, Walpole's main consolation was the prospect of their return. He had arranged for them to live at Little Strawberry Hill, otherwise known as Cliveden, where Kitty Clive had been his tenant until her death six years before; and he constantly visited their future home, fidgeting over the alterations and improvements which he was making for their comfort, and reckoning up the weeks and presently the days which must elapse before they were restored to him. Meanwhile his letters to them forced almost a continuous journal. The news of Twickenham and the surrounding district was retailed in minute detail. Mary and Agnes were informed of everything that occurred in their future neighbourhood; the tea-parties at Mr. Cambridge's, the gossip of certain old ladies known as "Lady Clackmannan" and "Tabor and Pipe," the rural breakfast that Mrs. Hobart—"nothing being so pastoral as a fat grandmother in a row of houses on Ham Common"—had given at her residence *Sans Souci*.[15] He told them all about his health, how he had gone to hear the Bishop of London preach and had caught rheumatism, how he had swallowed some violent medicine intended for the housemaid.[16] Amid floods of affectionate twaddle, his love and solicitude for his "beloved spouses" found ever stronger expression; and when he learnt that they proposed to return through France, his letters show that he was almost distracted with anxiety. At last, in November 1791, they arrived in England, and were presently settled at Cliveden. They lived there during the rest of Walpole's life. Every evening they went to Strawberry Hill, or he visited them at Cliveden. They became absolutely essential to his happiness, the willing victims of his exacting love.

This curious relationship, now advertised to an uncharitable world by the installation of the Berrys at Cliveden, was bound

[14] Walpole to Lady Ossory, January 29, 1793 (unpublished).

[15] *Lewis,* xi. 290 (Walpole to Mary Berry, June 14, 1791).

[16] *Ibid.,* 311, 316 (Walpole to Mary Berry, July 12 and 20, 1791).

to arouse a great deal of gossip. It was easy and inviting to ridicule Walpole's senile fondness, and equally so to censure the Berry family as a pair of mercenary girls, with their impoverished father, preying on a foolish old man. A newspaper attack of the latter kind, soon after their return to England, caused great unhappiness to Mary and Agnes. Mary wrote touchingly to Walpole: "If our seeking your society is supposed by those ignorant of its value, to be with some view beyond its enjoyment, and our situation represented as one which will aid the belief of this to a mean and interested world, I shall think we have perpetual reason to regret the only circumstance in our lives that could be called fortunate."[17] Naturally enough, people also speculated as to whether Walpole ever proposed marriage to Mary Berry. The greater part of his income came from his patent places, and lapsed at his death; but after his accession to the Earldom of Orford, he would have been able to charge the Norfolk estates with a substantial jointure. There is no evidence, however, to show that he ever attempted to make Mary his wife; and a passage in one of her letters, addressed to an unknown friend, seems definitely to state the contrary. After describing how desperate the financial position of her sister and herself would be after their father's death, she proceeds to discuss and dismiss some rumours that Lord Orford desired to marry her. "Why should he? when, without the ridicule or the trouble of a marriage, he enjoys almost as much of my society, and every comfort from it, that he could in the nearest connection? As the willing offering of a grateful and affectionate heart, the time and attentions I bestow upon him have hitherto given me pleasure. Were they to become a duty, and a duty to which the world would attribute interested motives, they would become irksome."[18] Moreover, she had long been attached to General O'Hara, a distinguished soldier and a *protégé* of Conway's. Walpole knew of this long-standing affection, but seems to have felt neither anxiety nor jealousy.[19] A middle-aged officer, who was obliged to spend almost all his life on foreign service in such arduous posts as Gibraltar and Toulon, did not

[17] *Ibid.*, 375 (Mary Berry to Walpole, December 9, 1791).

[18] *Berry*, i. 384–5 (Mary Berry to ——, August 20, 1793).

[19] *Lewis*, xi. 203, 246–7 (Walpole to Mary Berry, February 20 and April 15, 1791).

rank as a serious rival; and Walpole's references to O'Hara in his letters to Mary Berry indicate nothing but a friendly interest in his career. O'Hara was captured by the French at Toulon in 1793, and remained a prisoner until 1795; while the placid evenings at Strawberry Hill continued without a hint or threat of any change.

V

A few days after the return of the Berrys to England, Horace Walpole became the fourth Earl of Orford. His nephew had once again relapsed into insanity, and died after a short illness on December 5, 1791. Walpole had seen little or nothing of him for many years, and had thought it quite probable that he had been persuaded by his hangers-on to humiliate him by leaving the family property to strangers. Owing to the generous action of his uncles in 1778, it had become possible for Lord Orford to do this; but he had retained a sufficient sense of honour and family obligation to leave the whole of his Norfolk estates to his successor in the title. "I had reason to think that he had disgraced, by totally omitting me," the new Earl wrote to Lady Ossory: "but unhappy as his intellects often were, and beset as he was by miscreants, he has restored me to my birthright, and I shall call myself obliged to him, and be grateful to his memory."[20]

It was gratifying to Walpole's family pride that the ancestral estates should desçend to him; but in other ways his unexpected honours and possessions proved to be an almost overwhelming burden. He had been unwell during a great part of the year, and his anxieties about the return of the Berrys had put an additional strain upon his nerves. Now, when he had hoped to enjoy their company in tranquillity, he was obliged to spend interminable hours with lawyers and agents, to deal with a flood of tedious correspondence, to gauge the full extent of the confusion into which Houghton had fallen. He discovered that he was the poorest Earl in England.[21] The estate was loaded with debts and mortgages; Houghton, stripped of its pictures, surrounded by decaying villages and neglected farms, was "a mortifying ruin";

[20] *Toynbee,* xv. 93 (Walpole to Lady Ossory, December 10, 1791).
[21] *Ibid.,* 103 (Walpole to Lady Ossory, January 18, 1792).

among his nephew's latest achievements had been the gift to one of his satellites of the stately flight of steps which rose to the *piano nobile* of the house.[22] He was too old and infirm to visit Houghton; but he was determined to do his best for the tenants whom he would never see, and to restore, to the small extent in his power, the credit of the estate which had been his father's pride. So he grappled bravely with the mass of unfamiliar business: endless correspondence about the family boroughs, rebukes to clergymen who went to law with his tenants about their tithes, requests for the next presentation of livings, the distribution of venison and game; until the claims of his accustomed correspondents were almost forgotten, and he was obliged to risk the displeasure of Hannah More by writing to her on a Sunday.[23]

VI

In 1791 Walpole lost his "oldest acquaintance and friend," George Selwyn. "These misfortunes," he wrote, "though they can be so but for a short time, are very sensible to the old; but him I really loved, not only for his infinite wit, but for a thousand good qualities."[24] Of the people he had known in childhood and youth, scarcely any now survived. Lord Hertford died in 1794, and Conway in the following year. With the exception of his half-sister, Lady Mary Churchill, and of Lady Ailesbury, Walpole outlived the entire generation of his relatives and friends. To an immense circle of great-nephews and great-nieces—Cholmondeleys, Conways, Churchills, Waldegraves—he was almost the sole relic of the former age.

He made a few new friends, principally men of learned and antiquarian tastes, with whom he could gossip quietly among his books and prints. Foremost among these were the brothers Daniel and Samuel Lysons, the antiquarian and topographical writers. Daniel Lysons was curate of Putney; he frequently visited Strawberry Hill, and dedicated to Walpole his magnificent volumes of *The Environs of London*. Walpole's hospitality to another learned clergyman, the Rev. William Beloe, was less agreeably repaid. Beloe, in the course of an assiduous but ineffective literary

[22] *Ibid.*, 319 (Walpole to Lady Ossory, October 6, 1794).
[23] *Lewis*, xxxi. 363 (Walpole to Hannah More, January 1, 1792).
[24] *Ibid.*, xi. 182 (Walpole to Mary Berry, January 25, 1791).

career, had plagued Walpole with letters, which were always courteously answered, and bothered him about dedications, which were always politely refused. In *The Sexagenarian,* those dreary volumes of rancorous gossip in which Beloe avenged the accumulated hatreds of his life, Walpole fared as badly as the rest of the distinguished men who had gone out of their way to encourage or assist him.

In his old age, Walpole spent most of the winter at his house in Berkeley Square; but he returned to Strawberry Hill as soon as the weather allowed him. He was happiest in his Twickenham circle, with Lady Diana Beauclerk, and the Hardinges, and the Cambridges, always within reach; and with Mary and Agnes Berry in their charming villa a few hundred yards away. He grew more and more crippled with gout; often his servants would have to carry him from one room to another. For months at a time he was obliged to dictate every one of his letters to Kirgate, and his maimed fingers could hardly trace his signature in order to frank the covers. Yet his cheerfulness never left him.[25] He had not the slightest fear of death, and had long awaited its coming with perfect calmness. His extraordinary constitution frequently seemed to be on the verge of collapse. He would be taken acutely ill, and the doctors would shake desponding heads. Then his *"Herculean weakness"* would reassert itself; he would recover his strength and spirits, and would limp through the rooms at Strawberry Hill or be carried to little parties at the houses of his friends. He faced all the vicissitudes of his health with complete serenity. He had no pain; he slept like a dormouse; at the age of seventy-nine he had preserved his eyes, his ears and his teeth.[26] "My fingers are rather worse than they were, and my ankle so weak that I cannot rest upon it a moment, though held up by two servants. But I have all my playthings about me; and, when one is arrived at one's second childhood, is not one fortunate enough in having them and being able to be amused by them? How many poor old wretches are there who suffer more, and who have none of my comforts and assistances, though probably deserving them, which is not my case!"[27]

[25] *Farington,* i. 152. *Glenbervie,* i. 74.

[26] *Lewis,* xxxi. 402 (Walpole to Hannah More, August 29, 1796).

[27] *Ibid.,* 406 (Walpole to Lady Ossory, July 2, 1796).

An air of cheerlessness and neglect seems to have crept over Strawberry Hill in the final years of Walpole's life. Beloe complains that he grew extremely parsimonious in his old age, that his servants were kept on board wages and his dinners were remarkably meagre; a statement which he gravely substantiates by recording that Walpole made him dine on mutton, which he did not like, and omitted to offer him any cheese.[28] Such evidence by itself would be negligible; but it is corroborated to some extent by Pinkerton, and not very convincingly refuted by Miss Hawkins. The garden became neglected and overgrown; and the spires and pinnacles on the house were irresistible targets for the missiles of little boys.[29] There is an impression of inefficiency and disharmony among the servants: Margaret Young, that perfect housekeeper, had retired; Philip Colomb, "the sulky Swiss," his *valet-de-chambre* for many years past, had grown ill-tempered and tyrannical.[30] It was long a matter for general surprise that Walpole in his will had only left one hundred pounds to his printer and secretary Kirgate, apparently the most faithful and assiduous of all his servants. But Mr. W. S. Lewis has shown that for many years past Kirgate had been pilfering and hoarding up extra copies of the highly-priced Strawberry Hill editions on an almost startling scale; and it seems probable that Walpole had detected his thefts, and had adopted an appropriate if somewhat uncourageous remedy.[31] Mr. A. T. Hazen has further proved, in his bibliography of the Strawberry Hill Press, that Kirgate was responsible for a number of extremely skilful forgeries of the books and pamphlets issued by Walpole and in particular for those thick-paper copies of Gray's *Odes* which had so long been a subject of disagreement among bibliographers. In Mr. Hazen's opinion, Kirgate may be acquitted of having produced these forgeries in his employer's lifetime; he considers it more likely that they were all carried out during a few months of 1797, after Walpole's death and the disappointment of his unexpectedly small legacy, and before Mrs. Damer, the new owner of Strawberry Hill, decided that a resident printer was

[28] *Beloe,* i. 278–9, 293. [29] *Hawkins,* i. 87, 94.
[30] *Walpoliana,* xlvi.
[31] W. S. Lewis, *The Forlorn Printer* (privately printed 1931), *passim.*

a luxury which she could not maintain.[32] Our compassion for Kirgate must be qualified by the knowledge that he was singularly well able to take care of his own interests.

The twilight brooding over Strawberry Hill, the neglect of its garden and the imperfections of its staff, however obvious to others, seemed to be unnoticed by Walpole himself. His letters maintain a constant cheerfulness, an unchanging serenity almost to the end. With Mary at his side, with Agnes and Mrs. Damer within call, he was contented. If ever they neglected him, or if he fancied any neglect, he would be overcome with the knowledge of his age and loneliness; he would embark upon a letter of vehement and pathetic reproach, which would break off in helpless blots and scrawls. Their return would bring him instant consolation. The private passions and ambitions of these three women grew to mean less and less to him. Devoted and exacting, he demanded the whole of their attention and their love. He realized nothing of the burning devotion that Mrs. Damer, whose Sapphic inclinations were well-known to her contemporaries, conceived for Mary Berry; he never suspected the violent emotional storms, the sensibility and the tears, that agitated the little female group which ministered to him. And he ignored the brief and pitiable love-affair between Mary Berry and General O'Hara. "He does not *choose* to see," wrote Mrs. Damer to her friend, "and none, they say, so blind."[33]

In the summer of 1795 O'Hara, after two years' imprisonment in France, was exchanged for a French general and returned to England. He and Mary Berry at once renewed their old friendship, and soon afterwards became engaged to be married. For two happy months all went well. No other person shared their secret except Mrs. Damer, whose anxiety for Mary's happiness overcame all other feelings, and who fulfilled the part of a loyal and devoted *confidante*. Then O'Hara was appointed Governor of Gibraltar, and had to leave for his post in November. He urged Mary to marry him at once and go abroad with him. But she felt that her father and sister needed her; she felt that she could not expose Walpole, ill and enfeebled as he now was, to the shock and misery of a prolonged separation from her. The

[32] *Hazen,* 12–4, 24–31.

[33] *Berry Papers,* 150 (Mrs. Damer to Mary Berry, October 6, 1795).

marriage was therefore postponed until O'Hara's next visit to England, and he sailed for Gibraltar alone. At first he and Mary exchanged affectionate letters, discussed in detail the financial aspects of their married life, and considered the most suitable method of breaking the momentous news to Walpole when it should become necessary to do so. O'Hara fully realized that it would be kinder to keep from him as long as possible "the knowledge of an event that, separating you, will overwhelm him with sorrow and disappointment, and defeat all his views and only substantial comfort he enjoys and probably wishes to live for." He further anticipated "some sudden, peevish animadversions upon your marriage, some dictated by friendship, and others by resentment." But he concluded that Walpole would not be so selfish and ungrateful as to raise any obstacle to the happiness of his beloved Mary.[34]

In the course of the winter Mary did, in fact, "confide to my second father, to Lord Orford, that in a few months, as I then thought, I was to leave him for a still dearer friend and a nearer connection."[35] Nothing has been recorded as to the manner in which he received the news; but there was no real necessity for the concern which he undoubtedly felt and at times displayed. Mary's hopes of a happy marriage were about to collapse in a welter of misunderstandings, doubts and recriminations. She always believed that, if she and O'Hara could have met for twenty-four hours, all would have been set right. But it was not to be. By the summer of 1796, after months of epistolary wranglings and reproaches, they had managed to exhaust all their mutual confidence and love. "Alas, my dear friend," wrote Mary, "how you have trifled and *doubted* away both your own happiness and mine!"[36] O'Hara remained at Gibraltar until his death in 1802, settling down into an almost legendary figure, "the old Cock of the Rock," with a couple of mistresses and a flourishing family by each of them; while Mary turned mournfully back to the task of supporting and comforting Walpole during the few remaining months of his life.

[34] *Ibid.*, 171–2 (O'Hara to Mary Berry, October 31, 1795).
[35] *Berry*, ii. 320.
[36] *Berry Papers*, 185 (Mary Berry to O'Hara, July 16, 1796).

VII

Towards the end of November 1796 Walpole, still lingering at Strawberry Hill, was taken ill during a spell of bitterly cold weather, and was hurriedly brought to London. "This winter it is to be feared will be severe on the old and infirm," commented Lord Glenbervie, one of his more recent friends.[37] For a while his health improved; with the Berrys and Mrs. Damer in constant attendance, he still received company in Berkeley Square: and Glenbervie at the beginning of the new year found him as talkative and anecdotal as ever. On January 15 he composed his last letter to Lady Ossory, gently reproaching her for showing his "idle notes" to her admiring friends, and bidding her a simple and moving farewell. "Oh, my good Madam...pray send me no more such laurels, which I desire no more than their leaves when decked with a scrap of tinsel and stuck on twelfth-cakes that lie on the shop-boards of pastry-cooks at Christmas. I shall be quite content with a sprig of rosemary thrown after me, when the parson of the parish commits my dust to dust. Till then, pray, Madam, accept the resignation of your

Ancient servant,
Orford."[38]

Soon afterwards his health finally gave way. For two or three weeks he suffered considerably; but in the intervals of pain his old cheerfulness would return. Then fever came, and his memory began to fail; and if the women he loved were out of the room for a few moments, he believed himself neglected and deserted by them. Gradually he lapsed into a stupor of exhaustion, and died quietly during the afternoon of March 2.[39]

Eleven days afterwards his funeral procession passed through the park gates at Houghton. His tenants had assembled there, and hundreds of people came from the surrounding countryside. Few of them can ever have set eyes on Horace Walpole; but they pressed round the hearse and pulled away the funeral ornaments, the carvings and tassels and plumes, in their eagerness to obtain

[37] *Glenbervie,* i. 100.

[38] *Toynbee,* xv. 435–6 (Walpole to Lady Ossory, January 15, 1797).

[39] *Ibid.,* 433 n. (Miss Berry's account). *Farington,* i. 188, 191. *Glenbervie,* i. 131–2.

some memorial of the last of Sir Robert's sons, before he was laid with his father and his brothers in the vault beneath Houghton Church.

Bibliographical Note

A. Correspondence.

WALPOLE'S letters to West, Conway, Bentley, Gray, Chute, Lord Strafford, Lady Hervey, Lady Ailesbury and Hannah More were first printed in volumes iv and v of the edition of his *Works* published in 1798. The letters to Montagu and Cole first appeared in 1818; and those to Lord Hertford and Zouch in 1825. The first collected edition, in four volumes, was published in 1820. In 1813 Lord Dover edited the earlier letters to Sir Horace Mann in 3 volumes; and the later letters to Mann appeared in 4 volumes in 1843. A second collected edition in 6 volumes, edited by John Wright, was published in 1840. The letters to Lady Ossory were first published, under the editorship of the Right Hon. R. Vernon Smith, in 1848 (2 volumes). The correspondence between Walpole and Mason was published by the Rev. John Mitford in 1851 (2 volumes).

All these letters were included in a collected edition in 9 volumes by Peter Cunningham, which was published in 1857. This in its turn was superseded by the great edition by Mrs. Paget Toynbee, which appeared in 16 volumes between 1903 and 1905. Three supplementary volumes were added by Dr. Paget Toynbee in 1918 and 1925. In 1912 Mrs. Toynbee also published *Lettres de la Marquise du Deffand à Horace Walpole* in 3 volumes.

The Yale Edition of the *Correspondence,* now appearing under the editorship of Mr. W. S. Lewis, will supersede Mrs. Toynbee's volumes as completely as her edition replaced its predecessors. Besides the scrupulous accuracy of its text, the completeness of its annotation, and the remarkable number of new letters which it contains, the Yale Edition has the immense advantage that both sides of each correspondence are printed whenever this is possible.

At present (1963) thirty-one volumes of the Yale Edition have appeared. I have used the Yale Edition, referring to it in the footnotes as *Lewis,* in connection with these volumes. Elsewhere I have used the Toynbee Edition, referring to it as *Toynbee.*

B. Memoirs.

Walpole left his Memoirs ready for publication, together with many other papers, including the letters to Mann, in a sealed chest which was not to be opened "till the eldest son of Lady Waldegrave, or whichever of her sons, being Earl of Waldegrave, shall attain the age of twenty-five years, when the said chest, with whatever it contains, shall be delivered to him for his own." The chest was opened in 1818, when the sixth Earl Waldegrave reached the age of twenty-five. The Memoirs were then entrusted to the third Lord Holland, who published the *Memoirs of the last ten Years of the Reign of George the Second* in 2 volumes in 1822. I have referred to these as *Memoirs of George II.* In 1845 a further series was published by Sir Denis Le Marchant in 4 volumes, under the title of *Memoirs of the Reign of King George the Third.* This series was re-edited in 4 volumes by G. F. Russell Barker in 1894; and I have used the latter edition, referring to it as *Memoirs of George III.* The third series of Memoirs was edited by Dr. Doran in 1859, and was re-edited by A. Francis Steuart in 2 volumes in 1910, under the title of *The Last Journals of Horace Walpole.* I have referred to this edition as *Last Journals.*

C. Works.

During his lifetime Walpole had begun to print a quarto edition of his Collected Works; and although this was later abandoned, it served as the foundation of *The Works of Horatio Walpole, Earl of Orford* which appeared in five noble quarto volumes in 1798, the year after his death. These volumes were nominally edited by Robert Berry, who had been appointed Walpole's literary executor; but the work was almost entirely done, as Walpole had intended it should be, by his daughter Mary. As in the case of the Memoirs and much of the Correspondence, Walpole had left his Works carefully prepared for publication; and Miss Berry had little to do beyond the arrangement of the volumes. As she observed in the preface: "Lord Orford may still be considered as his own editor: every thing that he had selected is faithfully given to the public; and his arrangement, as far as it had gone, is in every respect strictly adhered to."

All my quotations from Walpole's miscellaneous writings, with the exception of *Aedes Walpolianae,* are taken from this edition. I have referred to it as *Works.*

D. Biographies.

The earliest memoir of Walpole was that prefixed to *Walpoliana,* a compilation of his table-talk by John Pinkerton (2 volumes, 1799). Biographical details were affixed to several of the collections of his letters. Macaulay's celebrated Essay was first published in the *Edinburgh Review* in October 1833, as a review of the first three volumes of the letters to Mann. Mary Berry's spirited reply to Macaulay, published in 1840 in Wright's edition of Walpole's *Correspondence,* deserves to be better known.

Austin Dobson was the author of the first formal biography of Walpole: it was published in America in 1890, and reissued in England in 1893; another edition, revised and enlarged by Dr. Paget Toynbee, was published in 1927. M. Paul Yvon's monumental work, *La Vie d'un Dilettante: Horace Walpole,* appeared in 1924. Miss Dorothy Margaret Stuart's study of Walpole was published in the English Men of Letters Series in 1927. Mr. Oswald Doughty prefixed an attractive memoir to his edition of *The Castle of Otranto* in 1929. There are also lives of Walpole by Lewis Melville (1930) and Mr. Stephen Gwynn (1932).

E. Authorities Quoted.

Reference has been made in the footnotes to the following works, by abbreviations as indicated:

Albemarle. Memoirs of the Marquis of Rockingham and his Contemporaries, by George Thomas, Earl of Albemarle. 2 vols., 1852.

From Anne to Victoria. From Anne to Victoria: Essays by Various

Hands, edited by Bonamy Dobrée, 1937. (Especially the article *Horace Walpole* by Romney Sedgwick.)

Beloe. The Sexagenarian, or the Recollections of a Literary Life, by the Rev. William Beloe. 2 vols., 1817.

Berry. Extracts from the Journals and Correspondence of Miss Berry, edited by Lady Theresa Lewis. 3 vols., 1865.

Berry Papers. The Berry Papers, being the Correspondence hitherto unpublished of Mary and Agnes Berry, edited by Lewis Melville. 1914.

Boswell Papers. Private Papers of James Boswell from Malahide Castle, in the collection of Lieut.-Col. Ralph Heywood Isham, edited by Geoffrey Scott and Frederick A. Pottle. 17 vols. 1928–34.

Chatterton's Miscellanies. Miscellanies in Prose and Verse by Thomas Chatterton (edited by John Broughton). 1778.

Clark. The Gothic Revival, by Kenneth Clark. 1929.

Coke. The Letters and Journals of Lady Mary Coke, edited by J. A. Hume. 4 vols., 1889–96.

Cole. A Journal of my Journey to Paris in the year 1765, by the Rev. William Cole, edited by F. G. Stokes. 1931.

Coxe. Memoirs of the Life and Administration of Sir Robert Walpole, Earl of Orford, by the Rev. William Coxe. 3 vols., 1798.

d'Arblay. The Diary and Letters of Madame d'Arblay, edited by her Niece. 7 vols., 1842.

Farington. The Farington Diary, edited by James Greig. 8 vols., 1922–8.

Genesis of Strawberry Hill. The Genesis of Strawberry Hill, by W. S. Lewis. New York: Metropolitan Museum Studies, 1934.

Glenbervie. The Diaries of Sylvester Douglas, Lord Glenbervie, edited by Francis Bickley. 2 vols., 1928.

Grafton. Autobiography and Political Correspondence of Augustus Henry, third Duke of Grafton, edited by Sir William R. Anson. 1898.

Gray. The Correspondence of Thomas Gray, edited by Paget Toynbee and Leonard Whibley. 3 vols., 1935.

Gray, Walpole, West and Ashton. The Correspondence of Gray, Walpole, West and Ashton (1734–71), edited by Paget Toynbee. 2 vols., 1915.

Grenville. The Grenville Papers: being the Correspondence of Richard Grenville, Earl Temple, K.G., and the Right Hon. George Grenville, edited by W. J. Smith. 4 vols., 1852.

Hanbury Williams. The Works of the Right Hon. Sir Charles Hanbury Williams, with notes by Horace Walpole. 3 vols., 1822.

Hartford-Pomfret. Correspondence between Frances, Countess of Hartford, and Henrietta Louisa, Countess of Pomfret. 3 vols., 1805.

Hawkins. Anecdotes, Biographical Sketches and Memoirs, by Laetitia-Matilda Hawkins. 3 vols., 1822–4.

Hazen. A Bibliography of the Strawberry Hill Press, by A. T. Hazen. 1942.

Hervey. Memoirs of the Reign of George II, by John Lord Hervey, edited by Romney Sedgwick. 3 vols., 1931.

Holland. Henry Fox, first Lord Holland, by the Earl of Ilchester. 2 vols., 1920.

Holland Letters. Letters to Henry Fox, Lord Holland, edited by the Earl of Ilchester. 1915.

Jesse. George Selwyn and his Contemporaries, by J. H. Jesse. 4 vols., 1882.

Mann. "Mann" and Manners at the Court of Florence, by Dr. Doran, F.S.A. 2 vols., 1876.

Meyerstein. A Life of Thomas Chatterton, by E. H. W. Meyerstein. 1930.

Montagu. The Letters and Works of Lady Mary Wortley Montagu, edited by Lord Wharncliffe, re-edited by W. Moy Thomas. 2 vols., 1887.

More. Memoirs of the Life and Correspondence of Hannah More, edited by William Roberts. 4 vols., 1834.

Nichols. Illustrations of the Literary History of the Eighteenth Century, by John Nichols. 8 vols., 1817–58.

Printing-Office. Journal of the Printing-Office at Strawberry Hill, edited by Paget Toynbee. 1931.

Pyle. Memoirs of a Royal Chaplain; the Correspondence of Edmund Pyle, D. D., edited by Albert Hartshorne. 1905.

Restituta. Restituta, or Titles, Extracts, and Characters of old Books in English Literature, Revived, by Sir Egerton Brydges. 4 vols., 1814–6.

Sedgwick. Letters from George III to Lord Bute, 1756–1766, edited by Romney Sedgwick. 1939.

Steegmann. The Rule of Taste from George I to George IV, by John Steegmann. 1936.

Stirling Taylor. Robert Walpole: and his Age, by G. R. Stirling Taylor. 1931.

Suffolk. Letters to and from Henrietta, Countess of Suffolk (edited by John Wilson Croker). 2 vols., 1824.

Tovey. Gray and his Friends, by Duncan C. Tovey. 1890.

Waldegrave. Memoirs from 1754 *to* 1758, by James Earl Waldegrave. 1821.

Archaeologia.

The Gentleman's Magazine.

The London Magazine.

The Monthly Review.

The North Briton.

The Town and Country Magazine.

The World.

F. Other Authorities.

Among other works used in the preparation of this book, but which are not directly cited in the footnotes, are the following:

The Glenbervie Journals, ed. Walter Sichel. 1910.

Hussey, Christopher: *The Picturesque.* 1927.

Ilchester, Earl of, and Langford-Brooke, Mrs.: *The Life of Sir Charles Hanbury Williams.* 1929.

Ironside, Edward: *History and Antiquities of Twickenham.* 1797.

Johnson's England, ed. A. S. Turberville. 2 vols., 1933. (Especially the articles "Taste" by Osbert Sitwell and Margaret Barton, "Painting" by the Hon. Andrew Shirley, "Architecture and the Garden" by Geoffrey Webb, and "The Interior of the House" by Oliver Brackett).

Kerr, S. Parnell: *George Selwyn and the Wits.* 1909.

Lewis, W. S.: *Notes by Lady Louisa Stuart on Jesse's "George Selwyn and his Contemporaries,"* 1928. *Horace Walpole's Fugitive Verses,* 1931. *The Forlorn Printer,* privately printed, 1931. *Bentley's Designs for Walpole's Fugitive Pieces,* privately printed, 1936.

Maurois, André: *Études Anglaises,* article "Madame du Deffand et Horace Walpole," 1927.

Mehrotra, K. K.: *Horace Walpole and the English Novel.* 1934.

Morley, Lord: *Rousseau,* 2 vols. 1886. *Walpole* (Twelve English Statesmen). 1889.

Namier, L. B.: *The Structure of Politics at the Accession of King George III,* 2 vols. 1929. *England in the Age of the American Revolution,* 2 vols. 1930.

Oliver, F. S.: *The Endless Adventure,* 3 vols. 1930–5.

Palmer, W. M.: *William Cole of Milton.* 1935.

Roscoe, E. S. and Clergue, Helen: *George Selwyn: his Letters and his Life.* 1899.

Saint-Beuve, C.-A.: *Causeries du Lundi,* 11 March, 1850; 9 May, 1859.

Sieveking, I. Giberne: *Memoir of Sir Horace Mann.* 1912.

Smith, Warren Hunting: *Architecture in English Fiction.* 1934.

Strachey. Lytton: *Books and Characters,* article "Madame du Deffand," 1922. *Portraits in Miniature,* article "Mary Berry," 1931. *Characters and Commentaries,* three articles on Walpole, 1933.

Strawberry Hill Sale Catalogue, 1842.

Tovey, Duncan C.: *Gray and his Friends.* 1890.

Toynbee, Paget: *Reminiscences written by Horace Walpole in* 1788 (Now first printed in full from the original), 1924. *Mason's Satirical Poems with Walpole's Notes,* 1926. *Strawberry Hill Accounts,* 1927. *Walpoliana (Blackwood's Magazine,* April 1927).

Tunstall, Brian: *Admiral Byng.* 1928.

Warburton, Eliot: *Memoirs of Horace Walpole and his Contemporaries,* 2 vols. 1851.

Whibley, Leonard: *Thomas Gray at Eton. (Blackwood's Magazine,* May 1929). *Thomas Gray, Undergraduate, (Blackwood's Magazine,* February 1930). *The Foreign Tour of Gray and Walpole, (Blackwood's Magazine,* June 1930).

Whitley, W. T.: *Artists and their Friends in England,* 2 vols. 1928.

Williams, Basil: *The Life of William Pitt, Earl of Chatham,* 2 vols. 1913. *The Whig Supremacy.* 1939.

Yvon, Paul: *Horace Walpole as a Poet.* 1924.

GENEALOGIC[A

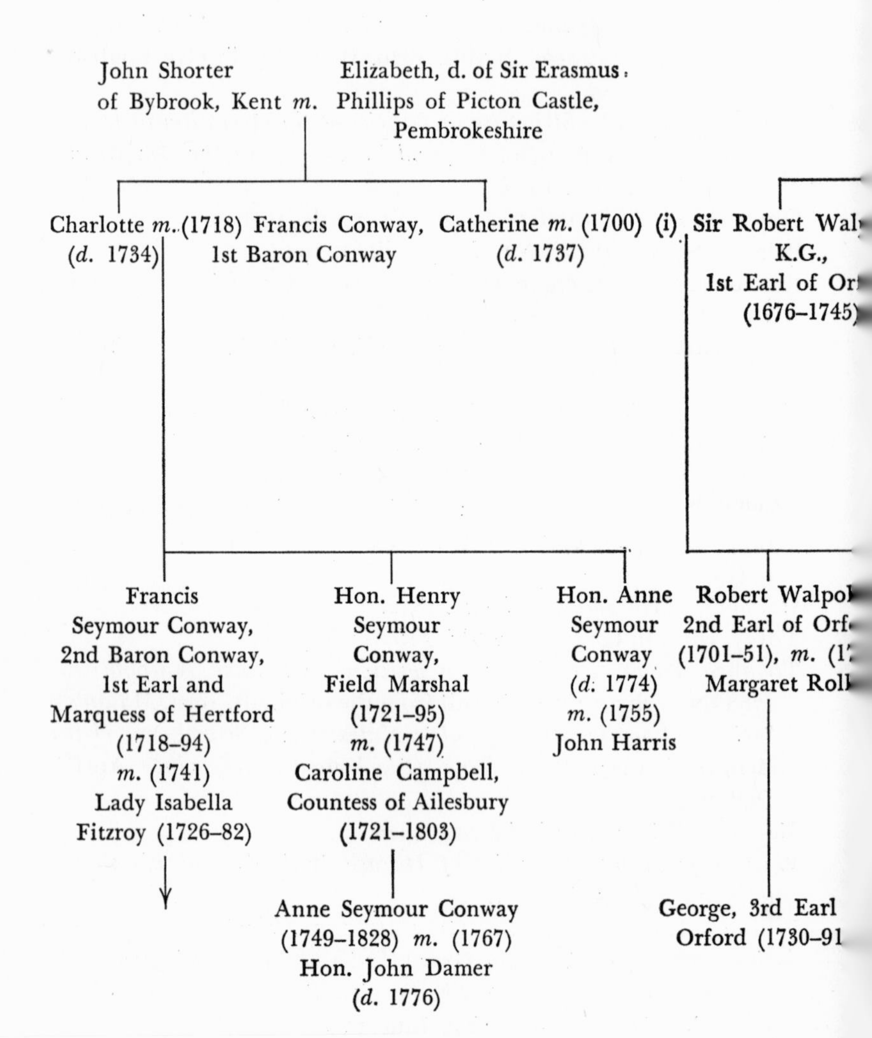

ABLE

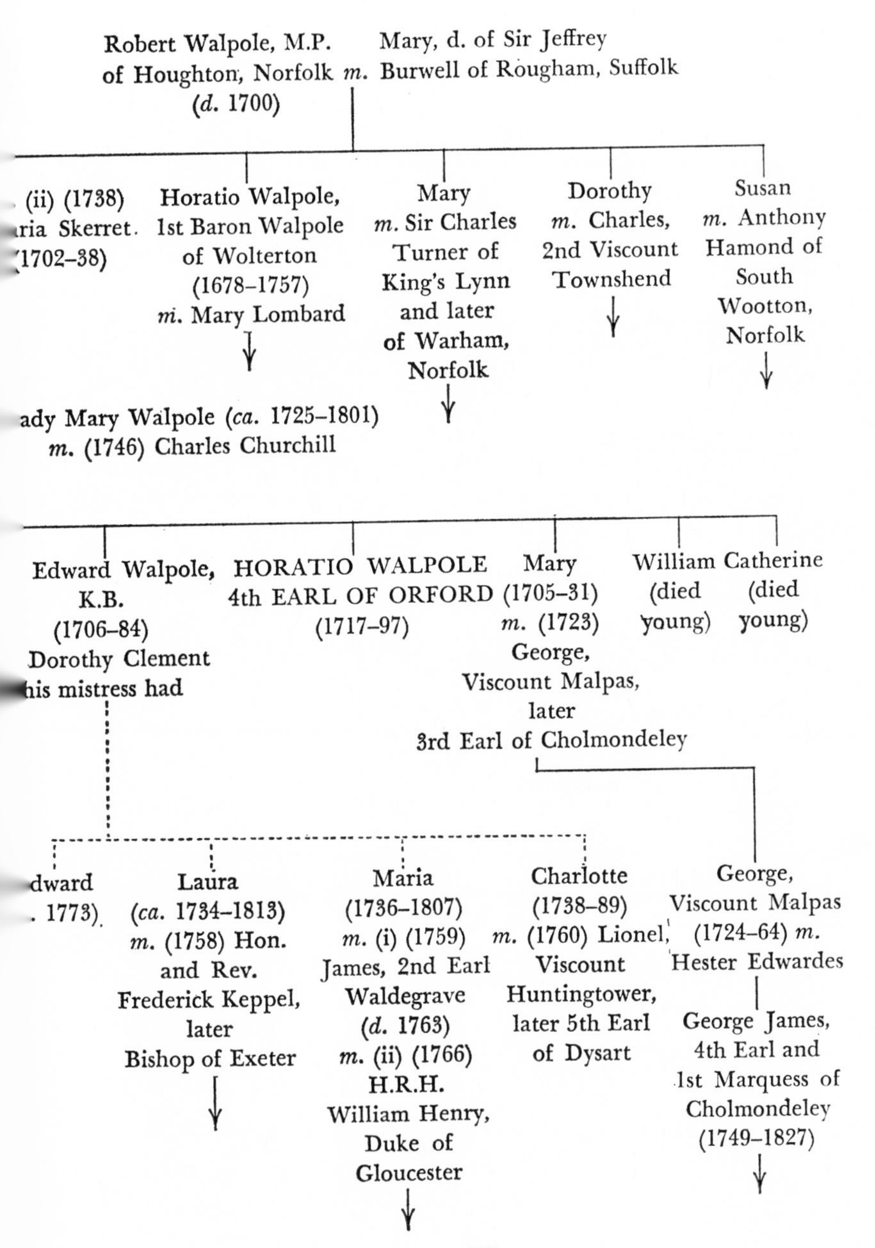

Robert Walpole, M.P. of Houghton, Norfolk (d. 1700) m. Mary, d. of Sir Jeffrey Burwell of Rougham, Suffolk
(ii) (1738)
aria Skerret
(1702–38)
Horatio Walpole, 1st Baron Walpole of Wolterton (1678–1757) m. Mary Lombard
Mary m. Sir Charles Turner of King's Lynn and later of Warham, Norfolk
Dorothy m. Charles, 2nd Viscount Townshend
Susan m. Anthony Hamond of South Wootton, Norfolk
ady Mary Walpole (ca. 1725–1801) m. (1746) Charles Churchill
Edward Walpole, K.B. (1706–84)
Dorothy Clement
his mistress had
HORATIO WALPOLE 4th EARL OF ORFORD (1717–97)
Mary (1705–31) m. (1723) George, Viscount Malpas, later 3rd Earl of Cholmondeley
William (died young)
Catherine (died young)
dward
. 1773)
Laura (ca. 1734–1813) m. (1758) Hon. and Rev. Frederick Keppel, later Bishop of Exeter
Maria (1736–1807) m. (i) (1759) James, 2nd Earl Waldegrave (d. 1763) m. (ii) (1766) H.R.H. William Henry, Duke of Gloucester
Charlotte (1738–89) m. (1760) Lionel, Viscount Huntingtower, later 5th Earl of Dysart
George, Viscount Malpas (1724–64) m. Hester Edwardes
George James, 4th Earl and 1st Marquess of Cholmondeley (1749–1827)

Index